A Seat of Popular Leadership

A Volume in the Series

Political Development of the American Nation:
Studies in Politics and History

Edited by   Sidney M. Milkis and
Jerome M. Mileur

A Seat of Popular Leadership

The Presidency, Political Parties, and Democratic Government

Michael J. Korzi

University of Massachusetts Press

Amherst and Boston

Library of Congress Cataloging-in-Publication Data

Korzi, Michael J., 1969–
    A seat of popular leadership : the presidency, political parties, and democratic
government / Michael J. Korzi.
        p. cm. — (Political development of the American nation, studies in politics
and history)
    Includes bibliographical references and index.
    ISBN 1-55849-450-2 (library cloth : alk. paper) — ISBN 1-55849-459-6
(pbk. : alk. paper)
    1. Presidents—United States. 2. Political leadership—United States. 3. Political
parties—United States. 4. Presidents—United States—Public opinion. 5. Public
opinion—United States. I. Title: Presidency, political parties, and democratic
government. II. Title. III. Political development of the American nation.
    JK516.K64 2004
    303.3'4'0973—dc22

                                                                                    2004005667

British Library Cataloguing in Publication data are available.

Contents

Acknowledgments

For his inspiration, insight, and patience, I am especially grateful to Bruce Miroff. My thanks also to Michael Malbin, who helped me refine and strengthen my ideas at early stages. Much of the research for this book was completed at the New York State Library, Albany, and credit is due its staff for their assistance. I also owe a great debt to the Towson University library staff, particularly Sharon Mollock, for tracking down numerous microfilm editions of nineteenth-century newspapers. Richard J. Ellis, professor of political science at Willamette University, generously shared his collection of nineteenth-century acceptance letters.

At all points along the way, working with the University of Massachusetts Press has been an outstanding experience. Sidney Milkis, series editor, encouraged the project from the beginning, offering key suggestions and theoretical refinement; the book owes much to his influence. Daniel Tichenor also offered useful commentary when he reviewed the manuscript for the press. Clark Dougan, senior editor, brought clarity, professionalism, and geniality to the publication process. Carol Betsch, managing editor, promptly and effectively addressed my concerns and questions throughout. I thank Patricia Sterling as well for her superb copyediting.

My colleagues in the political science department at Towson University provided a stimulating intellectual environment and through their experience were a rich source of information about book publishing.

As always, my mother and father took a great interest in my work and offered needed encouragement and support along the way.

I dedicate this book to my wife Dawn; for her tolerance, kindness, and perspective, I owe her more than I can express.

Portions of chapters have been previously published as articles and are used by permission. "The Seat of Popular Leadership: Parties, Elections, and the Nineteenth-Century Presidency," *Presidential Studies Quarterly* 29:2 (June 1999), and "Our Chief Magistrate and His Powers: A Reconsideration of William Howard Taft's 'Whig' Theory of Presidential Leadership," *Presidential Studies Quarterly* 33:2 (June 2003), both by permission of Blackwell Publishing; "A New Migration of Political Forces: Party Decline and Presidential Leadership in Late Nineteenth-Century America," *Polity* 36:2 (January 2004); "The President and the Public: Inaugural Addresses in American History," *Congress & the Presidency* 31:1 (Spring 2004).

A Seat of Popular Leadership

Introduction

The Presidency and Popular Government

Parties are unknown in despotic countries. They belong to the machinery of free governments. Through parties, public opinion is concentrated and directed. Through parties, principles are maintained above men. And through parties, men in power are held to a just responsibility.

Senator Charles Sumner, 1860

The relationship between the presidency and political parties has always been uneasy.[1] Particularly since the Progressive Era, we have tended to see political parties as impeding—rather than contributing to—effective presidential leadership. Political parties, on the Progressive view, were provincial and corrupt institutions that served local and state politicians' interests, precluding the possibilities for national presidential leadership that would serve the will of the people. Presidents could exercise effective democratic leadership only if liberated from these conservative and restraining organizations and brought into direct connection with the American people. The president, unfettered by party leaders and bosses—indeed, limited by nothing other than public opinion itself—would be free to do what was necessary to act as the "steward of the people," to use Theodore Roosevelt's language.[2]

These sentiments have remained so strong even into the twenty-first century that it runs against the grain to claim for political parties an important, even crucial, role in promoting democratic presidential leadership. An in-depth study of political parties and the presidency in the nineteenth century, however, yields precisely this conclusion. Although the assaults by Progressives and others were, to some extent, entirely condign, the critics failed to appreciate the virtues of political parties, particularly their role in creating a democratic presidential office that was capable of energetic leadership to address public questions but that was more generally held in check and tempered.[3] In fact, parties have been and, by implication, can be again bulwarks of effective yet restrained popular presidential leadership.

The Progressive critique of political parties surely contributed to their decline in the twentieth century. Although parties are experiencing an important resurgence in their organizational and governmental capacities, their ties to the American people, the party electorate, have undoubtedly attenuated, as the predominance of divided government in the last third of the twentieth century firmly attests.[4] More important to my purposes, in addition to shaping the politics of the twentieth century, the anti-partyism of Progressivism—and especially its understanding of presidential leadership—has colored, even jaundiced, our view of political parties and the possibilities for presidential leadership in the nineteenth century. Modern scholars, commentators, presidents, and presidential advisers have generally accepted the Progressive view that political parties contributed very little of positive value to the office of the presidency or to presidential leadership.

In fact, the modern preoccupation with presidential leadership of the Progressive stripe is so strong that few scholars and commentators see the point in even studying "premodern" or "traditional" presidents and their styles of leadership. The result has been a rich body of research on later presidents and very little work on earlier ones, with the exception of those, such as Jackson, Polk, and Lincoln, who manifested some "modern" leadership tendencies. What is more, the traditional presidents, when examined, are often dealt with in a cursory fashion and less on their own terms than in the ways they failed to be strong modern leaders. This approach to presidential history has produced a rather superficial picture of nineteenth-century presidents and presidential leadership.

An increasing number of writers, however, are challenging this uncritical view, calling attention to the drawbacks of the modern presidency and suggesting that the premodern presidency had important virtues.[5] Yet although more generous to the earlier presidents, most of these writers too do a disservice to the complexity and texture of the nineteenth-century presidency and its forms of presidential leadership.[6] They often completely neglect political parties and their influence, preferring to view nineteenth-century presidents as exhibiting predominantly "constitutional" behavior: that is, as acting for the most part consistently with the intentions and aims of the founders of the Constitution.

The contemporary debate over proper presidential leadership, therefore, revolves around the tension between two types: modern and traditional leadership—or, to use the idiom of political science, rhetorical, plebiscitary leadership and constitutional statesmanship.[7] Advocates of the modern style favor, in the Progressive tradition, a presidency that is front and center in the political system and that derives a significant supply of its power and authority from a strong relationship or connection with the American public. On this view, the president is T. R.'s "steward of the people," and it is his or her job to rally the populace and lead the nation to address the problems facing it. Demagoguery and constitutional imbalance are minor concerns, as the problem of American politics is that the government, with its many checks and balances, lacks the energy and dynamism to address the major issues and dilemmas of the day adequately. Theodore Roosevelt embodied this perspective well in the 1912 election, inveighing against the "overdivision of governmental powers" in his unprecedented campaign for a third term.[8] The only real likelihood of meeting the demands of the day is through reliance on a president who could command center stage in the political system and marshal the support of the people behind his policies and programs. Appealing not only to our demands for action, this view is also consistent with our democratic sensibilities, which are offended by any suggestion that leaders should be removed from the people.

Those preferring a constitutional or traditional style argue that presidents should be more aware of their place in the constitutional order and should generally refrain from the rhetorical public appeals that form the bedrock of the modern presidency. The twin dangers of demagogic excess and constitutional imbalance, the natural byproducts of a presidency wedded to public opinion, necessitate that the presidency be brought more in line with its originally prescribed constitutional role, thus protecting the nation from unbridled ambition and policy overreach or misdirection. This perspective is concerned less with bold presidential action than with a stable, constitutional regime and a presidential office that is able to resist, (in Alexander Hamilton's phrase) "every sudden breeze of passion."[9]

As presently framed, then, the debate over presidential leadership features a dynamic presidency that dominates the political landscape and harnesses public opinion to the service of broad goals and visionary leadership versus a constitutional presidency largely independent of public opinion and reserved in its use of powers. Yet this debate poses a false choice. Inattention to the richness and texture of presidential history, particularly the involvement of political parties, engenders neglect of nineteenth-century party leadership, which popularized and invigorated the presidency while it also restrained and limited it. As Marc Landy and Sidney Milkis have argued, "While checking unwonted ambition, party also provided a vital source of presidential authority. . . . It provided presidents with a stable basis of popular support and, episodically, during periods of realignment, with the opportunity to embark on ambitious projects of national reform."[10] Party leadership of the nineteenth and early twentieth centuries contained aspects of both the constitutional and plebiscitary models—it was popular yet restrained—but it was qualitatively different.

Putting an emphasis on the rise of mass political parties shows the development of the presidency in a different light and reveals in Stephen Skowronek's phrase, "other 'presidencies' worthy of consideration."[11] In fact, not two but three overlapping tendencies or "constitutions" in American political history guided and structured presidential leadership and behavior: falling between the traditional and modern periods is what I call, following Joel Silbey, the party era or party period.[12] Lasting roughly from 1836 to 1892, this party period constitutes a significant and yet rather neglected piece of presidential history. Although it has since been eclipsed by the modern era, there is today a residue of many of its assumptions, values, and structures, some of which are worth preserving and nurturing. Most notably, the popular leadership exercised by party-era presidents, and the values that guided this party leadership, need to be revisited and reexamined.

The Presidency, Party, and the Public—An Alternative View

Most commentators have regarded nineteenth-century political parties as either irrelevant or detrimental to presidential leadership. Yet not only did parties have a prominent influence, but their influence was, more often than not, a positive contribution to presidential leadership. There is no doubt that in nineteenth-century presidential practice, certain norms were working to constrain the presidents in their uses of the office and, especially, in their relations with the people. Direct appeals to "the people" were few and far between.[13] A constitutional norm worked to preclude direct popular appeals to the people—a main wellspring of power—by presidents in the nineteenth century, but this constitutional norm goes only so far in explaining the behavior of those presidents vis-à-vis the public. Indeed, the presidency became a seat of popular leadership in the nineteenth century. Presidents of the period were not plebiscitary leaders, but neither were they simply constitutional officers or "clerks." Approaching them with a distinct emphasis on that bugaboo of the founders, the party, permits a quite different perspective on the quality of their leadership, particularly its democratic character.

It has been fashionable for scholars to argue that American parties have been electoral machines largely devoid of any substance or principles.[14] Recent studies, however, have shown the importance of partisan and ideological differences in the nineteenth century, from the 1830s onward. In a major study of party ideologies in American history, for instance, John Gerring has pointed out the real differences and principles that separated the parties. The Whigs and Democrats, and after them the Democrats and Republicans, clearly espoused differentiated and competing principles and ideologies. In fact, writes Gerring, "American parties have articulated views that were (and are) coherent, differentiated, and stable. American party history and, by extension, American political history at large have been irreducibly ideological."[15]

Joel Silbey, further, has drawn attention to the vital impact that parties had not only on elite but also on mass political culture in the nineteenth century: "A politics largely rooted in elite-dominated factions gave way, by the late 1830s, to a populist-oriented, institutionally organized political nation dominated by a system of two-party politics 'unique in its power and in its depth of social penetration.'" As Michael Holt has noted, discussing the mass-based quality of the Democrats and Whigs: "Voters knew what the parties stood for in terms of both specific legislation and general goals. . . . And they responded in rational ways to the contrasting programs and party images presented to them." Partisanship was so pervasive that it infused social and political life to a great degree, affecting political institutions, norms and behavior. Many writers, however, have failed to follow through on this main point, failed to ask how partisanship actually affected political institutions, norms, and behavior in the nineteenth century. Or, if they do follow it through, they somehow exempt the presidency from analysis, focusing on state, local, or congressional offices. Yet Silbey rightly argues that presidents too were implicated in this partisan culture: "Presidents and governors were vigorous members of their party communities as well, in terms of both patronage and programs." "Not all matters divided clearly and consistently along partisan lines during this period," adds Gerring, "but the party label was a good predictor of the positions a presidential candidate might take on most issues of domestic policy."[16]

Despite these and similar insights, the impact of partisan culture on the nineteenth-century presidency has not been systematically explored. Particularly, the democratic nature of the office and the leadership styles of presidents in the party era need to be fully examined. Party should not be neglected when speaking of democratic or popular presidential leadership, given the party's traditional role as mediator between elites and masses.[17] In this media-saturated age it is easy to forget that parties, rather than television and mass-circulated newspapers, were the early linkage mechanisms developed to bring the mass and the leaders into more efficient and closer contact.[18] We tend now to speak of "public opinion" as an entity constituted most prominently by opinion polls, but nineteenth-century parties and public opinion were inextricably bound, nearly inseparable.[19] Senator Charles Sumner's statement of 1860 bears repeating in this context: "Parties are unknown in despotic countries. They belong to the machinery of free governments. Through parties, public opinion is concentrated and directed. Through parties, principles are maintained above men. And through parties, men in power are held to a just responsibility."[20] The contemporary scholar A. James Reichley, in more prosaic fashion, similarly captures the essence of parties: they "provided a foundation, both electoral and programmatic, on which coherent government policies could be built; and they served public accountability by giving voters a meaningful choice in elections." The party was the preeminent means for reaching and organizing the mass of people; it was the crucial linkage between the people and leaders, including presidents.[21]

The conception of the president as a "democratic" leader certainly squares with the excessive focus that was placed on presidential elections in the nineteenth century, especially in the partisan era (1836–1892). The extensive attention paid to presidential elections and candidates would be nearly incomprehensible had the presidency been a nonpopular and removed office. Would voters have viewed nearly every *presidential* election as a matter of grave concern if they had been choosing only a constitutional officer? More plausibly, participants in nineteenth-century politics saw the presidency as an important, at times crucial, popular office. Presidential elections were a major concern because people thought (or, at the least, hoped) that the principles articulated in campaigns and party platforms would be carried out when the president and his party were swept into office.[22]

Jeffrey Tulis has argued that two constitutions actually structure the conduct of the presidency. There is the original written Constitution, which suggests that the president be a constrained officer with minimal contact with the people and little flair for bold leadership. A second "constitution," emerging in the early 1900s, advocates a quite different role for the president, a strong leadership role anchored in public opinion. Another "constitution" should be added to the mix: a "party" or "people's" constitution, to use James MacGregor Burns's idiom. As Burns has put it, "the party constitution differed from the checks-and-balance constitution in its prime effort to supply teamwork and support collective leadership between the state and national levels of government and the three branches of each level of government."[23]

Burns dates the development of the so-called party constitution to the 1830s, with the work of Martin Van Buren and his party machine, the New York Albany Regency (though there were anticipations of party-building earlier). This party constitution is still with us today; it exists alongside the original Constitution and the later plebiscitary one, although its dominance has certainly been undercut by the latter. The party constitution guided and shaped nineteenth-century politics substantially. It valued the participation of the people and thus competed openly with the original Constitution's view of the proper relationship between public opinion and governance, differently outlining the role of the presidency and the parameters of leadership: the presidency and presidents, under this constitution, were to be more closely linked to the people than prescribed by the original Constitution but not quite as closely linked as under the plebiscitary constitution. Such linkage with the people afforded a democratic presidency that, at times, was capable of ambitious and bold leadership, but more regularly was moderated and held in check by what Burns calls the collective leadership of the political party. Presidential leadership under the party constitution provides a model for democratic presidential leadership that has distinct relevance to modern politics.

Clearly, this is a different interpretation of the function and role of political parties in the nineteenth century than that offered by the Progressives and many modern scholars and commentators. Preceding a fuller defense of political parties in my conclusion, two points need to be made at the outset. First, the picture of political parties presented in this book is not uncritical and, in fact, dovetails at times with the Progressive view. For example, it is unquestionable that profound corruption of the parties in the post–Civil War era prevented them from living up to their potential. I pay due deference to this and other drawbacks of the political parties. Second, aside from the Progressive critique of corruption and provinciality, I am also aware that at no time in the nineteenth century did political parties promote democracy in a complete sense. It is well known and granted that women and African Americans were not included in the political universe of the parties, the latter not even after the guarantees of the Fifteenth Amendment to the U.S. Constitution. Nevertheless, the openness of mass political parties in the nineteenth century to *all* white males, regardless of income, social standing, or religious affiliation, represented a truly important step toward the fulfillment of equality and democracy in the United States.[24]

Notwithstanding their drawbacks, parties helped to create a type of presidential leadership that had important virtues (though they will not be considered virtues by all readers and students of politics) and that needs to be revisited. The main values or virtues served by the party presidency are "representation," "accountability," and "deliberation." Indeed, one might say that the raison d'être of the party constitution was representation, linking those in government to public opinion through the instrument of the political party.[25] Instead of strongly mitigating the influence of the people on government (the aim of the original Constitution) or strengthening the government by wedding it to mass opinion (the thrust of the "plebiscitary constitution,") the party constitution democratized the national government to ensure representation of the diverse network of interests throughout the United States. These diverse constituencies, working through the parties, laid a strong claim on federal offices, including the presidency.

The resulting political structure produced a presidency that was far more in touch with the networks of public opinion, without question a more democratic office, than the one envisioned by the founders. As the guiding principles of this structure were representation, accountability, and deliberation, however, party presidential leadership was rarely bold and overpowering. The direction of governing was set through the collective of the political party, in all its diversity and decentralization. As Landy and Milkis have put it, "The party system made the executive accountable to a collective organization with a past and a future—to a national institution that enlarged even as it restrained presidential ambition." The president, though an important force in the development and advancement of the policy direction, was but one of numerous influential actors. Only in periods of party realignment could presidents become the towering and dominant figures so lauded by modern commentators.[26]

The values of representation, accountability, and deliberation today are often neglected or, worse, abandoned. A key irony of the modern presidency is that although it appears to bring the people closer to the office, the appearance may be at odds with actual reality. In fact, the modern presidency has strong similarities to the model of executive power outlined by Alexander Hamilton in the *Federalist*. Although jettisoning—at least publicly—Hamilton's rhetoric about the vices of the people and popular democracy, modern presidents do routinely bypass the normal channels of democratic action, most notably the U.S. Congress, to enact policies that they favor. In recent years, executive orders, unilateral military actions, and administrative decisions have constituted a larger and larger slice of presidential actions and conduct. One major ramification of this growing consolidation of power in the executive and administrative bureaucracy is that presidents become more and more removed from the public opinion that forms the bedrock of the political parties and their leaders in Congress and in state and local organizations. More and more decisions escape the purview of public debate and deliberation.[27]

Certainly, public opinion is a major force in politics today; however, the ubiquitous opinion polls—private and public—to which presidents, their advisers, and political commentators pay so much allegiance, are a hollow shell of the public opinion that parties, at their best, fostered and nurtured. Party institutions with multiple centers of power and constituencies created a rich and textured debate and brought many different voices to political issues and controversies. To be sure, party democracy did not always produce efficient or wholly desirable results, but the decisions reached were far more likely to be "representative" and "accountable" than executive, administrative decisions.

Surely few today would argue for a full return to the political structure of the nineteenth-century party era, and rightly so. Although it would simply be folly to recommend, much as the American Political Science Association did in 1950, a strengthening of political parties without addressing the necessarily expanded role of the presidency in the contemporary world, there should not be a complete rejection of the party-era model of presidential leadership.[28] Awareness should translate into caution when advocating reform, but it should not quash steps toward reform. There should undoubtedly be a "modern" cast to presidential leadership in the modern era, but there are no necessary reasons that modern presidential leadership cannot incorporate lessons, tactics, and values from the past, particularly from the party era. At the very least, a presidency that more fully respects representation, accountability, and deliberation—with or without the aid of the parties—would be a welcome development.

This book begins with a brief theoretical exposition of the "original" and "party" constitutions. First, I examine the founders' views of parties and the steps they took, via the Constitution, to preclude the influence of party and popular opinion and thereby to prevent presidents from assuming boldly popular leadership roles. Second, to this examination I juxtapose the conception of the "party constitution," described only briefly thus far. I focus on the writings of nineteenth-century figures, primarily Martin Van Buren, who helped to provide its theoretical and practical basis. Since no "convention" constructed this constitution, one must be content with discovering only the broad contours and directions of this "document." As with the original Constitution, I discuss specifically the relationships between people and president—and the implications for presidential leadership—that underpin the notion of such a constitution. This theoretical discussion sets the context for and provides a stepping-stone into the more empirical chapters of the book.

   If party presidential leadership merits attention today, one must get a sense of its actual, historical contours. Thus, with chapter 2, I begin examining the fit of the party constitution with nineteenth-century presidential practice, focusing on the electoral environment of the presidency. As the founders well knew, the way presidents are elected is fundamentally related to the functioning of the presidential office. Through an extensive analysis of campaign biographies from nineteenth-century elections and candidates' party nomination acceptance letters, I demonstrate the importance of party and party principles in the nomination and election of presidential candidates, beginning in the 1830s and 1840s. Most presidential candidates in the party period, much against the sentiment of the founders, willingly espoused fidelity to a party and its principles and were clearly expected to carry out these principles once they were in office.

   In chapter 3, I examine the change over time in the relationship between presidential candidates and their parties in nineteenth-century elections. Through further analysis of campaign biographies and candidates' nomination acceptance letters, I track the increasing importance of candidates vis-à-vis their parties as the nineteenth century wore on. By the 1880s and 1890s, parties were increasingly coming in for criticism and candidates were beginning to overshadow them in importance in campaigns. These changes portended the rise of the plebiscitary presidency and strongly suggest the key role of the decline of party in the rise of modern, rhetorical presidential leadership (and, obversely, the possible role for parties in circumscribing the rhetorical presidency today).

   Since elections can tell only so much about the American political system and presidency, the next three chapters seek to understand the roles of the presidency and parties in governing decisions in the party period. In chapter 4, through a diachronic examination of inaugural addresses, I show the levels of importance of parties and the people to presidents beginning in the 1830s and 1840s. Party-period presidents, as evidenced in their inaugural addresses, saw the presidency as a popular office and themselves as exercising democratic leadership via the political parties. In chapters 5 and 6, I examine five presidential administrations from the party period: those of James Polk, Zachary Taylor, U.S. Grant (first term), Benjamin Harrison, and Grover Cleveland (second term). Systematic and idiographic analyses show the strong "pull of party" on the nineteenth-century presidency at the governing stage.[29] Also in these chapters I begin to examine the nuance of party leadership along an "agent-leader" continuum. From the five case studies, one can see that presidents varied considerably in their relationships with their parties, some preferring to be "agents" and instruments of their parties and others exercising a more prominent "leader" role. The leader models of Polk and Cleveland, with some modifications, I argue, have continuing relevance to contemporary politics and debates over the proper role of the presidency in a modern democratic polity.

Throughout chapters 4 and 6, I also continue to track the decline of party and the concomitant elevation of the person of the president over the last third of the nineteenth century. Paralleling developments at the electoral stage was a notable shift over time in the importance of presidents relative to parties at the governing stage. Particularly with Grover Cleveland one notices the declining significance of the party vis-à-vis the presidency and the simultaneously increasing emphasis on the person of the president.[30] Given that these changes were antecedent to the "modern" presidencies of Teddy Roosevelt and Woodrow Wilson, one is again forced to consider the role of party decline in the development of modern presidential leadership and thereby the importance of party renewal to curbing the ill effects and excesses of the rhetorical presidency.

I conclude this book by addressing the larger implications of the party presidency model for contemporary presidential leadership. First, I make a sustained critique of the modern presidency and clarify the reasons for reconsidering the party presidency as a model for democratic presidential leadership today. Second, I treat head-on the numerous criticisms of political parties in the nineteenth and twentieth centuries, particularly the claim that they have been merely "electoral machines" (and not "responsible") throughout their history. Acknowledging the very real problems with parties in America in the nineteenth century—especially in the Gilded Age—and historically, I nonetheless maintain that at their best, American parties have approximated a democratic ideal that is worth revisiting. Finally, I address the possibilities for a renewal of parties in the American polity and confront the skeptics who assert that the days of strong parties are long gone. Emphasizing impressive signs of renewal in recent years, I argue that the death knell of political parties has been sounded prematurely. Given the resurgence, admittedly uneven, of political parties, the time is right to reconsider the relationships among presidential leadership, political parties, and democratic government.

Chapter One
The Constitution and the Party Constitution

The presidential candidate has a double character. He is put forward as being individually qualified for the great place of executive head of the nation, because he is a man of integrity, energy, firmness, intellectual power, experience in affairs. He is also recommended as a prominent member of a great national party, inspired by its traditions, devoted to its principles, and prepared to carry them out not only in the proper executive capacity, but, what is more important, as the third branch of the legislature, armed with a veto on bills passed by Congress.

James Bryce, *The American Commonwealth*

Antiparty sentiment was dominant at the time of the republic's founding and maintained a hegemonic hold on the political philosophy of most American leaders, especially presidents, until at least the mid-1820s. A decided break with this tradition occurred, however, in the late 1820s and the 1830s. By then, parties were more generally accepted in the American political milieu (although they still had their prominent detractors) and, once established, would dominate the political landscape of American politics through the 1890s. This change was due in no small part to the influence of Martin Van Buren and his colleagues in the Albany Regency. While Andrew Jackson was indeed important to the development of the party system, he was quite like Machiavelli's prince in that he was crucial to the *founding* of the political system, but thereafter, the system did not depend on him; it had its own justifications and purposes, separate from his personality, which were to a significant extent the work of the New York Republican Party and especially Martin Van Buren. Van Buren had not the charisma or brazenness to be a prince, but (albeit somewhat reluctantly) he found a vehicle for his designs in the person of Andrew Jackson.

It was Van Buren's (and his colleagues') designs that ultimately established the place of party in American politics. To be sure, he can hardly be credited with consciously masterminding the establishment of the two-party system—that development was not a completely clear-cut or continuous phenomenon—but he and other local party leaders can be thought of as at least "half-consciously" framing a "people's" or "party" constitution, a solid understanding of which can be obtained from his writings and recollections.[1] But first it is necessary to consider briefly the antiparty context of the founding era.

"Talents for Low Intrigue"

It is well known that most of the founders were versed in classical history and politics and that John Locke and Montesquieu were important influences on American political thought. The impact of the English thinker Bolingbroke is less well known, yet his writings helped to shape the understanding of parties current in America during the founding period.[2] A controversial political figure in eighteenth-century England, Bolingbroke wrote a number of important political works, including *A Dissertation upon Parties* and *Idea of a Patriot King*. He was deeply skeptical of the influence of parties, which, "even before they degenerate into absolute factions, are still numbers of men associated together for certain purposes and certain interests, which are not . . . those of the community."[3] One would hardly be surprised to be told that James Madison or another of the founders wrote these words.

An even more integral aspect of Bolingbroke's thought which the founders, especially those who became president, to various degrees espoused is outlined in *Idea of a Patriot King:* his belief that only through a virtuous leader could the evils of faction and party spirit be thwarted and overcome.[4] This style of leadership, hinted at in the Constitution and the *Federalist,* is clearly a prominent aspect of the early presidencies. But specifically why were the founders so distrustful of party, and what did they propose for mitigating its nefarious effects?

For Madison and the other founders, the participation of the people in government was far from an innocuous affair. Popular governments, like all governments, were prone to certain problems, and the downfall of popular governments was almost always faction. Madison defined faction as "a number of citizens, whether amounting to a majority or minority of the whole, who are united and actuated by some common impulse of passion or of interest, adverse to the rights of other citizens, or to the permanent and aggregate interests of the community." Faction was always present in a popular government where liberty was valued, for it was "sown in the nature of man" and would manifest itself if given freedom.[5] Thus, it must be tolerated, but because it could be pernicious, it must be controlled. The idea that a faction (or, what was same thing in the idiom of the founders, party) or a contest between factions could possibly work toward the public good was really not conceivable to Madison: "The public good is disregarded in the conflicts of rival parties."[6]

The founders' solution to the problem of faction, the preeminent problem of popular government, was predominantly an institutional one: tailoring the institutions of the republic to mitigate the deleterious effects of faction, while being careful not to squelch liberty. The founders hoped that enlightened statesmen would guide the republic, and they created mechanisms such as the electoral college to facilitate the election of such men. But because they were not sanguine about the likelihood that virtuous leaders would continually occupy office, the constitution they created provided for a number of institutional checks on the exercise of power by persons or, more likely, factions animated by passions hostile to the public weal.

In *Federalist* No. 10, Madison defends the idea of a "large republic" or "extended sphere" as a way to mitigate the evils of popular majorities actuated by tyrannical impulses. In a "small republic" (a state) a majority would have little problem in coalescing to abridge the rights of a minority; at the level of the national government this danger would be much less a possibility, primarily because of distance and communication obstacles to majority formation. Moreover, the institutional construct of separation of powers worked to prevent one dominant passion from overtaking the whole of government. If government comprised merely the legislature, the chances of a dominant impulse taking over would be great; with three separate institutions constituting the government, the likelihood that popular prejudices could hijack it was significantly decreased.

The presidency had a particularly important role in the founders' scheme. The electoral college was created, in part, to ensure that popular passions and the spirit of faction would not infiltrate government through the election of a demagogue. Ideally, for the founders, a presidential candidate would not campaign openly and vigorously for the office on the basis of political issues or popular appeals; rather, he would allow his character, experience, and reputation to speak for him. If a candidate contravened this desideratum, the electoral college would work to prevent his election. Electors were given independent judgment in case the people were swayed by the wiles of a leader out for self-aggrandizement or the abridgment of the rights of certain groups in society. Moreover, that electors would vote in their respective states, rather than in a common location, was a further obstacle to passions of a national sort gaining control of a major organ of government. As Hamilton put it: "Talents for low intrigue, and the little arts of popularity, may alone suffice to elevate a man to the first honors of a single State; but it will require other talents, and a different kind of merit, to establish him in the esteem and confidence of the whole Union, or of so considerable a portion of it as would be necessary to make him a successful candidate for the distinguished office of President of the United States."[7]

Once a candidate had been elevated to office, further contrivances would keep factions and popular passions at bay. The president held the office for a significant period of time, four years. For some critics of the Constitution, this tenure was far too long; the president could not be readily accountable to the people. From the founders' point of view that was precisely the point: distance between the people and the president was the four-year term's key attraction. The president would not have to kowtow to "every sudden breeze of passion," as Hamilton put it, yet he would ultimately have to be responsive to the people. The president would act his conscience as against the sentiments of the people, whether a factious majority or an especially vocal minority, but because of the lengthy term would then have time to persuade the people that he was correct in his actions and that they were misguided in their factious sympathies.[8]

Further, the president was given the powers of the qualified veto and appointment. The veto "establishes a salutary check upon the legislative body, calculated to guard the community against the effects of faction, precipitancy, or of any impulse unfriendly to the public good, which may happen to influence a majority of that body."[9] As the legislative body was quite closely linked to the people, especially the House of Representatives, with its direct elections and two-year terms, the veto would be necessary to squelch any divisive spirit that existed in the broader society and manifested itself in the legislature.

If a congressman acted contrary to the public voice—even a pernicious, shrill one—he could count on being quickly unburdened of his seat. The president, on the other hand, was given the luxury of a longer term during which passions would likely cool and reason would putatively illumine the rectitude of a particular veto. It is important to note that the power was not absolute; the veto could be overturned. The founders, still worried about executive tyranny and the absolute veto of the king of England, were reluctant to give too much power to the president. Moreover, though distrustful of the legislative body in the main, they held it quite improbable that "improper views will govern so large a proportion as two thirds of both branches of the legislature at the same time; and this, too, in spite of the counterposing weight of the Executive."[10]

The appointment power vested in the president was similarly important to the founders. As Hamilton argued, the president would be much better suited than the assembly to appointing good individuals.[11] The assembly, being more susceptible to factious spirit and divisiveness, would be predisposed to base appointments upon the prevailing political winds of the day. The president, however, would be more likely to choose on the basis of merit and character, not party affiliation. In the case that the president made a poor choice or a partisan choice in appointment, the required approval of the Senate, markedly more insulated from the people and party than the House, would be the fail-safe of the system.

This view of parties as articulated in the *Federalist,* primarily a "Madisonian" or pluralistic view, sees parties as inevitable in a free society; what is more, it holds that though somewhat pernicious, parties are ultimately tolerable if kept in check.[12] The president's role, on this view, is largely to protect the public good and the Constitution by seeing that the machinations of factions are kept in check and mitigated. Yet another view of parties hinted at in the Federalist—a "Hamiltonian" view— would have particular influence on the behavior of the early presidents. The Hamiltonian view of parties, rather like Bolingbroke's in that it does not want to tolerate party but seeks to transcend it, envisions the president as key to uniting the people against the divisive effects of faction. As Ralph Ketcham has argued, the first six presidents were, in their own ways, trying to be national leaders who would unify the people and transcend the divisiveness of party, even if that required the aid of an ostensible party of national unification. The Hamiltonian view explains the willingness of Jefferson and even Madison, that most astute critic of majority tyranny, to abandon their fears of party majorities when it came to making the Democratic-Republicans the dominant political party.[13] Thomas Jefferson and James Madison, and for that matter James Monroe and John Quincy Adams, saw the Democratic-Republican Party as a party of national unification or, to put it another way, as a party to end all parties.[14] Parties, on the Hamiltonian view, haggle over the fundamentals of politics and hence are dangerous, for the passions they arouse could lead to the downfall of the republic.

The experiences of George Washington are particularly relevant here, for he, if anyone, was the ultimate patriot leader. In his famous farewell address (drafted, not coincidentally, by Alexander Hamilton), he summed up his feelings about party after having served his country as president for eight years. It is well known that Washington was surrounded by factional disputes, primarily the one between Hamilton and Jefferson, and that he can be said to have reluctantly taken sides in the matter. Yet doing so was not a duty that he relished. He did not preach a reluctant tolerance for parties in the farewell address; Washington acknowledged the inevitability of faction but suggested that the people must "discourage and restrain" it and that "the effort ought to be by *force* of public opinion to mitigate and assuage it [party]."[15] This interesting language intimates that the people ("public opinion") may quell the spirit of party—certainly not the same thing as the institutional checks on faction outlined in *Federalist* No. 10. Rather, there is the suggestion of a unified people opposing (and, preferably, squelching) the evils of faction.

In his farewell address, then, Washington played the role to which he aspired throughout his service to his country, the role of the patriot leader. Although he might seem to suggest that the people should unify *themselves* to transcend party, in fact, he was making one last pitch as patriot leader to unify the people against the deleterious effects of party. The five presidents who followed him all continued, more or less, in this tradition of striving to be a leader who would unify the nation and transcend faction.[16]

It is important to note that neither the early presidents nor any of the founders ever consistently or coherently conceived of parties as beneficial organizations that could contribute to the health of the body politic. They found it difficult to conceive of parties as revolving around issues that were not regime-threatening. Moreover, they had no clear under-standing that the early "parliamentary" parties that developed in the colonial and then state and federal legislatures were functional, helping to promote unity and bridge the gap between executive and legislature. As Ralph Harlow has put it, the founders, in developing the Constitution, "disregard[ed] the very agency that made possible the successful working of the whole system."[17] They saw the development of parties as perhaps inescapable but nonetheless, unfortunate and potentially troublesome. Indeed, the president was either to fulfill the largely negative role of pro-tecting the Constitution and the public interest from parties or the more positive role of unifying the nation and overcoming the divisive effects of faction. The Madisonian and Hamiltonian views were really the only available party views for the founders at this time. It was left to Martin Van Buren to develop a richer and more affirmative understanding of party.

"Political Parties Are Inseparable from Free Governments"

In the 1820s, Martin Van Buren gradually emerged as a critical pro-party figure in American politics. Although numerous events and experiences helped to solidify his advocacy of political parties—such as President Monroe's nonpartisan patronage policies—the most notable event was the election of 1824.[18] Critical of Monroe's nonpartisan presidential conduct, Van Buren believed there would always be party competition and conflict: "The two great parties of this country, with occasional changes in their names only, have, for the principal part of a century, oc-cupied antagonistic positions upon all political questions."[19] What is more, partisanship and party conflict, Van Buren came to believe, were actually positive goods to be maintained and nurtured.

Monroe's biggest failing, on Van Buren's view, had been not choos-ing a successor, a failure that created the volatile and dangerous political context of the 1824 election. It had been the practice since Jefferson for the president to select a successor: Jefferson had designated Madison; Madison, in turn, had chosen Monroe. Monroe, however, declined to name anyone, and the ensuing scramble for nomination had dire effects on the Democratic-Republican Party. When a successor is known ahead of time, the party can rally around that figure, and the president can lend his power and name, helping to ensure the unity of the party behind the chosen man. Monroe's failure to choose would result, Van Buren feared, in an undercutting of the Democratic-Republican Party and a concomitant revitalization of the Federalists. But more problematic than a resurgence of the Federalists—an inevitability from Van Buren's perspective—was the volatile, personality-driven politics that would surely result. And, indeed, the 1824 election was dominated by personal factions. As Van Buren put it: "In the place of two great parties arrayed against each other in a fair and open contest for the establishment of principles in the administration of Government which they respectively believed most conducive to the public interest, the country was overrun with personal factions. These having few higher motives for the selection of their candidates or stronger incentives to actions than individual preferences or antipathies, moved the bitter waters of political agitation to their lowest depths."[20]

The 1824 election confirmed Van Buren's fears of personal ambition and factionalism, the so-called corrupt bargain with Henry Clay that put John Quincy Adams in the White House being the last straw. An administration chosen on the basis of personality factions would naturally tend, on Van Buren's view, to privilege the elite interests that conspired to place it in office—which is exactly how he thought of Clay's plan for national economic development, the American System: as an attempt to consolidate power in the federal government, that is, away from the people and into elite hands.

Van Buren was not alone in opposing the John Quincy Adams administration: after the congressional session closed in 1826, writes R. V. Remini, "an opposition had been formed, along rather indefinite lines, which was ready to challenge every move the administration made."[21] Van Buren resolved that he needed now, more than ever, to launch a party movement. He knew that this opposition movement must be organized along national lines. Drawing upon his work with the party machine in New York, the Albany Regency, he reckoned that the most effective way to unify the movement was through the establishment of a newspaper. He pressed Vice President John Calhoun on this issue but was rebuffed: Calhoun thought that the *United States Telegraph* was doing a sufficient job in opposing the administration.[22] Although Van Buren disagreed, he was unable to get a thriving newspaper off the ground and had to find some other method to organize and unite the opposition groups. Finally, and somewhat reluctantly, he turned to Andrew Jackson, Adams's rival in 1824, as the solution to his problem. He hoped to draw on Jackson's immense popularity with the people to unite the antiadministration groups in a viable party organization.

Van Buren was reluctant to harness the opposition to Jackson because he did not want the party to be merely an extension of Jackson's personality. Although Van Buren wanted the people to have a larger role in politics (indeed, this was the wave of the future), he also wanted to restrain and control their involvement, fearful that the people could potentially be rallied to support ambitious politicians and devious ends. Just as he worried about the election of 1824 being dominated by personal factions, he also worried that a party with Jackson as the figurehead would risk becoming merely a tool for the furtherance of Jackson's ego and would therefore not serve the public interest. Thus when Van Buren joined forces with Old Hickory, he wanted to be assured that certain principles and ideas would be upheld and espoused by Jackson and the party. Indeed, he admonished Jackson not to affirm "*any opinion upon Constitutional questions at war with the doctrines of the Jeffersonian School.*"[23]

Van Buren's criticisms of the election of 1824 and his relationship with Andrew Jackson evidence certain substantive principles that informed his thoughts on party. The first and most fundamental point is that he did not see parties as necessarily nefarious or even disruptive, as did the Madisonian and Hamiltonian views. Even the far more tolerant Madisonian view did not envision a very positive role for parties in the political system; they should be kept within boundaries and certainly not be unnecessarily encouraged or promoted. The Van Buren view, on the other hand, did not equate parties with factionalism per se.

There is little distinction between the terms "party" and "faction" in the Madisonian and Hamiltonian views. To them, a party, just like a faction, was a grouping of individuals whose intentions were invidious and anathema to the public good. Moreover, there is an assumption of crass instrumentalism in their definitions: individuals form parties to benefit themselves materially or selfishly. Although Van Buren did not entirely disregard such motives, he did not hold that parties were necessarily driven by selfishness.[24] Parties could instead be made up of individuals whose goal was the general good of the community. He distinguished between factions as groups that were partial, pernicious, and destructive, and parties, which were better thought of as principled organizations seeking to hold the reins of government and acting in the public interest.

A second important aspect of Van Buren's thought on parties was the belief that there always had been, and always would be, principled divisions in American politics, clustering mainly around two poles. He was not of the opinion, as were so many of the earlier American statesmen, that national unification was possible. Rather than a faux national unity that would degenerate into personal factionalism, he preferred a contest between two sets of party principles. That Van Buren prized one party (the Democratic-Republicans) over the other (Federalists) did not mean that he hoped the Federalists would eventually be overcome or eradicated: "Knowing, as all men of sense know, that political parties are inseparable from free governments, and that in many and material respects they are highly useful to the country, I never could bring myself for party purposes to deprecate their existence."[25]

What Van Buren was articulating was the importance of a two-party system. Parties are crucial to free government because of their place within a party *system*. The idea of a system is crucial here, for a party that has as its goal the general interests of the community, as in the Hamiltonian notion of party, would be very similar to the "temporary party of national unification," which, after it triumphs, is no longer necessary and presumably dies away. Van Buren's view calls instead for a permanent system whereby two or more parties espousing opposing principles and ideas compete openly for the people's favor and thereby control of government. Those parties not in control of government do not waste away but thenceforth assume the position of a "formed opposition."[26] This arrangement is important because the people are presented with principled alternatives from which to choose their government and, hence, have an important say in the workings of government beyond the conventional choice of leaders only. (This is why, for example, Van Buren was not disturbed by Jackson's statement of political principles in the elections of 1828 and 1832; it is also why he did not hesitate to publish his own political principles when running for the presidency.) Furthermore, the government in office, under the watchful gaze of a formed opposition, is presumably less inclined to pursue invidious policies and compelled to chart a reasonable governing course in line with its promises to the people. The people are thus protected from abuses of power by the vigilance of the opposition.

Third, Van Buren was wary of the demagogic politics that would too easily fill the void if dominant political conflicts were downplayed in the name of national unity. As James Ceaser has noted, he was quite concerned with controlling political ambition.[27] If party organizations were weak, factions based upon personalities would begin to predominate and demagoguery become more likely. Particularly in an era when democratic suffrage was being extended markedly, something had to be done to moderate and restrain both candidates and the electorate and thus prevent demagogic appeals. True to his Jeffersonian roots, Van Buren welcomed the participation of the people in the choices of government, but, wary of the possibilities for demagoguery that popular participation held, he tried to temper the popular voice through competition between principled parties.

Fourth, since Van Buren clearly favored principled party contests over personality-based factional disputes, he focused much attention on party unity and discipline. The only way that a party could stay "principled" was by disciplining its members and striving for unity. In the absence of discipline and unity, party contests (within and between parties) could degenerate into personal clashes having little redeeming public value—hence Van Buren's stubbornness in trying to organize a caucus in 1824 to select the Democratic-Republican candidate, notwithstanding the ill repute into which the congressional caucus system had fallen. That Van Buren has often been labeled a mere power politician concerned only with the spoils of office is certainly not the whole of the story. Indeed, he was concerned with patronage. But for him, patronage was inextricably tied to party unity, and that unity was crucial to a principled party system; patronage could thus actually be construed as (among other things) a key to the survival of "free governments."

Finally, he thought, the party system would serve the end of democratization in two important ways. Through loyalty to the party, rather than personal reputation or fortune, members could attain positions of power as representatives in the government. Parties would allow less well-known figures who were better connected with the people (who were "of the people," we might say) to aspire to office; still, by remaining tied to party principles, these men would not have carte blanche once in office.[28] Without party discipline, those promoted to office would usually be elevated precisely because they had made a reputation for themselves as wealthy or elite individuals. Not surprisingly, according to Van

Buren, when these elites attained office, the usual course of events would be self-aggrandizement or aggrandizement of elite interests as against those of the people. Even more important, beyond merely promoting "lower-born" men to office, the party system was democratic in a very straightforward sense: it connected the government with the mass public.

It is perhaps obvious that Van Buren's party system was not the same as the elite, parliamentary-based party system of earlier times, but the point merits elaboration. Although, to be sure, "the people" did not include blacks and women, restrictions that barred some white men from voting were removed over the first several decades of the nineteenth century in nearly all the states; moreover, the electoral college system was assuming a more popular cast at this time. The party system that Van Buren favored would be responsive to and would cultivate this expanding electorate, not simply an elite class of voting white men who met certain property qualifications or who occupied positions in state legislatures. As Robert Wiebe has put it, "The parties congealing in the late 1820s and 1830s affirmed and reaffirmed the common sovereignty of all white men."[29] By contrast, "the party Jefferson headed," Burns observes, "was still mainly organized from the top down. It was not a mass party in the modern sense, with several cadres of leadership pyramiding up from an organized, grass-roots party membership, through county and state organizations to the national."[30] The earlier party system, while flirting with a mass character, had been predominantly responsive to notables and elites throughout the nation. The new system would be based upon, if not always direct participation by white men (regardless of class) at the grassroots of the party system, then at least far broader participation at the electoral stage in casting ballots for a party.

The Party Constitution and the Presidency

Martin Van Buren, then, much at odds with the norms and beliefs of the founding generation, helped to create a mass-based party system in the United States in the 1820s and 1830s. But more than just a party system, according to James MacGregor Burns, Van Buren helped to develop a whole new conception of political life in the "party constitution,"[31] based on a notion that political parties not only helped to sustain democracy but were critical to its very existence. The people would choose between parties (and their respective principles), and the winning party would work to carry out these principles once its candidates were in office. With party unity and discipline, the restraints of the checks-and-balances system would be eased and the people, the majority, would have their will carried out. The rival party, far from being anathema (although sometimes portrayed this way for political reasons), would be a watchdog to make sure that the party in office was adhering to its promises to the people. Thus, the party constitution infused the nineteenth-century political world with its participatory emphasis and competed openly with the original Constitution's unflattering view of the people and their place vis-à-vis government. It extolled the virtues of the people, although within particular limits, and sought to bring the public into closer contact with governmental leaders.

This constitution also defined differently the role and functions of the presidency. Although Van Buren did not articulate and defend a new role for the president very explicitly, there were, nonetheless, important changes in the president's function under the party constitution. First, the manner of electing the president was quite different from that prescribed under the original Constitution. The founders, wary of giving the people too great a say in the election of the president, provided certain checks on their involvement: the informal taboo against presidential candidates presenting themselves to the public and discussing issues; the electoral college. On the party view electors were to vote not according to their independent judgment but according to the party line of those from the state legislatures (or voting public) who selected them.[32] Moreover, the candidates for office were not to remain completely removed from the people—although some continued to do so throughout the party era—and were not required to remain silent on political principles and issues.

The most important change came at the nominating stage with the development of the party convention and the party platform. Once the convention system was firmly established, by the 1840s, presidential nominees were chosen through competition of the various interests and groups within each party. The ideal nominee was one who was acceptable to most if not all of the diverse groups and interests, one who represented the middle ground of party opinion. (Less ideally, a candidate would be nominated who was either not well known or so bland as to offend no major faction of the party.) This candidate, furthermore, was expected to pledge allegiance, as nearly all did, to the definition of principles articulated in the party platform, which was also a product of the party convention and the clashes and compromises between interests and viewpoints.

The electoral process under the party constitution, then, much against the intentions of the framers, tied a presidential candidate to party support and principles articulated by the party's diverse representatives at the party convention. The founders thought that presidents should be chosen on the basis of their experience, reputation, and character; the party view held that these things should form only part of the decision; another part should be based upon the candidate's identification with a specific party and a set of political principles. Whereas the founders wanted to assure the president leeway to act as he saw fit once in office, the party view tied the president to a specific course of action, to certain principles, and, importantly, to individuals of the same party in the legislature.

This method of selection had a considerable impact on presidential action in office. Given the decentralization inherent in the party system and the nominating process, presidents were compelled to respect the variety of opinion within the party and particularly in Congress. Because presidents depended so heavily for nomination and renomination on state and congressional party leaders, they were generally respectful of local and state opinion, especially as made manifest through representatives in the House and Senate. But respect did not take the form of subserviency. Presidents were not merely servants of congressional partisans; within the collectivity of the party they were important figures, armed with influential and persuasive powers, especially the veto and appointment powers.

The party view had clear prescriptions for the employment of those powers. The veto was not something to be used only (or primarily) to combat the legislature and its factions or to uphold the dignity of the presidential office and the Constitution. Rather, the veto likely would be used for policy reasons, though not surprisingly, the policies that a president would be advocating in his use of the veto would often be those to which he and his party were pledged. The veto was the president's way of enforcing the party principles on which he had been elected. In this way the veto would encourage deliberation not only within but also sometimes between parties, depending on the party composition of the executive and legislative branches. The partisan use of the veto was inaugurated in the presidency of Andrew Jackson, particularly with his veto of legislation to recharter the national bank. Jackson boldly positioned the president as an important player in the process of legislating, and thenceforth, write Sidney Milkis and Michael Nelson, the Congress would have "to consider the president's opinions about bills before enacting them or else risk a veto."[33] Although presidents might, of course, continue to the wield the veto for "constitutional" reasons, policy and partisan motivations would increasingly dominate.

Parenthetically, it is worth noting that the battle over the rechartering of the bank illuminates the power that party (and partisan interpretation of politics) began to assume in the 1830s. Political parties opposed each other and mobilized the electorate around differing explanations of the political world and political values. The Constitution itself was subjected to partisan debate and interpretation: the bank battle positioned Democrats in support of a strict interpretation of national governmental power but also a strong executive presence, whereas the Whig support of stronger national power would put Congress, not the president, in the lead. These were differences of political values, to be sure, but they were also differences over the very nature and scope of constitutional powers and structures. Many modern scholars have made much of nineteenth-century presidents' concern with constitutional questions; their rhetoric putatively demonstrates how much influence constitutional forms and norms had on their conduct.[34] The picture is more textured, however. The Constitution did engender much respect and reverence from nineteenth-century leaders, but it was not free from the considerable pull of the popular politics established by the party system.

The appointment power was another way for the president to maintain party strength and unity. By appointing good party men to positions within his government, the president could assure, as far as possible, that his administrators were beholden to the party and to himself as its titular head. Furthermore, by dispensing patronage according to the party line, the president could accommodate state, local, and congressional leaders whose support was crucial to the unity and power of the party. Gaining the support of the local and state leaders was always important to campaigns, presidential, state, and congressional. And, it goes without saying, the party loyalty of members in Congress was critical to the administration's effort to advance party principles.

In sum, the party view saw the president as the head of a political party that had as its mission the charge of government according to its political principles. The president would act in concert with party leaders at national, state, and local levels to mitigate the institutional obstacles of federalism and especially separation of powers in order to see that the party's principles were followed. Whereas the original Constitution expressed a more than moderate distrust of the people and sought to limit their influence and their relationships with government officials, the party constitution did not express nearly as deep a distrust of the people. Presidential candidates pledged themselves to certain issues and ideas, and the people were expected to make a wise decision between them. There was no great fear that the people were incapable of or unqualified for making decisions on policy and principles.

Still, the party view was not "democratic" by today's standards, for the relationship between presidents and the public was managed and moderated by the parties. There was no great probability, when there were strong parties, that a demagogic figure would arise and mislead the population, because candidates and presidents owed their success (or failure) to their fellow partisans. Even if political ambition did harness itself to a political party, the decentralized nature of the party system would likely thwart excessive presidential action; that is, gaining support of a varied and diverse party would never be easy, even on small-scale issues and policies. What is more, the opposition party would also serve as a protector of the public interest by alerting the people to any dangers at hand. Although the party view in many ways advocated more democratic forms of government and leadership than the original constitutional view, popular influence was channeled through the political parties and their many centers of power and influence and therefore it was tempered, allaying Madison's fear of the tyranny of the majority. The party view tried to carve out a relationship between presidents and the people falling somewhere between the extremes of minimal participation and direct democracy.[35]

The party constitution held certain political values—notably, representation, accountability and deliberation—to be preeminent. In fact, the raison d'être of the party constitution was representation: namely, tying those in government to the popular voice through the instrument of the party. Rather than insulating the government from the people (as in the original constitutional blueprint), or strengthening the government by harnessing mass opinion (the thrust of twentieth-century politics), the party constitution popularized the federal government to ensure representation of the multiplicity of interests throughout the United States. With political parties controlling access to government offices and with parties owing their power to a network of state and local constituencies, these constituencies had a strong claim on the officers of the federal government, including the president. Thus would political parties and their presidents and presidential aspirants be held accountable to a panoply of interests and viewpoints. And because the parties were tied to numerous centers of power, they helped to create and cultivate a moderate, deliberative democracy. Deliberation characterized the process at several stages. Nomination of the president and the setting of party policy would emerge through deliberation at the convention stage, and the normal course of legislating would favor deliberation in Congress and between the president and the Congress. Although parties facilitated action, it would be moderate and principled action, anchored in a decentralized and deliberative party system. The party constitution, then, even as it competed with some values of the original Constitution, worked to complement certain other values, particularly those of deliberation, moderation, and institutional balance.

Because the other guiding principles of this constitution were representation and accountability, party presidential leadership was popular and democratic but not given to dramatic displays or bold actions. The political party, as a collectivity, established the general policy contours of the government, the president being an important force in their development and advancement but only one of numerous important players. Public policy at the federal level emerged through a messy process of give-and-take among local, state, and especially federal party members; there were rarely directives from the presidential office. Only episodically, in periods of party realignment, were presidents able to exercise the bold and dominant leadership so characteristic of modern presidential leadership.[36]

The Party Constitution: Theory and Practice

It is the argument of this book that the pro-party view, of which Van Buren is the archetypal exponent, had become largely accepted in American politics by the late 1830s.[37] To be sure, just as the Constitution was never completely accepted by all groups, neither was the party constitution. The Whigs, for example, at times openly argued against party spirit and ironically drew their strength as a party, to some extent, from the antiparty sentiment still alive and well in the country. Indeed, the Constitution's values and those of the party constitution remained in tension throughout the nineteenth century. As the famed English commentator James Bryce noted of American presidential elections in the post Civil War period:

> The presidential candidate has a double character. He is put forward as being individually qualified for the great place of executive head of the nation, because he is a man of integrity, energy, firmness, intellectual power, experience in affairs. He is also recommended as a prominent member of a great national party, inspired by its traditions, devoted to its principles, and prepared to carry them out not only in the proper executive capacity, but, what is more important, as the third branch of the legislature, armed with a veto on bills passed by Congress. . . . In America, therefore, we have a source of possible confusion between issues of two wholly different kinds—those which affect the personal qualifications of the candidate, and those which regard the programme of his party.[38]

Nevertheless, if the Madisonian and Hamiltonian views were not eradicated from the American political lexicon after the 1830s, their place was quite diminished; the party view had attained parity at least, if not hegemony. Yet the fact that the party view gained acceptance in nineteenth-century political rhetoric does not necessarily mean that the organizational and structural reality of the American party system allowed the party view to predominate in practice. It is important to avoid reifying the idea of a party constitution. After all, since the American political system was specifically engineered to confound the smooth workings of majorities, that a majority party could assume charge of government and institute its principles is certainly not a foregone conclusion. Particularly, one must take into account the separation of powers and the decentralization of the American political system when assessing the compatibility of the party view with the reality of nineteenth-century politics. To fulfill the majoritarian purposes that the party view carves out for them, parties must overcome the institutional tensions between president and Congress; moreover, they must link their many local and state units together somewhat coherently—no mean task—to be a formidable majoritarian agent.

Dealing with the latter first, one certainly cannot deny that a crucial feature of the American political system is decentralization. Moreover, de-centralization seems to have loomed especially large in the nineteenth century, absent today's centralizing communication and travel technologies. Local clubs, state delegations, and particularly local and state bosses had considerable control over the political system; Michael McGerr has estimated that more than one-fifth of northerners were members of local political clubs in the nineteenth century. And as E. E. Schattschneider has pointed out, local leaders were often interested only in their own locales and were often unwilling or reluctant to go along with the more national concerns of the parties. Or, as Wiebe more strongly states, "Democracy [in the nineteenth century] was an agglomeration of innumerable self-protective groups of white men who restricted membership, suspected outsiders, and defended the status quo."[39]

Nevertheless, important as it is to give decentralization its proper due, it would be a mistake to conclude that there were no strong connections between the sundry local and state party organizations. While not really "centralized," the parties did establish common links. As Wiebe has put it, "Large loose leagues of loyalty [parties] were held together by pride in a common name, shared heroes and memories, a few deeply felt party truths, occasional puffs of news about lodge victories elsewhere, and the quadrennial mobilization for a national campaign."[40] Local clubs, or lodges, while exhibiting many provincial characteristics, were far from being sui generis; indeed, many local party clubs resembled one another, discussed many of the same issues, and rallied around the same candidates. The most important "connective" (or networking) forces were the presidential elections held every four years; elections were the lifeblood of the nineteenth-century political system. Most white men who were able to vote did so, in local, state, and national elections, but most important for party unity was the presidential election, the only fully national election. This was a time for party contingents from all over the country to come together in all their diversity to stake out common positions and principles, which were then vested in the presidential candidate, the standard-bearer for the party in all its manifestations. During presidential campaigns the decentralized local and state parties in a very important sense became The Party.[41]

Whereas the parties would break up into local and state contingents (with less than strong concerns for national affairs) between presidential elections, every four years the emphasis was on commonality, connectedness, and, especially, unity. Furthermore, after years of congregating for presidential elections, a party develops a history and culture that become part and parcel of the party's identity, insinuating themselves even into the most local manifestations of the party. As Joel Silbey has suggested, the local milieu, then, becomes informed and influenced by the same principles and issues that have dominated the national contests.[42] One cannot make cut-and-dried distinctions between wholly local affairs and more national affairs; they become largely bound up with one another. As a result, the parties in the nineteenth century were able to resist the centrifugal pull of the American political system and undertake more or less collective, common actions.

But even though the problem of decentralization was brought under some degree of control through the "magnification" of presidential elections, the party system still had to deal with the separation of powers between Congress and the presidency.[43] Indeed, with Congress and the president constitutionally in tension, there would naturally be some conflict, even if the Congress was teeming with the president's partisans. That tension, however, could certainly be mitigated by the bonds of party, especially in eras of strong party loyalty. Undoubtedly, even presidents and Congresses of the same party could disagree, but nineteenth-century nominating conventions generally worked to choose moderate candidates acceptable to a majority of the state and local party groupings. Hence, presidents were usually at least marginally acceptable to a majority of the party's members in Congress, who largely reflected the major factional variations within the party. Moreover, in a system where voters frequently cast straight tickets, the party winning the government, securing the presidency and a majority in Congress, was expected to do more than degenerate into warring factions, for intraparty bickering was an invitation to the opposition party to assume charge of the government for the next four-year period.

Even when nineteenth-century presidents and their partisans were unable to enact all or most of their principles into law, the party constitution continued to hold an important place in the political culture. To be sure, the connection between the government and public would be somewhat attenuated if party leaders were unable to redeem their pledges to the people. Yet the parties would nonetheless be operating largely according to the party view; they were still working to institute the ostensible will of the people, even if they sometimes failed in their attempts.

The idea of a party constitution, then, is not, prima facie, at odds with what is known about the actual structures and actions of the nineteenth-century political and party systems. Decentralization and separation of powers did pose problems for the party view—as Richard P. McCormick has said, it is a wonder that parties "were able to operate as effectively as they did in the face of such . . . institutional inhibitions"[44]—but connective devices and structures were in place, and it is not unreasonable to think that the parties could unite nationally. It is at least plausible that the party view well characterizes the functioning of the nineteenth-century parties and party system.

This book demonstrates that the idea of a party constitution does indeed capture an important part of nineteenth-century political behavior; that presidential candidates and presidents acted in ways consistent with the dictates of such a "constitution"; and that presidents had a closer relationship to the people than that prescribed by the Constitution, party being the key to this more substantial relationship. What is more, this relationship was the basis for a new style of democratic leadership that had considerable merit. To be sure, there was never a complete domination of the party view over the original constitutional one, but in their uneasy coexistence the party view held a prominent place.

Chapter Two
Presidential Elections and the Party System

Being the representative of the great Democratic party, and not simply James Buchanan, I must square my conduct according to the platform of the party, and insert no new plank, nor take one from it.

James Buchanan, "Speech to the Keystone Club of Philadelphia, June 9, 1856"

Elections became popular partisan contests beginning in the 1830s. As the American political system in general was popularized by mass political parties, so was the presidency, a change made clear by the elections of 1836–1892. Through examination of what party-period presidential candidates said (if anything) during the course of the campaign, what was said about the candidates, and how they were characterized, I address the following questions: Were candidates as distanced from nineteenth-century campaigns as conventional wisdom has it? Were appeals to the people based upon a candidate's background, character, and reputation, as the founders desired, or on party affiliation and policy pledges? Were parties merely "electoral machines" attaching themselves to a candidate simply for the sake of winning office?[1] Or did candidates have a stronger relationship with the parties and thus the people? Were candidates' principles and political opinions made known before the election and were campaigns organized around these points? Were candidates identified with parties and were they pledged to obey party principles once in office? In short, did the presidential office, at least at the electoral stage, become more partisan and popular in the nineteenth century? And, if so, what were the contours of this newly popularized office?

"He Stands Free and Untrammeled"

Drawing on presidential campaign biographies from the party period, and also nominees' letters of acceptance, one can gain a rich understanding of the political values of the nineteenth-century party era and chart its prevalent and cohesive assumptions, with particular regard for the predominant understanding of the presidential office.[2] That amid the notable changes there are also significant continuities with the constitutional values of the founding period is not at all at odds with the major arguments of this book. My aim is not to say that the constitutional understanding of the presidential office played no important role in nineteenth-century political culture after the 1830s but rather to suggest that constitutional norms and ideas were not the only important and major ones at work at that time; ideas consistent with what I call the party constitution are significantly represented in the campaign biographies. They do, however, reflect constitutional norms in several ways.

First, the layout of many of the biographies is consistent with constitutional norms. They often discuss events in the candidates' lives which are not very "political" but are important to the development of their character, patriotism, firmness, or intelligence. In biographies of military heroes especially, the bulk of the text relates heroic or patriotic instances in the candidate's life. Those of Winfield Scott, Zachary Taylor, Ulysses Grant, and William Henry Harrison contain little besides a retelling of the heroics of these men on the battlefield and their consequent love of country and public good. Other biographies too seek to emphasize defining events in a candidate's life, to the neglect of discussions of political principles or pledges. A common theme in the antebellum period is support of the United States in the war with England. As a congressman, the gallant Henry Clay, for instance, supported all the measures of the Madison administration and stood at its side to the end of the war.[3] After the Civil War, of course, support of the Union is championed. Another theme, although less prominent, is the important legal case that the candidate tried at some point in his professional career and that provides crucial information about his character. For instance, Theodore Cook's life of Samuel Tilden has a full chapter titled "Mr. Tilden as a Lawyer—The Flagg Case" and asserts that "the Flagg case and the Burdell-Cunningham case attest Mr. Tilden's greatness as a lawyer of mathematical precision and deep penetration of character."[4]

Second, beyond simply the choice of emphasis and the composition of the biographies, in nearly all actual discussions of the qualities necessary for the presidency there are claims very consistent with constitutional values. A popular way of describing the candidates is as "statesmen" who will dutifully man the "ship of state." A biography of William Henry Harrison declares that his military and civil career has been marked by firmness and integrity and that as president "he will be still more conspicuous for his republican principles, his moderation in office, his firm integrity, and his extended and enlightened views as a statesman." Franklin Pierce's past record evidences "patriotism, integrity, and courage" as well as "natural authority." Lincoln will bring to the office "ability that men can never question, firmness that nothing can overbear, honesty that never has been impeached, and patriotism that never despairs." A section of his campaign biography titled "The Statesman" declares that General Winfield Scott Hancock, "if he was not born a statesman . . . certainly developed into one." And James Blaine, "ripe in judgment, prompt in action, patriotic always . . . deserves to be the Head of the Republic of which he has been so long the pride."[5]

Furthermore, these heroes are said to be quite reluctant to campaign for and occupy public office; they agree to run because of their sense of duty and because "the people" have enlisted them. Following the model that George Washington established in the very first presidency, they are seeking office not to serve private goals and ambitions but rather to serve the public good. Prominently situated in William Holland's biography of Van Buren in 1836 is a letter in which the candidate strenuously argues against his having sought the nomination and says that no one "can truly say, that I have entered or sought to enter with him into any arrangement, to bring about the nomination which I have now received, or to secure my elevation to the Chief Magistracy of my country." Zachary Taylor expresses his reluctance to run but then admits that "if I were called to the Presidential Chair by *the general voice of the people, without regard to their political differences,* I should deem it my duty to accept the office." Franklin Pierce's modest and retiring ways recall "the early days of our republic, when offices sought men—not men offices." And Grover Cleveland has "thrice . . . received the great honor of nominations to high positions—those of Mayor, Governor, and President—without seeking it."[6]

Third, and putatively most damning to the argument of this book, are the passages, not uncommon, that discuss party. In not a few, the candidates are distanced from the parties and valorized as "independent" leaders. William Henry Harrison's "public service has been rendered to his country rather than to a party," and "he stands free and untrammeled."[7] Obversely, Martin Van Buren's crime as president was that he "sacrificed his independence as a statesman, by promising to follow blindly in the footsteps of his predecessor." Zachary Taylor is quoted: "I need hardly add that I cannot in any case permit myself to be brought before the people exclusively by any of the political parties that now so unfortunately divide our country, as their candidate for this office."[8]

And the list goes on. Lincoln "is no longer the representative of any particular political party, but comes before the loyal voters of the country as an indefatigable, incorruptible, public servant, whose multi-form and perplexing duties have been faithfully performed, and who has no other ambition than to so administer the affairs of the nation as will be most conducive to its welfare." Horace Greeley, since he claims "for himself the right to vote for or against any candidate of his party as his own sense of right and duty shall dictate . . . very freely accords to all others the same liberty, without offense or inquisition." Grover Cleveland, upon hearing of his renomination for the presidency in 1888, announces that "I will not be denied the privilege of asserting at this time that in the exercise of the functions of the high trust confided to me, I have yielded only to the Constitution and the solemn obligation of my oath of office."[9]

And why do candidates not always hold close ties with the parties? Because the parties are no great bulwark to democracy; in fact, they are detrimental to the political system. The "baneful spirit of party animosity" is something that candidates should triumph over or at the very least eschew: "We consider it a strong circumstance in favor of General Scott that he has not mingled at all in the bitter party strife which has characterized in a marked degree the political movements of the country for many years." Party activity is divisive and unproductive; a president is needed who is removed from partisan bickering and who can transcend the narrow interests of the parties. A major problem with the parties, especially in the postwar period, is that "principles have been lost sight of, in trying to keep pace with party sectionalisms."[10] Parties are more concerned with patronage and the satisfying of sectional and factional elements within their ranks and thus, principles are far less important than the spoils of office.

The foregoing excerpts from the campaign biographies, hardly sentiments that evidence a strong party system, are thoroughly out of accord
with the party constitution's notion of the presidency. Biographies that
are thin on policy or party references, cast candidates as reluctant heroes
and statesmen, and, when they do discuss party, rail at its evils add much
fodder to the argument that the nineteenth-century presidential office
was construed as a constitutional clerkship. Yet the continuing allusions
to constitutional norms are only a piece of the story told through
campaign biographies; party constitution norms and values also occupy
a prominent place. Indeed, although the founding norms are there, a
closer and more systematic look at the campaign biographies yields
a much more complicated and rich picture of nineteenth-century political culture.[11]

The Pull of the Party Constitution

For every biography containing little but discussion of military victories
and heroic episodes, there is a biography that is quite content to discuss
the candidate's partisan affiliation, political pledges, and views of matters
political. For every instance of the virtuous and independent statesman,
there is a competing instance of the good party man who has worked his
way up through the party channels to the nomination and who will,
upon assuming the office, act consistently with the party. Further, although antipartyism is, at times, common, it is not predominant, not
spread evenly or thickly across the whole of the party period; rather, it
manifests itself in particular party ideologies (Whigs) and movements
(Mugwumps), in grave circumstances (the Civil War), and in specific per-
sonages (such as Grover Cleveland). Much more common across the period are references to the democratic utility of the parties, to the idea that
parties are conduits for the people's will. The campaign biographies exhibit a distinct tension between the original Constitution's notion of the
presidency and the party constitution's presidential norms.

Clearly, the ideas of the party constitution are not simply a random
blip on the nineteenth-century political radar screen; they comprise a
coherent set of assumptions across the period. There were, of course,
changes within the party period—particularly between the ante- and
postbellum eras—and the beginnings of the decline of party in the latter
stages of the period. But underlying those differences was a common po-

litical culture that distinguishes the party period from both the constitutional era (1787–1832) and the modern period (1896 and thereafter).

The conception of the candidates and the parties garnered from the campaign biographies is quite similar to that of the party constitution view.[12] Across the party period there is significant evidence that candidates actually were expected to present their political opinions and pledges to the people. Either through the campaign biographer's assertion or through the inclusion of "political" speeches, candidates' own views are often highlighted in the biographies. Herein lie the seeds of the more "modern" conduct of presidential candidates in their direct, plebiscitary appeals to the people along policy lines and stances; however, these political opinions and principles in the party period are almost always associated, by either the candidate or the biographer, with one of the major parties. The parties channeled the appeals of candidates to the public and were seen by many candidates, biographers, and other political leaders whose speeches appear in biographies to be conduits for the people's will.

"A More Full and Reliable Account of His Political Opinions"

Of the sixty campaign biographies I used for this study, few would fully qualify as having no discussion of political issues and the political viewpoints of the candidate; indeed, often their aim was to provide the public with a record of their candidates' political opinions. For instance, a James Buchanan biography proclaims: "The object of this volume is very simple and definite. When the Hon. James Buchanan was nominated on the sixth of June as a candidate for the Presidency, the public of course became interested to receive a more full and reliable account of his political opinions, than is usually afforded them in the various newspapers of the day."[13]

The meaning of political "viewpoints" and "issues" needs to be specified carefully. As already noted, the founders did not want candidates to pledge to courses of action before their election, for they wanted officials to maintain independence once in office. A campaign pledge to the people about a policy direction or even the declaration of substantive political opinions would indicate a break with these norms. Yet a distinction must be made between pledges and political principles that are simply vacuous expressions—providing no role for the voter in controlling government, no clear constraint on an official once in office—and those that are more substantial and prescriptive, binding the candidates clearly to a course of action. The former are the expression of "hollow" issue positions, and the latter, "substantive."[14]

Hollow issues, of course, abound in all the biographies, but substantive issues and principles surprisingly appear, albeit in differing quantities, in nearly all of them. Only two of the biographies I examined have no discussion of political principles, contain no discussion of "substantive" issue positions. As William Burlie Brown has said, "It is the rare campaign biography that is completely silent on the candidate's views on current topics."[15] This point can be further demonstrated with a closer look at the biographies over time. The contests between Martin Van Buren and William Henry Harrison in both 1836 and 1840, are an appropriate and illustrative starting point.[16] In the Van Buren biographies there is no hesitation to identify the candidate with opposition to "internal improvements": as a senator, Van Buren had "called the attention of the Senate to the alarming assumption of power, by the General Government, in regard to internal improvements."[17]

By contrast, William Henry Harrison, Van Buren's opponent, is one of the few candidates across time about which there is little discussion of political principles and issues. Such statements as that he has always "endeavored to ascertain the wishes of the people, to comply with their instructions, and to advance their interests" are standard fare for the Harrison biography—the essence of the hollow issue. But even Harrison could not be completely free from more substantive pledges and statements of political principle, saying that if elected president he would do his "utmost . . . to carry out the principles set forth in their [Anti-Masons] resolutions [of 1838]."[18] These resolutions called for, among other things, a one-term rule for the presidency, a pledge to use the veto power sparingly, and a resistance to allowing the executive branch to become the seat of legislation—very much Whig as well as Anti-Mason policies. Furthermore, Harrison did craft a letter to the Whig convention (not excerpted in his biographies, which were published earlier) directing attention to two public letters he had previously written, because "it may perhaps be expected that I should embrace this occasion to declare the principles upon which the administration will be conducted, if the efforts of my friends to place me in the presidential chair should prove successful."[19] What is more, when Harrison directly canvassed the voters in 1840 (a dramatic break with tradition), he identified himself with Whig programs even more closely: he said he would, if elected, act to "carry out the doctrines of his party" on such things as banking and paper money.[20]

For the election of 1844, between James Polk and Henry Clay, the biographies are *predominantly* discussions of political principles and contemporary issues. Clay is unabashedly cast, through his own words and those of the biographers, as the representative of the "American System" and, consequently, a friend of the protective tariff, a national currency and national bank, and internal improvements by the federal government. According to George Collins, an "Irish Adopted Citizen" and Clay biographer, the "Tariff is not oppressive but remedial; it is not vindictive, but merciful . . . [and] Mr. Clay is its supporter and defender." Moreover, Clay "is the father of the Internal Improvement System."[21]

Similarly Polk's (opposing) views are made clear. He is cast as a "strict constructionist" and one who has always been against the federal government's appropriating money for "what he deems the unconstitutional purpose of constructing works of internal improvements within the States." Also, he opposes both a national bank and an "oppressive tariff for protection." Moreover, in George Hickman's biography, following a nearly identical text there is an appendix with copious extracts from Polk's major speeches as a member of the House and as governor of Tennessee. These are not hollow or vacuous speeches conveying only platitudes or efforts to demonstrate the virtue and character of the speaker. Rather, they declare Polk's decisive stands on a national bank, the "Maysville Veto," the protective tariff, the annexation of Texas, and the abolition of slavery.[22]

The remaining antebellum elections continue this trend, that of 1856 between James Buchanan and John Charles Fremont being typical.[23] Although there are, to be sure, platitudes and hollow issues in the biographies, there are also significant expressions of the political opinions. One cannot get much clearer than the statement that Fremont, if elected, would pursue a policy to ensure the "triumph of free labor—the natural capital which constitutes the real wealth of this country, and creates that intelligent power in the masses, alone to be relied on as the bulwark of free institutions." Buchanan, on the other hand, is a "true and consistent advocate and defender of that great principle of popular sovereignty and State rights."[24] These passages convey a definitive sense that a candidate was to be associated with substantive political principles that would have an important effect on how he would act in office. For what other reason would such statements be offered? If the voters elected Buchanan, they would presumably be giving themselves a president who would act sympathetically toward the South and slavery. They would be giving themselves precisely the opposite with Fremont. Among other things, then, the election of the president was to be a monumental policy decision. The election of a mere clerk would seem hardly to warrant such interest and excitement.

Not surprisingly, the 1864 election, miraculously held in the midst of a Civil War, was rather an outlier election; candidates are not linked strongly to political principles, at least not to controversial and divisive ones. Abraham Lincoln's and George B. McClellan's biographies both tend to broad generalities and patriotic sentiment—and, indeed, this state of affairs would last for several elections thereafter. "Waving the bloody shirt" is particularly notable during this period, U. S. Grant's campaigns being the epitome of using sympathy for the Union effort to gain the presidency. Grant is often portrayed as a Washingtonian figure who, because virtuous and true to country, will be the ideal president. Yet even Grant did not escape the established trend of candidates being associated to some degree with political principles and issue positions. He was, during Andrew Johnson's duration in office, quite opposed to Johnson's policies and much in favor of the Reconstruction policies of the Congress: he "was for crushing the Rebellion, not merely by armies in the field, but by such acts of reconstruction as would prevent the rebel element from regaining ascendency in the Government."[25]

Grant's opponents in 1868 and 1872 were undoubtedly taking positions opposed to his. Horatio Seymour's "protest against the banishment of Mr. Vallandigham [a Democratic congressman critical of Lincoln], his earnest appeals to the people not to sustain the central Government in the assaults they were making upon State rights and individual liberty," clearly mark him off as alternative to Grant. Horace Greeley's "policy of reconstruction is summed up in four words, a thousand times repeated in the Tribune: 'Universal Amnesty—Impartial Suffrage.'"[26] With regard to reconstructing the South, federalism is the key issue animating the campaigns immediately following the war (1868, 1872, and 1876), and the expectation was that candidates would speak (or that others would speak for them) about this issue and how they might act on it once in office. The competing candidates, amid the usual quota of vacuity, did manifest differing opinions.

Through the 1880s to 1892, the last presidential election of the party period, the protective tariff dominated the political discourse. To be sure, racial matters were a continuing concern, and civil service reform was also on the public mind, but the tariff for the most part dwarfed these issues. Of James Garfield it was said that "protectionists of the country who have kept watch over tariff legislation during the past twenty years, and who have assisted to shape and maintain the present tariff, are perfectly satisfied with his tariff votes and speeches." James Blaine had protected labor "not only by maintaining the duties on imports which protect the American manufacturer and mechanic against ruinous competition from abroad . . . but also by opening new fields for enterprise in the direction of ship-building, the ocean-carrying trade, and commerce of countries which need our products."[27]

Grover Cleveland's opinions on the tariff were not only made known in the 1888 campaign but largely formed the basis of the whole campaign. His third annual message as president, in 1887, was precisely directed to the issue of the protective tariff. This was "a message to the Democratic and Republican parties, outlining to both of them the political battlefield selected by Field Marshall Grover Cleveland for the great Presidential battle of 1888." Benjamin Harrison, Cleveland's opponent in 1888 and 1892, was likewise not reticent on the tariff; his biographies are not silent on this issue or on a host of lesser issues animating the political environment, for, as General Lewis Wallace's biography says, "a biography of him would be inexcusably imperfect if it failed to give the reader a view of his opinions in this connection."[28]

The quotations above, by no means an unrepresentative sample, suggest that campaigns in the nineteenth century, beginning in the 1830s, were to an important extent events in which the political opinions and principles of candidates were expected to be espoused publicly.[29] Much against the constitutional norms of the founders, party-period candidates did make pledges and offer platforms to the voters.

"He Has Always Acted with His Party"

These opinions and principles are not presented simply as statements by individual candidates who would reach their stations and act on these principles as individuals. Rather, the political principles of the candidates are, almost without exception, portrayed as being consistent with those of one or another of the major political parties. Once in office, the successful candidate would act alongside a group of like-minded individuals of the same party. A candidate did not yet appeal to the people in his individual persona, extricated to a large degree from partisan affiliation; rather, the appeals were carried by the vehicle of a party with which the issues and principles were identified. A candidate's stand on an issue or principle per se was to some extent secondary in importance to its function in demonstrating that the candidate was a "good party man" and would, if elected, work for the party.

In each of the cases already outlined, the issues or principles that the candidates espoused can be easily identified with a major party and its political platform. For instance, Polk's association with strict construction, opposition to a national bank, and internal improvements places him solidly in the Democratic fold. Henry Clay's support for the tariff and the American System clearly puts him in the Whig camp. Cleveland's suspicion of the tariff and Harrison's and Blaine's support of the tariff can also be seen as patently staking out positions consistent with the Democratic and Republican stands, respectively, on the tariff issue. Thus, through their association and attachment to principles consistent with their parties' ideological predilections, the candidates are identified as party men and loyalists to one degree or another. Moreover, in addition to revealing his political stands, biographers often went out of their way to stress that the candidate was a "good party man."

Notwithstanding the inchoate form of the mass party system in 1836, even then there was evidence of at least one candidate being cast as a good party man. William Holland wrote of Martin Van Buren, "It has not been the design of the writer merely to contribute to the political elevation of any man; he has aimed, rather to display the spirit and principles of the republican party of this country, and to exhibit, by the history of an individual, the nature of the relation which that party sustains to its public men."[30] The biographer was grouping Van Buren intimately with the party to which Andrew Jackson was ostensibly the contemporary heir; indeed, he discussed the Democratic-Republican party and Martin Van Buren almost interchangeably.

With William Henry Harrison, Van Buren's opponent in 1836 and

1840, the story is different. It is common in the Harrison biographies to come across either absolutely no references to party or references that are hostile to party, with the recurring phrase that he stands free from party influence, "free and untrammeled." Only rarely is Harrison identified with a political party, and that is almost without fail the patriotic "democratic" party of Jefferson and Madison: Harrison "has always been a democratic republican, of the school of Washington, Jefferson, and Madison; he detests the agrarian, infidel principles which are gaining power and influence at the present day."[31] But, even within this seemingly empty statement lay the seeds of a more substantial party association. Both Democrats and Whigs laid claim to the heritage of Jefferson, but they differed in tracing it. Van Buren was clearly associated with the Republican (also sometimes called "Democratic" and "Democratic-Republican" at this time) wing, which traced its descent down through Jackson. Harrison obviously contested this lineage and hence allied with the "republicans" (i.e., the incipient Whig Party) opposed to the "agrarian, infidel principles" of Jackson.

Once a two-party system was in high gear, with distinctions between Whigs and Democrats firmly in place, candidates associating in clear-cut fashion with parties became more the norm, as the 1844 election aptly reflects. Collins begins his apologia on Clay with a discussion of his own early support of the Democrats and consequent dislike for the Whigs and Henry Clay. Collins quickly adds, though, that he thereafter discovered Clay and the Whigs to be the true "democratic" party and the Democrats the "aristocrats."[32] Leaving aside the banality of Collins's comment, the important point is that Clay is very much identified with the Whigs. This biography of Clay takes as its point of departure a defense of the Whig Party and its principles.

As for Clay's opponent, James Polk, "From his entrance into public life, his adherence to the cardinal principles of the Democratic creed has been singularly steadfast," writes Hickman. Polk was a warm supporter of Jackson and Van Buren during their tenures and always fought for Democratic principles; in fact, he was so staunch a supporter that some wondered if he was not too partisan: "It is true that, despising the cant of *no party*, which has ever been the pretext of selfish and treacherous politicians, and convinced that in a popular government nothing can be accomplished by isolated action, he has always acted with his party, as far as principle would justify."[33]

Zachary Taylor, the Whig candidate in 1848, like William Henry Harrison, was somewhat reluctant to declare his affiliation with the Whigs, and his biographies reflect this disposition. Yet the pull of the party system and party fealty manifest themselves in an interesting manner with his candidacy. Taylor had expended much energy, before and after his nomination, decrying the party system and partisan affiliations, only to be pressured by the strength of that very system into declarations of loyalty to the Whig Party. Taylor could be pressured only so far; nonetheless, the felt need of a biographer (and the Whig platform of 1848) to inform readers that if Taylor had voted in the presidential election of 1844 (he had never voted), he would have voted for Henry Clay seems to imply that candidates were expected to affirm some minimal attachment to parties. More explicit evidence of the pull of the party system is a catchphrase (from a letter of Taylor's) that played an important part in the campaign: Taylor is "a Whig but not an ultra Whig."[34]

Taylor's opponent in 1848, Lewis Cass, not only is identified with patently Democratic issues but has ostensibly distinguished himself as a good Democrat: "He is, in every sense of the word, a Democrat" and is, in fact, so well thought of by Democrats that he stands "invested with the confidence and the regard of the entire National Democracy." Furthermore, since "General Cass has always been of the Democratic school," he is no Johnny-come-lately to the Democratic cause but has been a stalwart Democrat throughout his whole life and will presumably continue to be a Democrat once in the presidential station.[35]

Franklin Pierce, the Democratic candidate in 1852, has "always voted strictly with the Democratic party."[36] Winfield Scott, the Whig candidate in 1852, like Harrison in 1840 and Taylor in 1848, is not strongly associated with the Whig Party, yet "from his political affinities and connection we may anticipate that he will endeavor" to protect industry and foster growth. Moreover, "With a man at the head of the Government . . . [who is] favorable to the development of the resources of the country, by a proper system of improvements and reasonable protection to our industry and particularly agriculture, and maintaining our peace both externally and internally, how con [*sic*] the country fail to be prosperous?"[37] Though not repeatedly declaring Scott a "good party man," the biographies nevertheless are clear as to his "political affinities and connection." Their authors presume that as president, Scott will act in a manner consistent with these Whig principles.

James Buchanan, the Democratic standard-bearer in 1856, is seen as the epitome of a good party man, one who "has unwaveringly adhered to the doctrines of the Democratic party; accepting, sustaining, and endeavoring, by all suitable measures and efforts, to carry out the views of the party in relation to all great and national questions which have agitated the people of this country."[38] His major opponent, John Charles Fremont, was in a slightly different situation as the candidate for the newly created Republican Party. As the Republicans were not merely Whigs in a new garb, there was no pantheon of figures or party history to which Fremont could show allegiance, but there was a history of antislavery agitation to which he could pledge allegiance and thereby cement himself to the new party and its major ideas. Thus, when Fremont settled in the California territory, he made known "his decided stand on the side of free labor, and against all forms of servitude, except for crime" and his support for a "constitution which should prohibit slavery altogether."[39]

By the time 1860 rolled around, the Republicans had become a more established party with a bonafide, if short, history. Lincoln, then, had a better opportunity to be a "long-standing" supporter of the Republicans. Indeed, it was said, he "always acted with moderate Whigs of the Henry Clay school, and since the former parties of the country committed themselves fully to the interests of the Slave Propaganda, he has been found working with the party of free labor."[40] Stephen Douglas, the national Democratic candidate in 1860, is also claimed as a firm supporter of his party: "Equally in harmony with the known doctrines of the democratic party have been all the doctrines of Mr. Douglas."[41]

Even in the outlier 1864 election, a biographer writes, the "Democratic party, speaking through General McClellan, its candidate, while it demands the restoration of peace, and the integrity of the Union has not made the condition of the abandonment of slavery essential either to peace or Union."[42] Moreover, Lincoln's famous speeches defending the Republican Party and its principles are not neglected in the biographies. Yet these candidates were much less associated with the parties than the preceding ones—not surprising, considering the circumstances.

With a large contingent of the Democracy bolting the party for the Confederacy, playing up a strong association with the Democrats was not a very wise policy for the Democratic candidate in the election. Indeed, the Democrats nominated not a "good party man" but a prominent Union general, George McClellan, to convey the idea that the

Democrats were not a treasonous party. But party took a back seat to the heroism of the candidate. On the Republican side, Lincoln was primarily concerned with the ultimate survival of the American political system; he was clearly prepared to transcend partisan politics and rally the nation as one people, with little regard for the "minor" issues that are the stuff of party politics. According to one biographer, "Long habit had accustomed the American people to the notion of a party in power, and of a President as its creature and organ, while the more vital fact, that the executive for the time being represents the abstract idea of government as a permanent principle superior to all party and private interests, had gradually become unfamiliar."[43] Abraham Lincoln, one is left to infer, had broken with that "long habit." Indeed, transcending partisan politics was the impetus behind the Republicans' casting of their party as the "Union" party in the 1864 election.

By 1868, with the war over, many former Democrats who had supported Lincoln were making their way back to their party, at least in the North (the South being in an unsettled condition at the time). The Democratic Party had shown surprising resilience, and with the question of loyalty to the Union no longer paramount, Union or Disunion—about which there could be little room for disagreement—did not dominate the political realm. As the smaller, less grave issues surrounding Reconstruction cropped up in partisan debate, it was more acceptable to be a good, strong Democrat. Horatio Seymour, for example, was said to have been "educated a Democrat and an Episcopalian, and to his party and his church he has ever adhered with unwavering fidelity . . . [although] he is never impatient of opposition, nor unjust to others."[44]

The situation was different for the Republicans, who, not surprisingly, saw no reason not to capitalize on their perceived status as the party that had saved the Union, had transcended "politics" in the interest of the country. They therefore nominated Ulysses S. Grant, a military hero and general largely "untainted" by party. There is little sense in searching campaign biographies for references to Grant as a "good party man"; there are none. Grant did not, in fact, display fealty to either major party before his nomination. Perhaps even more than William Henry Harrison and Winfield Scott, he constitutes a partial exception to the pull of the party system and party loyalties in the era. To be sure, Grant is identified vaguely with some notably Republican policies, yet the relationship was somewhat attenuated, and there was no attempt to cast Grant as even a moderate party loyalist.

Grant's second campaign was very similar. In 1872 he was still billed as the patriotic leader, the heir to Washington, one largely removed from party and politics. His opponent, Horace Greeley, was the nominee of both Democrats and Liberal Republicans, a group of Republican bolters who were dismayed by Grant's ineptitude and Republican corruption. Democrats, believing—disastrously for them—that they could defeat the Grant Republicans through a coalition with the Liberal Republicans, adopted the platform of the splinter group and nominated Horace Greeley as the Democratic standard-bearer.[45] Greeley was certainly not a good Democrat: "From the days of his apprenticeship [as an editor] he had observed the course of 'Democratic' administrations with disgust and utter disapproval, and he had borne his full share of the consequences of their bad measures."[46]

Greeley had, indeed, been associated with the Republican Party. But having always been intrigued by new ideas, he was quite open-minded and not against "bolting" when he thought it proper. Yet he did not refrain from articulating party principles in 1872. He campaigned as the representative of a party, albeit a new (and ultimately temporary) coalition party, and its principles. In fact, he gave some two hundred public speeches (replete with discussions of the political issues surrounding Reconstruction) in an electioneering canvass of several states.[47] Quite important to these speeches, which were circulated during the campaign, was the Cincinnati platform adopted by both the Liberal Republicans and the Democrats, and to this platform Greeley paid heed. He did, then, represent the party style, although in an unorthodox manner, pledging to a platform of principles created by a new movement claiming to represent the public.[48]

By 1876, things were back to normal in that two party loyalists were nominated by the major parties. Samuel Tilden, although a reformer, was very strongly identified with the Democratic Party; he had been accepted early on—by Martin Van Buren, no less—as "one worthy to *think* for the party": "If the Democratic party had not been convinced that he was the best representative of its best ideas, he would not have been nominated."[49] Rutherford B. Hayes had a long and distinguished career of party service. In the antebellum period he had been a warm supporter of Henry Clay and the Whigs, and after the Civil War he was a strong Republican, especially when he served in Congress. According to William Dean Howells, "He voted with his party on all the measures of reconstruction" and was intimately involved "in securing passage and ratification of the thirteenth and fourteenth amendments."[50]

The 1880 election featured two more military heroes, but these heroes were also allied closely with the parties. Winfield Scott Hancock, namesake of the famous general and former presidential candidate Winfield Scott, was the candidate for the Democracy. His military service is played up by his biographer, but so is his party allegiance: "It was as a Democrat that he hastened to the preservation of this Union, gave his best energies, and shed his blood in its preservation."[51] James Garfield, the Republican nominee, was even more closely identified with his party. In fact, a "Publisher's Note" preceding one biography informs the reader that "the Republican Party presents a man for the suffrages of the nation, who fitly and fully embodies in his public services the grand principles for which the party has victoriously striven during a deserved ascendancy of twenty years."[52]

As the final three elections of the party period offer only three different candidates among them—Grover Cleveland (1884, 1888, 1892), James Blaine (1884), and Benjamin Harrison (1888 and 1892)—I can treat them all together. Cleveland is frequently affiliated with the Democratic party. His uncle had joined up with the Republicans in 1860, but Cleveland himself "was faithful to the doctrines he had already imbibed, and he acted with the party which, in his opinion, offered the only hope of escape from the evils threatened by a Republican success." Blaine and Harrison, closely allied with the Republican Party, strove to see that it did not hand over control of the government to the Democrats. "Without his [Blaine's] courage and fertility of resources the old Republican party would have been doomed to a long eclipse." Harrison was similarly devoted: "In his public life General Harrison has been an unswerving and earnest Republican from the first, and always on the side of the best and worthiest elements in the Republican party."[53]

In general, then, candidates were associated with political parties in the party period of the nineteenth century. Not only were their (quite consistently partisan) political principles made known, but it was conventional to cast the candidates as party men, if not "good" party men. But why was it important to be a "good party man"? What was the importance of party allegiance? The biographies also provide a glimpse of what nineteenth-century candidates, political leaders, biographers, and others thought about political parties and what roles they should play in the political system.

"Parties Were Made for the People"

In the main, candidates were cast as good party men because most nineteenth-century politicians accepted that parties served a central democratic function in the American political system. Unquestionably, there was always a healthy dose of skepticism toward party, a sentiment that did not completely die out even at the apogee of the party period. Moreover, there were clearly variations, depending on the sort of candidate running for the presidential office, the particular events surrounding the election (war, for instance), and which party was running the candidate.[54]

What is more, there is some tendentiousness in the party descriptions of the period, each one thinking of itself as a vehicle for the people and the other as a cover for narrow interests. Democrats often criticize Whigs as being "Federalists" who are not really concerned with the will of the people but try to prevent public influence: "The anti-democratic party [Whigs], regarding government as a matter too important and intricate to be trusted to the integrity and capacity of common people, cast around for *great men* to sustain its functions and regulate its principles."[55] The assumption in that comment is that only one party, the Democracy, is legitimate and that the other does not really represent "the people."

Still, amid this political cant and rhetoric one finds a different, more tolerant notion, even of opposition parties. Parties would allow the people to assume the reins of government: "The [Albany] Regency may be described as an honest ring, which sought the promotion of worthy ends through the power of party discipline. . . . The Regency guided the currents, and, by forecasting public opinion, brought about the results with almost unerring accuracy." Even the Whigs, a somewhat "reluctant" party, tended to see the election of their candidates as allowing the people to speak at the ballot box: William Henry Harrison was "the great instrument elected to carry out the desired reform" expressed by the public in 1840; by voting for Harrison and Whigs, the voters were deciding on issues of public policy. Harrison had a "mandate" to take certain actions. Later on, Andrew Johnson would be chastised for "defection" from "the party which elected him." Presumably, Johnson had violated the will of the people as expressed in the 1864 election.[56]

That was why knowing the political viewpoints and opinions of candidates before an election was so important: "Such information is needed to enable political parties to ascertain if their principles and views of public policy will be properly presented in the Government before casting their votes."[57] The parties offered pledges and platforms to the people for validation through suffrage. The founding norm, which had held that candidates would stand before the people simply as virtuous and reputable men, was openly rejected. As James Buchanan put it when campaigning for Franklin Pierce in 1852: "Principles rather than men ought to be our motto. . . . In voting for these candidates, then, every Democrat will be voting for his own cherished principles, and sustaining the platform of his party."[58] Simply electing great men would not give the people nearly as much input in the management of the government as the party model demanded.

Pledges by the parties and their candidates to do certain things once in office were not taken lightly but were expected to be honored. A speech by a "Senator Spooner" on Benjamin Harrison's presidency illustrates this importance: "He has been free from 'variableness or shadow of turning' in his devotion to the principles of the Republican party, and to the redemption of the pledges made by it to the people."[59] Lincoln perhaps best articulated this philosophy of party pledges and the public suffrage in one of his 1858 senatorial debates with Douglas: "And I say here to you, if any one expects of me, in the case of my election, that I will do anything not signified by our Republican platform and my answers here today, I tell you very frankly that person will be deceived."[60]

Parties were perceived as the means by which the people could control government, the presidency included. They were seen as democratic devices that acted in the public interest, not narrow interests. They were the natural outgrowth and yet also the protectors of our liberties and freedoms. As Lewis Cass described the American political culture to French leaders: "We are indeed, divided into parties, and this, perhaps, is one of the conditions of the preservation of freedom." Benjamin Harrison's biographer was even more forthright: "The best evidence of genuine popular liberty is the existence of political parties. They are in fact the organized expression of opinion permissible only in a state of freedom." And parties that became narrow and acted against the public interest needed to be chastened. Grover Cleveland very much believed one of his jobs to be chastening the Democratic Party: "Parties were made for the people, and I am unwilling, knowingly, to give my assent to measures purely partisan which will sacrifice or endanger their interests."[61] It hardly needs mentioning that these conceptions of party would have been virtually unthinkable to the founding generation.

"To Carry Out the Pledges Made to the People"

Quite prominently displayed in nearly all the campaign biographies were candidates' letters accepting party nominations. These letters, to be sure, tend to be somewhat rhetorical and formal, but they are a telling manifestation of the pull of party in the nineteenth century. They demonstrate all three of the major threads of argument presented above: that candidates were expected to indicate political principles and stands, that they were to profess loyalty to a party, and that parties were vehicles for the people's control of government.

Letters of acceptance, considered quite important by political contemporaries, were eagerly awaited. It is perhaps a bit much to say, with Henry Ramsdell, that "a CANDIDATE'S letter of acceptance is justly deemed a matter of momentous importance. It is an utterance made in full view of the facts in the case. Omissions of valuable points, or unhappy statements of any points, are damaging beyond recall." Probably more realistic is Edward Mansfield's statement regarding the letters of Grant and Colfax (the Republican vice presidential candidate): "They made written replies, which I add here, that the reader may see the positions of the candidates in reference to the platform adopted."[62]

Candidates themselves undoubtedly saw the letter of acceptance as important. Some candidates labored over them so much that they often made a brief "informal" response to the nomination, putting off until later—likely to allow time for deliberative thought—the release of the formal letter. Lincoln, for one, did not take the acceptance of his nomination lightly. Upon being informed of his renomination in 1864, he responded: "I know of no reason to doubt that I shall accept the nomination tendered; and yet, perhaps, I should not declare definitely before reading and considering what is called the platform."[63]

Letters of acceptance did not become a standard part of campaigns until the 1852 election; those written in the 1830s and 1840s assumed only an episodic place in the campaigns or the biographies of the candidates. For example, Holland's biography of Van Buren includes his letter accepting the nomination of the Democratic-Republicans, and William Henry Harrison's acceptance of the Anti-Mason nomination in 1838 appears in several of his biographies, but these letters do not take on a central role, as they would in later biographies. What is more, no prominent letters of acceptance were written by Henry Clay, James Polk, Lewis Cass, or Zachary Taylor.[64] Their letters are, in fact, difficult to track down: one must search party newspapers of the time or their collected papers to secure them. There was evidently no imperative to include such letters in biographies or to make them the centerpieces of the campaigns in those elections.

The scarcity of earlier letters does not mean that candidates before 1852 were not expected to honor the principles of and be loyal to the parties; the party platforms in the years where there are no prominent letters of acceptance clearly do the talking for the candidates, making any wide publicity of acceptance letters redundant. The first official national platform of principles was adopted by the Democrats in 1840. They had adopted a statement of principles in 1836, but in 1840 they designed and submitted to the people a formal platform.[65]

Until 1852, the Whig and Democratic platforms usually contained the names of the candidates for president and vice president. For instance, the Whig platform of 1844 begins: "Resolved, That, in presenting to the country the names of Henry Clay for president, and of Theodore Frelinghuysen for vice-president of the United States, this Convention is actuated by the conviction that all the great principles of the Whig party—principles inseparable from the public honor and prosperity—will be maintained and advanced by these candidates." The Democratic platform of 1848 conveys a similar sentiment. Not only does it speak of the nominee, Lewis Cass, but it lauds the service of President James Polk and Vice President George Dallas as having "fulfilled the hopes of the Democracy of the Union." The platform goes on to expound a number of Democratic principles and issues that Polk and Dallas upheld when in office.[66] Thus, although the letter of acceptance was not an important aspect of the early canvasses, the platforms performed a functionally equivalent role in identifying the candidate with the party and the party's principles.

A quick look at two of the letters from this interstitial period further reinforces the point. In 1844, neither Clay nor Polk attempted to augment or expound upon his party's platform. Henry Clay simply thanked the convention for the nomination and their unanimity; he did not endeavor to set the terms for the campaign or even comment on Whig principles.[67] Polk's letter was also very demure. He did not speak of the resolutions in the Democratic platform, but it was clear that he would honor them: he said that he would not seek reelection, to thus "enabl[e] the democratic party to make a free selection of a successor who may be best calculated to give effect to their will, and guard all the interests of our beloved country."[68] The presidential candidate, on Polk's view especially, was the tool of the party; he should be deferential to its will and not try to elevate himself above it. There was no need to make such pro forma letters centerpieces of the campaign.

By 1852, though, it had become conventional for candidates to issue formal letters of acceptance, and thenceforward a formal acceptance was expected. A delegation from the convention would generally provide the candidate with a formal solicitation for his services as nominee and, importantly, with a copy of the platform resolutions drawn up by the convention. For instance, Lincoln's notification of his nomination in 1864 states: "On its [the Republican Convention's] behalf I have also the honor of presenting you with a copy of the resolutions or platform adopted by that Convention, as expressive of its sense and of the sense of the loyal people of the country which it represents, of the principles and policy that should characterize the administration of Government in the present condition of the country."[69] The candidate would then be expected to respond to the nomination and the resolutions, at times even articulating the sense of his relationship and the party's with the people.

Franklin Pierce's response to the convention is characteristic of the tone and range of acceptance letters: "I accept the nomination upon the platform adopted by the Convention, not because this is expected of me as a candidate, but because the principles it embraces command the approbation of my judgment, and with them I believe I can safely say there has been no word, nor act of my life in conflict." James Buchanan's letter puts the formulation in even more dramatic form: "Being the representative of the great Democratic party, and not simply James Buchanan, I must square my conduct according to the platform of the party, and insert no new plank, nor take one from it."[70] This statement, demonstrating the popular Democratic mantra "Principles Rather Than Persons," subordinates Buchanan's individuality or personality to the identity and principles of the party. It manifests that under the party constitution the candidate was closer to the public, through embracing a platform that was then offered to the people, than under the original constitutional system. Yet it also shows that the candidate was constrained from making personal appeals to the people by his fidelity to the platform.

Lincoln's 1860 response echoes these sentiments but goes further to articulate clearly what is implicit in many of the acceptances, that the candidate will strive to act on the principles of the convention once in office: "The declaration of principles and sentiments, which accompanies your letter, meets my approval, and it shall be my care not to violate or disregard it, in any part. . . . I am most happy to co-operate for the practical success of the principles declared by the convention."[71] This form and sentiment is pervasive throughout the party period. In 1880, for instance, James G. Garfield's acceptance declares that "in my judgment these principles [of the convention] should control the legislation and administration of the Government. In any event, they will guide my conduct until experience points out a better way."[72]

Perhaps most interesting is the following letter by an incumbent president, Benjamin Harrison, accepting renomination by the Republican Party in 1892: "I have endeavored without wavering or weariness, so far as the direction of public affairs was committed to me, to carry out the pledges made to the people in 1888."[73] Harrison was undoubtedly articulating the major ideas of the party constitution, demonstrating his sense of obligation in being chosen to represent the Republican Party and its platform or "pledges made to the people," as he frames it. Clearly, the parties are intended, at least ideally, to be the vehicles of the people's active influence on government.

To be sure, the letters of acceptance did not always evince unqualified support of the notion of the party constitution. Some candidates were more and some less likely to espouse loyalty and fidelity to the parties and platforms. Although Ulysses S. Grant's 1868 letter says that "I indorse their resolutions," it continues: "In times like the present it is impossible, or at least eminently improper, to lay down a policy to be adhered to, right or wrong, through an administration of four years. New political issues, not foreseen, are constantly arising, the views of the public on the old ones are constantly changing, and a purely administrative officer should always be free to execute the will of the people."[74] Grant was distancing himself from the resolutions adopted by the Republican convention, carving out a position of independence for the executive, free from the influence of party. What was good for the people and the country, regardless of the party platform, would be his pursuit. Horace Greeley's letter of acceptance to the Liberal Republicans in 1872 voices a similar concern. After espousing their platform, he incongruously adds, "In this faith, and with the distinct understanding, that, if elected, I shall be President, not of a party, but of the whole people, I accept your nomination."[75]

Even in the face of these variations (and others discussed in the next chapter), the case for the party constitution as evidenced in the acceptance letters is strong. Most candidates expressed an obligation to embrace the principles of the convention and to carry them out once in office. It is clear that such pledges to the people through the acceptance of the party nomination and platform of principles are at odds with the original constitutional relationship between the office of the presidency and the people.

In short, presidential elections during the party period, 1836–1892, were conducted in a manner rather consistent with the provisions of the party constitution. Campaign biographies and nomination acceptance letters show that candidates were expected to identify with certain political principles; that candidates' political views and principles were channeled largely through the parties; and that parties were thought of as affording the people a significant role in the governing of the nation. Still, although elections provide a substantial window on the American political culture of the nineteenth century, the rhetoric of campaigns may be at odds with the reality of governance. Chapter 4 commences an examination of the governing stage through study of that transition between electoral and governing stages, the inaugural message.

Meanwhile, chapter 3 briefly detours to talk about the secular decline of parties during the nineteenth century, as brought to light by both campaign biographies and nomination acceptance letters. Despite the numerous and weighty similarities across the party period that justify my periodization, there were also differences too significant to be neglected.

Changes particularly in the later part of the period suggest the logic underlying the development of the plebiscitary presidency: the decline of political parties. In an inversion of the old mantra, the motto of the later nineteenth century might rightly be seen as "Persons Rather Than Principles, Men Rather Than Measures."

Chapter Three

Persons Rather Than Principles?
Changing Trends in Presidential Elections

The platform of resolutions adopted at Chicago was felt to be altogether incomplete until it could be printed with an appendix from the cautious pen of the Governor of New York.

William O. Stoddard, *Lives of the Presidents: Grover Cleveland*

Although political parties loomed large in the nineteenth century after the 1830s, their strength and dominance were uneven across the party period. In post-Civil War America, previously held views about parties, candidates, and their relationships to the people began to erode, especially at the presidential level. By the 1890s the parties had come in for much criticism as corrupt and stagnant institutions; simultaneously, presidential candidates and presidents had become more important vis-à-vis their parties, forging closer and more direct ties with the public.

These trends were directly at odds with the forces at work in the antebellum period. In that era, even candidates who wished to distance themselves from—or place themselves above—the parties were strongly encouraged to pledge their allegiance, and antiparty venom even from the Whigs began to wane in the early 1840s. As the editor of the *American Review,* a Whig journal, put it in 1845, "We regard the presence, activity and vigilance of great political *parties,* in this country, as alike essential to the permanence of liberty and the best security for the virtual and beneficent dominion of constitutional government."[1] The presidential candidate, quite important in the pre-party era, became less so;

beginning in the 1830s, parties assumed a dominant role as candidates receded into the background. This shift was, after all, a key purpose of the party system, according to Martin Van Buren: the establishment of a system that would mute the influence of individual presidential candidates and thereby reduce the possibilities of demagoguery and personal factionalism.[2] Focus on candidates and antiparty spleen at the presidential level, then, waned over time in the antebellum period, whereas in the postwar period, parties gradually assumed a less dominant role as candidates started to move into the foreground and antiparty rhetoric began to return.

Evidence of these trends can be found by tracing nineteenth-century presidential elections throughout the party period. Campaign biographies and nomination acceptance letters offer further support for this rise and subsequent decline of political parties at the presidential level.[3] In the antebellum period the case of the Whigs is illustrative. Initially and ostensibly a "party against parties," they in time became a full-fledged, although sometimes reluctant, party. Their eventual acceptance of the party logic indicates the gradual strengthening of partisanship and partisan norms in the years before the Civil War—in contrast to the vitriolic terms with which party began to be discussed in the 1870s, by, for example, independent newspapers and candidates who declared their independence from party (particularly Horace Greeley and Grover Cleveland). This incipient overshadowing of the parties by presidential candidates and presidents in the postwar period, reflected in the increasing length and importance of nomination acceptance letters, helps to explain the political development of the modern, plebiscitary presidency.

"A Whig but Not an Ultra Whig"

Before the Civil War there were important differences between Whig and Democratic understandings of the relationship between presidential candidates and the people. The Democrats' conception was often in nearly perfect accordance with what I have termed the party constitution: candidates pledged themselves to a platform of principles espoused by a party and agreed to carry them out if elevated to the office of the presidency. Candidates subsumed their personalities and ambitions to the dictates of the party and—through the party, its functionaries, and its principles—of the people.[4]

The essence of the party constitution was contained in the nineteenth-century mantra, often voiced by Democrats, "Principles Rather Than Persons, Measures Rather Than Men." The principles and measures of the party, in other words, were more important than the personality or even the principles of the candidates. It was the duty of the candidates, on this view, to be largely deferential to the will of the party, to be an agent of the party (and, ideally, of the people).[5] The Whigs, however, did not accept the party system as quickly or as wholeheartedly as the Democrats. As demonstrated in chapter 2, Whig campaign biographies hark back to a founding ideal far more than do Democratic campaign biographies. The Whigs generally were more interested in nominating heroes and military men, and in presenting their candidates as men of courage, character, and rectitude, than in putting the political opinions of these candidates before the people or identifying them as partisans. Whereas Democratic candidates were almost universally presented as individuals holding firm political principles on specific issues, the political principles of the Whig candidates were sometimes downplayed, elided, or even completely eschewed in campaign biographies. What is more, their relationships to political parties were often portrayed as tentative at best. But even the Whigs eventually, if reluctantly, accepted the dictates of the party constitution.

Although at times closely associated with the Whig Party, William Henry Harrison, Whig candidate in 1836 and 1840, was more often cast as a nonpartisan military hero. With Henry Clay, in 1844, the party association was much stronger; there were few attempts to portray Clay as a nonpartisan statesman. But Zachary Taylor's candidacy in 1848 again shows the schizoid character of the Whigs and illustrates their reluctant acceptance of party. Before his nomination, Taylor distanced himself from partisanship and sought to portray himself as a leader who would transcend the parties. Yet when many Whigs became upset by his anti-party stance and by the suggestion that Whig principles were unimportant to him, Taylor began to characterize himself differently. Thus, a biography referred to the general as indeed a "Whig but not an ultra Whig," quoting a prenomination letter Taylor had circulated to that effect, the so-called First Allison Letter.[6] This was Taylor trying to satisfy the demand for candidates to declare their political principles and party affiliations, since the parties had by that time exerted a penetrating hold on the American political culture, and even many Whigs had come to accept the importance of party discipline.[7] That preeminent Whig, Henry Clay, remained concerned about Taylor's candidacy, lamenting in June 1848 that the "Whig party has been overthrown by a mere personal party. . . . Can I say that in [Taylor's] hands Whig measures will be safe and secure, when he refused to pledge himself to their support?"[8]

With some prominent Whigs such as Clay still troubled about the candidate's fidelity to the party and its principles, Taylor in September 1848 released a "Second Allison Letter," again addressing the issue of his Whig allegiance. Explaining his initial reluctance to affiliate with a party and his subsequent embrace of the Whig Party, in a cunning strategic move he appeared to square the circle saying that he had been adhering to "good Whig doctrine" all the while in that he "would not be a *partisan* president, and hence, should not be a party candidate."[9] Thus, even as he affirmed his party allegiance, he also called attention to his removal from "partisanship." Although by "partisan president" Taylor may have meant simply that he would not be unduly or crassly partisan, his seemingly contradictory stance illustrates the necessarily schizoid character of a "party against parties" in an increasingly partisan era. Certainly in line with the conventions of the party era was his deference to Whig politicians and partisans in allowing them to run his campaign. With the exception of the Allison letters (and a few others) that Taylor wrote and released, Gil Troy relates, he largely "avoided the limelight after the nomination, deferring to advisers like [Thurlow] Weed, [Horace] Greeley, and [William] Seward. . . . Whigs showed their loyalty to the party, not the man. . . . The party machine worked."[10]

In 1852 the Whigs faced a similar dilemma when they again nominated a military hero, Winfield Scott. Although he had a stronger tradition of service in the Whig Party, several Whig biographies appeal unabashedly to the old style, mentioning very little of Scott's political opinions or partisan affiliations. Yet other tracts clearly identify Scott as a Whig politician who would oversee a Whig administration if elected. For instance, one Whig pamphlet, largely a savaging of Democratic opponent Franklin Pierce and Democratic policies, ends with this unambiguous statement: "With a man at the head of the Government, knowing no distinction of section or birth, favorable to the development of the resources of the country, by a proper system of improvements and reasonable protection to our industry and particularly agriculture, and maintaining our peace both externally and internally, how can the country fail to be prosperous?"[11] Presented directly in association with Scott are the twin pillars of Whig policy, improvements and protection, both of course devoted to that Whig summum bonum, prosperity.

But "Old Fuss and Feathers," as General Scott was called by his foes, was not content to be a "mute candidate," deferring to the party and allowing it to take the case to the people. Instead, he engaged in a summer tour and made political speeches under the hollow pretense of military duty.[12] Whig leaders worried that, if elected, he might "be apt to say 'my own right arm hath gotten me the victory.'"[13] As with Clay's concern about Taylor, Whigs were again concerned for the success of their principles with a candidate who might be too removed from the party or too far out in front of it. Their original creed of a nonpartisan presidency had been politically and ideologically attractive, but Whigs increasingly understood its undesirability and its potentially deleterious ramifications.

Whether the Whigs would eventually have embraced the party system wholeheartedly cannot be known, since the party had utterly collapsed by the 1856 election. Still, their reaction to the antebellum party universe is instructive. Starting out largely as a "party against parties," they gradually developed a distinct appreciation for the unity of party and the utility of a president who would act with partisans in Congress.[14] Although they retained some of their antiparty rhetoric throughout their existence, later Whig fulminations against parties can be seen as to some extent "purely ceremonial," a piece of tradition that had lost much of its relevance in a highly partisan era.[15]

The death of Harrison and the ensuing party debacle were strong galvanizing events, moving the Whigs toward the Democratic notion of party organization and unity.[16] They were shocked at the abandonment of the party by John Tyler after he assumed the presidential office; as a "spokesman for the planter elite in the Old Dominion," he had been chosen for the vice presidential slot on the Whig ticket in an attempt to draw votes away from the Democrats in the South.[17] As a former Democrat, Tyler did diverge naturally in his views from the mainstream of the Whig Party, yet the Whigs certainly did not expect that as president, he would consistently run afoul of their party leaders in Congress. Having been nominated by the party, Tyler was expected to act consistently with the Whig program; Henry Clay in particular saw the nomination as binding on the candidate.[18]

The bank bill was "a keystone of the party's program for economic recovery, and Tyler was duty bound to sign it," according to most Whig leaders.[19] The collective resignation of Tyler's cabinet (except for Daniel Webster) after his second bank veto markedly reinforced this point. This striking show of party unity by the standards of the day, particularly on the part of the Whigs, writes Daniel Walker Howe, "reflected something of the British example of collective responsibility."[20] And two days after the cabinet resignations, adds Michael Holt, "Whig congressmen adopted a manifesto written by John Pendleton Kennedy, the novelist and Baltimore Whig congressman. Gathering in the public gardens outside the Capitol, they literally read Tyler out of the party."[21] This move indicated that many Whigs, by 1841, had assumed that the presidency would in fact be implicated in the partisan universe. In any case, the extended conflict between Whigs in Congress and the "Whig" in the presidential office was enough to disabuse many party members of the utility of a "nonpartisan" president. In their very next campaign, Whigs offered a readily distinguishable party man—Henry Clay.[22]

Whig reaction to the Tyler apostasy demonstrates the richness and nuance of the Whig conception of the presidency. Although often cast as a nonpartisan conception, emphasizing presidential deference to Congress, it reveals itself to have been more complicated. The Whigs did not, indeed, accept the Democratic, Jacksonian conception of the president as an active and even dominating force in the service of the popular will, but their president was not merely a nonpartisan clerk.

To be sure, the Whig president was expected largely to follow the lead of Congress. As Howe has put it, the Whigs were skeptical of the executive as a "court party" and clearly favored the "country party" or the legislative majority. Yet this view did not necessarily mean that the president would have no role in national politics, or that he should actively rise above party. The expectation of the Whigs, a reasonable one, was that a president would be of the same party as the majority in Congress. Most Whigs, for instance, saw the 1840 election of Harrison as part of a national directive from the people to change governmental policy; campaign biographer George Collins said, "There was never before a more decided expression of its [the people's] will given." Harrison was to be "the great instrument elected to carry out the desired reforms" that the people had demanded at the ballot box. He was not expected to be a Jackson-like strong president, but he was to be a supporter of this new direction in national affairs that Whigs were ostensibly elected by the people to initiate. And Harrison's short administration suggests that he was not insensible of this Whig understanding of the presidency: he repeated campaign pledges in his inaugural address, replaced numerous Democratic officeholders with Whigs, and called a special session of Congress to deal with the Whig economic program. Yet at the same time he strove to exercise executive restraint in appointments and steered clear of the more crass forms of partisan politics, such as "assessments" (kickbacks to the parties) of federal employees.[23]

Being deferential, if not subservient, to Congress would still mean being a player in the collective of the party. In their rush to criticize executive dominance and usurpation, Whig rhetoricians sometimes overstated their case, but it should be recognized that their response to executive tyranny was not legislative tyranny. Rather, they were ultimately concerned with "balance" in the system, a balance they believed had been egregiously upset by the Jackson administration.[24] Congress would be the presumptive leader in the relationship, but the presidency would have an important role in the collectivity of the political party. Although the Whigs accepted the party universe only grudgingly and never completely, most of them eventually came to realize that "without organization, method, discipline, agreement, in short, *without party*," politics would degenerate into factionalism and stagnation.[25]

Over time, then, the Whig view converged with the Democratic view, both accepting that the presidency was to be tied to the political parties and, through them, to the public will; it would no longer be largely an independent office removed from the people and political parties. Democrats *and* Whigs, albeit to different degrees, followed the party model's understanding of the presidency and presidential leadership. The nonpartisan norms that had assumed hegemony for much of the life of the American political system were now clearly subordinate if not extinguished.[26]

"A New Migration of Political Forces"

The rise of the Republicans nearly overnight to full-fledged party status demonstrated that the concept of party was well accepted and sanctioned by the political culture. As James MacGregor Burns put it: "Would the demise of the Whigs in the early 1850s be followed by another long

period of one-partyism and no-partyism, as occurred with the decline of
the Federalists earlier? The Republicans answered this question by building a party strong enough to challenge the national Democracy in 1856
and to win the presidency with Abraham Lincoln four years later."[27] Republicans quickly inserted themselves into the party system in opposition
to the Democrats, equipping themselves with all the language, customs,
and behaviors of both the Whig and Democratic Parties—not surprising, given the many former Whigs, and also some Democrats, in the new
party.

What is interesting is the Republicans' self-portrayal. They did not,
for the most part, criticize the Whigs and Democrats qua parties; they
did not see themselves as a party to cast away all other parties. Instead,
they mimicked closely the forms and traditions of the earlier antebellum
parties. As early as 1858, in his famous debates with Stephen Douglas,
Abraham Lincoln, the former Whig, could be found conforming to the
conventional party understanding of political, popular leadership: "I
have supposed myself, since the organization of the Republican party at
Bloomington, in May, 1856, bound as a party man by the platforms of
the party, then and since."[28] When Douglas and Lincoln again squared
off in 1860, even with war clouds looming on the horizon, both men
generally embraced the party model of presidential leadership. Of the
former it was said that "equally in harmony with the known doctrines of
the democratic party have been all the doctrines of Mr. Douglas"; of the
latter, that "the [party] platform will be found satisfactory, and the nomination gratefully accepted."[29]

The 1864 election concluded a far-from-normal partisan campaign,
with Lincoln forming the "Union" party to transcend divisions among
northerners; the Democrats nonetheless mounted an important challenge.[30] Furthermore, by 1868 the two-party competition of the antebellum period was back in full swing, with the Republicans taking the
place of the Whigs. Democrats would not win the presidency for some
time after the war (although they polled more popular votes and initially
more electoral votes than Republicans in the disputed 1876 election),
but they won back control of the House of Representatives in 1874 and
thereby demonstrated their staying power and the voters' continued acceptance of the party tradition. Republicans did try to capitalize somewhat on their status as the party that had saved the Union, but they were
ultimately unable to parlay this advantage into a one-party domination

of American politics. The Democrats and the two-party tradition were too strong.

Yet even with the two-party system intact, important new challenges to it began to build in the postwar period. A main reason, of course, was the alleged (and often very real) corruption of the parties following the war. Perhaps the most significant event galvanizing public sentiment against the spoils system and, by extension, party was the assassination of James Garfield by a disgruntled office-seeker. As Matthew Josephson has put it, "From its mood of apathy or knowing cynicism public opinion veered to intense sympathy with the stricken Garfield; it expressed itself in demands for the punishment of the clique of Stalwart bosses whose partisan excesses had loaded the pistol of the deranged assassin."[31] This push culminated in the Pendleton Act of 1883, which put a number of federal positions out of the reach of partisan politics. Another major reason for the backlash against parties was the influence of an industrial class dissatisfied that national economic policies were subject to the vicissitudes of the party system. "The new economic system," writes Joel Silbey, "was too complex and their own political fate too precarious to be left in the hands of the masses and their party managers."[32]

The major postwar challenges were concomitant with and contributed to the rise and growing importance of independent-minded voters and, particularly, reformers. As Michael McGerr has observed, the "efforts of the [postwar] liberal reformers redrew the boundaries of partisanship, fostered new political ideals and techniques, and helped start the decline of popular politics."[33] The new political ideals included, most notably, "independence" in voting and a disdain for party loyalty, a push for neutrality and objectivity in newspaper reporting, and an increasing emphasis on candidates and their individual personalities as opposed to parties and platforms.

Analyzing campaign biographies from the party period, one is immediately struck by the marked rise in references to independent voters and their importance in the postwar years. For instance, in Governor Samuel Tilden's informal acceptance of the Democratic nomination in 1876, he opined that perhaps this "popular movement . . . should not extend by contagion to that large mass of independent voters who stand between the parties in our country." And Cleveland, it was said, was chosen to appeal not only to Democrats but also "to the large and increasing number of independent, unattached, or semi-detached voters."[34] Although somewhat hyperbolic and self-serving, a statement by the independent Republican Carl Schurz, talking about party in American politics in 1884, does capture the changing environment: "But happily, what an impotent cry it [party] is in these days! Look around you and see what is going on. The time of a new migration of political forces seems to have come. The elements are restlessly moving, in all directions breaking through the barriers of old organizations."[35]

Dissatisfaction with the parties was expressed even by party loyalists and by biographers who were working in concert with a major party and its candidate. A strong concern of many was that their parties were degenerating. Tilden, the Democratic reformer nominated for the presidency in 1876, had fought corruption in order "to save from degradation the great party whose principles and tradition were mine by inheritance and conviction."[36] In 1880, according to Hancock's biographer, "Principles have been lost sight of, in trying to keep pace with party sectionalisms." The nomination of James Garfield was applauded because he was distinguished "from the common run of party men by broader views, a more liberal mind, and a more intelligent statesmanship." One of Cleveland's main selling points was that he had never been a party manager or chairman and that, moreover, "he had never made any [office], whatever its character, a partisan position, and its use for personal ends was entirely foreign to his nature and his ideas."[37] Many political observers, regardless of party, were concerned about the potentially nefarious influence of party and partisanship on American politics.[38]

A notable early instance of dissatisfaction with the parties and flirtation with independence after the war was the rise of the Liberal Republicans in the 1872 election. Bolting from the Republican Party because of its abuses and direction, the Liberal Republicans formed a third party.[39] Although their nomination of Horace Greeley to head their ticket was electorally ruinous, it was an apposite choice. Greeley had been identified with the Republicans but had always expressed an independence in his political leanings and advocated bolting whenever a party's decisions disagreed with those of the individual party member. Nevertheless, he and the Liberal Republicans were not inveighing against party per se (although some of Greeley's rhetoric lent itself to this interpretation); their formation of a third party was an attempt to bring the Republicans into line and curb their corruption more than to wipe them out or to eliminate the notion of party.[40] As the liberal reformer Theodore Dwight Woolsey said of "independence" in 1878, it "is the great purifying agency in politics."[41] But these attacks by independents on the parties would eventually cut more deeply into the system than most reformers perhaps initially envisioned.

After the resounding electoral defeat of Greeley, many independents and reformers did not again follow the third-party route (even though there were quite a few third-party movements in the latter stages of the nineteenth century).[42] Nonetheless, independents and reformers remained a vital force and managed to have an impressive effect on the party system in other ways, helping to foster, by the mid-1870s, a political environment wherein, writes Troy, a "growing spotlight on the candidate undermined the party."[43] Perhaps the event that most signaled the influence of independent-minded reformers and voters and trends for the future was the election of Grover Cleveland in 1884.

It is difficult to achieve a coherent understanding of Cleveland's relationship with the Democratic Party from the campaign biographies of 1884 (or of 1888 and 1892, for that matter), or to find a clear-cut evaluation of the party system. At times, the biographies validate the strength of party by identifying Cleveland as a strong Democratic supporter and an avowed partisan, yet at other times they stress his independence from party and his popularity with independents and Republicans, implying that party is not so crucial after all. Thinking of Cleveland as either a strong partisan or an independent-minded politician ultimately proves impossible; one must see in him a combination of these seemingly incongruous stances. Indeed, Cleveland's presidency marked a time when party was still strong but no longer hegemonic, being challenged to a significant degree by independent and antiparty sentiment.

The election of 1884 featured the good party man James G. Blaine for the Republicans and Grover Cleveland for the Democrats. Blaine was inextricably tied to the Republicans, having been, among other things, Speaker of the House of Representatives. As a campaign biographer put it, without a hint of the changing tenor of the times, "It is more as a party leader and organizer than as a statesman in the strict sense of the term that Mr. Blaine has been most successful."[44] But Blaine was too much of a party "organizer" for his times, too closely associated with the corruption of the party machines. He himself had engaged in dubious financial deals over the years and was reputed to have used his position as Speaker for personal gain.[45] Because of this shady past, Blaine was anathema to liberal reformers (inside and outside of the Republican Party) who were already skeptical of parties; to them, his nomination only further proved their suspicions that parties were, in fact, corrupt. Democrats, seizing the opportunity, nominated Grover Cleveland, a man associated with the Democratic Party, yet one who had an unblemished record of probity and a reputation for independence in the political realm.

Democratic Party leaders sometimes complained of Cleveland's independence. "He is above all a Cleveland man and he has no use for any who are not like himself, Cleveland men," lamented one.[46] Yet precisely his independence and willingness to flout party constraints were key features of Cleveland's appeal. The *New York Times* said in his praise that he was above "partisan bias, indifferent to such party interests as are in conflict with official probity and the public welfare."[47] Carl Schurz pointed out approvingly that Cleveland "need only follow his own example in order to adopt from any party what is good, and to reject, even coming from his own party, what is bad." Pendleton King, a Cleveland biographer, summing up Cleveland's virtues, said that "he probably rests under fewer obligations to his own party than any other prominent man in it; as President he will therefore be able to follow out thoroughly the principles of reform in selecting his Cabinet, in making appointments to office, and in outlining his policy."[48] And Cleveland would not disappoint as president, working to elevate his person above his party. Indeed, according to a recent biographer, Richard Welch, "Grover Cleveland's tenure provides the essential preface to the evolution of the modern presidency in the McKinley-Roosevelt administrations."[49]

This trend toward independence and antipartyism in presidential electoral politics had a distinct counterpart in the realm of journalism. Evident in the postwar period was the rise of independent journalism and the subsequent decline of the party presses and newspaper partisanship. These developments are salient, for the rise of independence in journalism was influenced by and, in turn, fueled the decline of partisanship in the electorate and government, particularly at the national, presidential level. The nature of the newspapers changed substantially. Important technological changes coupled with new ways of presenting the news raised their circulation rates and their prosperity. Whereas many antebellum newspapers had had to be sustained by party subsidies or government contracts, postwar papers were more profitable and run like businesses.[50] In fact, newspapers *became* businesses instead of largely the organs of parties or of editors with political agendas. As Michael Schudson explains, "When Lincoln broke from the policy of maintaining a semiofficial organ among the Washington newspapers, the traditional link between paper and party, at least on the national level, was conclusively broken."[51] One important reason was editors' discovery that they could sell more newspapers by focusing less on politics and more on human interest stories; hence, with politics a smaller concern, partisanship was also less prominent. Further, a significant number of editors and a rising class of professional journalists believed that the people no longer wanted partisan coloring of the news and, in any event, that slanted reporting was unprofessional.[52]

Interestingly, more than a few members of the postwar liberal reform movement were editors and journalists—Horace Greeley and Whitelaw Reid only the most prominent among them. These reformer-journalists were instrumental in developing a style of news reporting that veered from the strict party standard of the antebellum years: "Re-examining the relationship of the press and the parties," writes McGerr, "these men promulgated a new code known as 'independent journalism.'"[53] Still, as with the independent movement in general, there was an ambivalence to independence in journalism. The original concern was to discipline or "purify" the parties, rather than abolish them. Gradually, though, independence came to mean, for many, more than a cleansing of the parties; it came to mean a denouncing of parties as such—which others found unsettling. As Whitelaw Reid commented, "It never occurred to me that in refusing to obey blindly every behest of party it was necessary to keep entirely aloof of party—to shut one's self from the sole agency through which, among a free people, lasting political results can be attained."[54]

Of course, editors did not fashion out of thin air the declining partisan culture; they responded to, reinforced, and to an extent, abetted the trend toward independence. As Frank Luther Mott has put it: "Doubtless the widespread loosening of party bonds and relaxation of party loyalties contributed to newspaper 'independence,' though it is probable that the contribution was reciprocal—that is, the changing function of the newspaper, caused by the advent of the popular cheap press, probably did much to weaken the old party solidarity. After all, the partisan newspaper had been one of the leading means of keeping party members convinced and faithful." None of this should be taken to suggest, however, that papers did not still lean toward one of the major parties. Even though, as Mott reports, "by 1880 one-fourth of the newspapers were listed in the directories as 'independent,' 'neutral,' or merely 'local'; and by 1890 the proportion had reached one-third," a sizable majority of papers in the postwar period were still partisan; the pull of party was still extensive.[55] But it is plain that many major news organs were growing skeptical of blind loyalty to party, and more than a few questioned wholesale the idea of party. Moreover, these trends toward independence among reformers, newspapermen, and (increasingly) voters were having significant effects on the political system. In particular, the presidency was becoming a far more important institution in U.S. government and society.

"To Place the Party under His Leadership"

Accompanying the postwar trends toward antipartyism and independence at the polls and in the news was an increasing competition between candidate and party for the political limelight. In the antebellum party period, candidates for the presidency had generally stayed out of the public eye, relying on party workers and leaders to broadcast their names and candidacies. Moreover, a candidate usually refrained from issuing even broad *written* statements to the public; his views would reach the people through campaign biographies, through the party newspapers, and through the candidate's acceptance of the party platform. According to Gil Troy, "The party model worked best with a mute candidate. The party machinery selected, the party newspapers promoted, and the party members elected, the president."[56] In short, most communications with the public were undertaken on behalf of the candidates by their partisans. The party was at the center in conducting the campaign, showcasing the candidate, and broadcasting the message.

After the Civil War, however, candidates became more likely to present themselves to the people. Where stump speakers and party workers had carried on the campaign, candidates gradually began to assume a larger role. By 1860, Stephen Douglas had already canvassed the country extensively in his bid for the presidency.[57] Horatio Seymour and Horace Greeley followed suit in 1868 and 1872, respectively. James Garfield developed a new method in 1880 (later used by other presidential hopefuls): in his "front-porch" approach, writes Robert Dinkin, he "offered a few well-chosen words to some of the many groups of visitors who journeyed by rail to his home in Mentor, Ohio."[58] And, of course, by the first decade of the twentieth century, William Jennings Bryan had completed three major speaking tours of the United States on behalf of his own presidential bid. With their increasing public involvement in campaigns as the nineteenth century came to a close, candidates were starting to rival their parties.

One gauge of this competition between candidate and party is the increasing length and prominence of presidential nominees' letters of acceptance in the postwar period. Party nominees crafted longer letters of acceptance over time, and after Cleveland in 1892, they would also "appear at a public notification ceremony to deliver an acceptance speech."[59] Additionally, the letter of acceptance, largely a formality in the antebellum period, began to assume a chief place in the campaign; in it the presidential candidate could sharpen the party platform and in some cases set the terms for the upcoming campaign. In a sense there were increasingly two platforms: the original party platform and the presidential candidate's letter platform.

As table 1 indicates, letters of acceptance increased in length markedly over time. Before 1868, none of the sixteen major party candidates crafted a letter of more than two thousand words. Indeed, ten of the sixteen letters are less than a thousand words, Henry Clay taking the prize for least prolix. From 1868 through 1892, however, seven of fourteen candidates wrote letters exceeding two thousand words (Blaine commanded the top spot with a dilatory letter of well over five thousand), and only three are under one thousand words—two from General Grant, a man reluctant to expound on party matters and notorious for his reticence, and the third by Winfield Scott Hancock, which was roundly derided in newspaper accounts for its lack of substance.

Furthermore, there seems to be a relationship between the length of letters and their prominence in the campaigns. Many of the shorter letters written before the Civil War were not given any space in campaign biographies or even mentioned. Brief and reserved acceptance letters were the antebellum convention, even in the face of grave circumstances. There were, of course, exceptions. For instance, James Buchanan's relatively long letter in 1856 did stress several planks of the Democratic platform, particularly the slavery plank. Most likely, though, had not it been

Table 1. Length of Nineteenth-Century Major Party Nominees' Acceptance Letters

Election	Candidate	Party	Number of Words[a]
1836	Harrison	Whig	N/A[b]
	Van Buren	Democratic	1,360
1840	Harrison	Whig	400
	Van Buren	Democratic	N/A[c]
1844	Clay	Whig	130
	Polk	Democratic	330
1848	Taylor	Whig	190
	Cass	Democratic	1,320
1852	Scott	Whig	720
	Pierce	Democratic	400
1856	Fremont	Republican	1,110
	Buchanan	Democratic	1,460
1860	Lincoln	Republican	140
	Douglas	Democratic	780
1864	Lincoln	Union/Republican	200
	McClellan	Democratic	800
1868	Grant	Republican	220
	Seymour	Democratic	2,300
1872	Grant	Republican	250
	Greeley	Joint Nomination[d]	1,020
1876	Hayes	Republican	1,410
	Tilden	Democratic	5,240
1880	Garfield	Republican	1,890
	Hancock	Democratic	850
1884	Blaine	Republican	5,450
	Cleveland	Democratic	1,400
1888	Harrison	Republican	2,830
	Cleveland	Democratic	3,860
1892	Harrison	Republican	2,330
	Cleveland	Democratic	2,530

[a]Letters with fewer than five hundred words were precisely counted and rounded to the nearest ten. Word counts for those letters of more than five hundred words are approximate: average words/line (×) number of lines, rounded to the nearest ten.

[b]Whigs did not hold a convention in 1836.

[c]No record exists of a letter from Van Buren accepting the nomination in 1840. It must have been considered unnecessary, as he would clearly seek the office for a second term. See Elizabeth West, ed., *Calendar of the Papers of Martin Van Buren* (Washington, D.C.: Government Printing Office, 1910).

[d]Greeley ran jointly as a Liberal Republican and a Democrat. The word count for his letter is an average of his acceptances (similar in length) to both parties.

for the turmoil over slavery at the time, Buchanan would have found it unnecessary to expostulate in his letter. Moreover, he took pains to stress his fidelity to the platform of the Democratic Party: "To this platform I intend to confine myself throughout the canvass, believing that I have no right, as the candidate of the democratic party, by answering interrogatories, to present new and different issues before the people."[60]

Lincoln certainly could have used pressing events to justify lengthy letters in 1860 and 1864, but he opted to produce very short and reserved acceptances.[61] Douglas as well could easily have justified a lengthy outline of his principles and ideas, yet he kept his letter rather brief. He did mention the conflict over federal intervention with slavery in the territories and advocated noninterference, but he did not outline a plan or list his principles or in any way augment the platform of resolutions. He primarily laid emphasis on its overall direction and sense. After the Civil War, though, candidates' letters would become practically obligatory in the campaign biographies and eagerly awaited, for in an important sense they set the terms for the upcoming campaign; the person was beginning to vie with the party for the political spotlight.[62]

With George McClellan in 1864, one starts to see not only the importance placed by political observers on the letter of acceptance but also a candidate distancing himself from a platform. McClellan was unhappy with the Democratic Party platform's suggestion that peace should come before a reunion of the states, and he made his opinion known in his letter of acceptance: "The Union is the one condition of peace—we ask no more."[63] McClellan, then, distinctly disavowed one plank of the platform and put himself into competition with the platform. What is more, during this election the Democrats circulated a campaign tract called *The Democratic Platform*, which was in fact not the party platform at all but McClellan's letter of acceptance.[64] Although this publication was perhaps an aberration—the result of McClellan's need to distance himself from a Democratic Party that was perceived in some circles as treasonous—it would not be long before all candidates and their letters of acceptance assumed much more importance and began to compete with the party platform for attention in the campaigns.

In the immediate postwar period, in 1868 and 1872 particularly, the candidates' letters were either very short and to the point (simply affirming the platform), or they first commented on the state of political affairs but then affirmed the platform without much ado. Grant, for instance, was very brief; his letters simply acknowledged the nomination and accepted the resolutions of the convention. Yet even as Grant accepted the resolutions, he also distanced himself from them, playing in part the role of the patriot leader. In 1868, for example, after endorsing the resolutions, he contradictorily added: "In times like the present it is impossible, or at least eminently improper, to lay down a policy to be adhered to, right or wrong, through an administration of four years. New political issues, not foreseen, are constantly arising, the views of the public on old ones are constantly changing, and a purely administrative officer should always be left free to execute the will of the people."[65] Thus, even as Grant accepted the resolutions, he appeared to undermine the idea of accepting them and acting with his party. This style of Grant's was clearly an anomaly, however, for the patriot leader was an anachronism.

Although Horatio Seymour in 1868 and Horace Greeley in 1872 both adhered quite closely to the traditional form in their acceptance letters, Seymour pushed against the boundaries, his fairly lengthy letter commenting rather extensively on the contemporary political environment. Seymour said that he delayed sending the letter "for the purpose of seeing what light the action of Congress would throw upon the interests of the country."[66] He thus assumed an important position for himself in the Democratic Party: he was surveying the political landscape so as to comment on the magnitude of the current election and the necessity of a Democratic victory. Seymour seemed to place himself in the role of Democratic leader, acting for the party in interpreting the political environment. But he did not stress any particular issues for the campaign or suggest new issues to the party and voters. He merely recorded some recent political events, criticized the Republicans, and suggested that a change in the parties was necessary. Nevertheless, however modestly, Seymour carved out a new and broader role for the candidate.

Greeley's letter accepting the Liberal Republican nomination was unusual in that he rewrote the party's resolutions.[67] Yet he did not vary the sense and principles of the platform; moreover, his inclusion of it, even if rewritten, demonstrates that Greeley took seriously his acceptance of a nomination based upon these resolutions. Certainly his rewriting was brazen and may indeed have implied a changing role for candidates; his letter, nevertheless, was essentially consistent with the previously established conventions in acceptance letters.

In the 1876 election, candidates continued to push against the conventions of the acceptance letter. Both Hayes and Tilden crafted rather long letters that expounded on and clarified their platforms, Tilden requiring over five thousand words for his exposition. By the 1880s the trend was widespread: candidates were consistently writing longer and more involved letters, and the public and politicians were paying more attention to them. James Garfield's acceptance of the Republican nomination in 1880 went on at length about the various planks in the Republican platform: "I cordially indorse the principles set forth in the platform adopted by the convention. . . . I venture, however, to make special mention of some of the principal topics which are likely to become subjects of discussion."[68] Although somewhat similar to Seymour's survey of the political landscape, Garfield's letter actually addressed the platform point by point, expostulating on nearly all the planks rather than simply restating them, as Greeley had done. That Garfield felt the need to discuss the provisions in the platform (and "make special mention" of some) is telling: it indicates that candidates increasingly felt obligated to speak with their own voices rather than let the platform speak for them. Evidently, it was no longer sufficient solely to affirm the resolutions of the convention. Increasingly, a candidate would carve out a special place for himself and help to shape the upcoming campaign by giving attention to certain planks.

Further evidence for this felt need was the reaction to General Hancock's letter accepting the Democratic nomination in 1880. Hancock wrote a very vague and short letter espousing fidelity to the Constitution, articulating his philosophy of government, and discussing recent political history; he did not address the principles of the platform or even his own political views. What is interesting is that Hancock was lambasted for *not* discussing political principles and mapping out his relationship to the issues. Leonard Dinnerstein reports, "*Harper's Weekly* thought that the speech had 'a certain child-like innocence' while the other national news weekly, *The Nation,* opined found [*sic*] that 'no one but a scoundrel or a person of defective understanding would dispute a single proposition contained in it.'"[69] But because Hancock had not talked about his views on serious issues or principles, he was extensively criticized.

Later in the decade, candidates and their letters of acceptance assumed even more prominent roles in the campaigns. British commentator James Bryce, surveying the American political system at the turn of the century, explained: "The first step [of the campaign] is for each nominated candidate to accept his nomination in a letter, sometimes as long as a pamphlet, setting forth his views of the condition of the nation and the policy which the times require. Such a letter is meant to strike the keynote for the whole orchestra of orators. It is, of course, published everywhere, extolled by friendly and dissected by hostile journals. Together with the 'platform' adopted at the national party convention, it is the official declaration of party principles, to be referred to as putting the party case, no less than the candidate himself, before the nation."[70] No longer would candidates get away with merely endorsing the resolutions in the platform; additionally, they would without fail, take care to discuss them more deeply, to clarify their own views on various planks, and to highlight certain issues for the campaign. This highlighting of issues was perhaps the most notable development. More and more, candidates were to be proactive in the campaign, especially in setting the terms for the upcoming canvass, a task previously left in the hands of the party convention and the platform committee; it was a far larger role than candidates had traditionally assumed. A Blaine biography of 1884, published before his formal acceptance, speaks of Blaine's letter as being eagerly awaited. It is as if the party platform of resolutions was no longer sufficient; the presidential candidate had to put his individual stamp on them. Indeed, says the campaign biographer, Blaine's "aim [in the forthcoming letter] will evidently be to place the party under his leadership upon the platform of American destiny in the fullest sense of the term."[71]

Notice the phrase "place the party under his leadership," for it indicates a changed understanding of the candidate's relationship to the party. No longer simply subservient to the platform, he was beginning to vie with the party and the platform; otherwise, why would he need to do more than merely affirm the resolutions and agree to honor them if elected? Blaine did not disappoint: he wrote a very lengthy letter (the longest in my sample) in which he "venture[d] to accompany the acceptance with some observations upon the questions involved in the contest."[72]

The acceptance letter of Blaine's opponent, Grover Cleveland, was treated as a similarly important pronouncement. According to William Stoddard, a Cleveland biographer, "The platform of resolutions adopted at Chicago was felt to be altogether incomplete until it could be printed with an appendix from the cautious pen of the Governor of New York."[73] Stoddard may have been exaggerating, but there was surely a kernel of truth in the statement; the platform *was* felt to be "altogether incomplete" until Cleveland's letter was appended. In the antebellum period, acceptance letters had not been taken to hold such importance to the campaign. For a party to wait until a candidate had set the terms of the upcoming canvass would have been quite out of character; it likely would have been thought insolent for a candidate or his admirers to place so much emphasis on the individual nominee, rather than on the decided "will of the people" expressed in a party convention.

The sentiment conveyed in this Cleveland biography, then, was a far cry from the "Principles Rather Than Persons" sentiment that was prominent in the antebellum period. Cleveland was expected to stress certain points, expound on others, and set the tenor of the upcoming campaign. Like Blaine, Cleveland (as well as Harrison in 1888 and 1892) was expected to put the party under his leadership to some degree, rather than subordinate himself to the party and its platform and recede into the background, letting the party drive the campaign.[74]

As a culmination of the growing emphasis on candidates, notification ceremonies that included public acceptance speeches by the nominees became the norm in the 1890s. These affairs were watched closely—further evidence that the conventional relationship between candidates and their parties was changing significantly. Whereas Lincoln took umbrage at the notion of a candidate veering from a party platform, the later candidate would sometimes seek to grab attention away from the platform, weave his own interpretation of it, or even address different issues. Little by little, postwar candidates assumed a larger role in campaigns vis-à-vis their parties; increasingly, they would forge direct relationships with the American public and undercut the role of the party as connector between government and people. As Gil Troy has said, "Over the years, the notification committee grew to represent the party, in all its diversity. In the public notification, the active candidate embraced the people and the nation."[75]

The Progressive movement brought further evidence of the growing tensions between candidates and parties, between direct and mediated forms of popular control of government. According to Sidney Milkis, "Progressive democracy would reach its fulfillment in an alliance between public opinion and the autonomous executive . . . freed from the constraints of localized party organizations and practices."[76] Although the development of the modern, plebiscitary presidency was clearly uneven (witness the presidencies of Taft, Harding, Coolidge, Hoover, and even Eisenhower), by the turn of the century, parties and their candidates (and presidents) were in serious competition for the political limelight, a competition that would continue for many years. In time, however, the contest had a clear victor: "persons" so triumphed over "principles" (read "parties") that in 1996, Republican nominee Bob Dole could say he had not read the party platform upon which he was nominated. More to the point, very few political observers noticed or cared about this apostasy.

The evidence, then, suggests that the nineteenth-century understanding of the relationship between party and candidate (and, by implication, party and presidency) began to change in the twilight of the century; that candidates, hitherto subservient to the party, were now competing with their parties for the political limelight and, to a certain degree, were becoming independent of the parties as well. This behavior is of a piece with the trends toward reformism and antipartyism in the postwar period: as parties came in for criticism and "independence" was on the rise, it was natural for candidates to assume a greater role in campaigns and politics. Parties dominated the political scene for nearly forty years, but as they began to lose their power, presidential candidates, and the presidency, moved in to fill the void.

Gil Troy has captured the essence of this development when discussing William Jennings Bryan and Theodore Roosevelt: "Born nearly twenty years after McKinley, they grew up in a political culture increasingly skeptical of parties and cordial to bold democratic leadership. They excited the people, not merely the partisans."[77] Presidential candidates writing longer and longer letters of acceptance (that is, candidates taking on a larger role in the campaign) is part and parcel of these trends toward independence, denigration of the parties, and praise of direct, democratic leadership.

None of this however, should be taken to imply that the end of the nineteenth century signaled a triumph of "personality" over "principles"; that antinomy is something of a red herring as far as this argument is concerned. To be sure, a shift of emphasis to "persons" rather than "parties" was a necessary preliminary in the movement toward the personality politics of the twentieth century but did not in any necessary or immediate sense imply the dominance of personality and the absence of issues in presidential campaigns.[78] As Michael McGerr has demonstrated, the partisan style of nineteenth-century campaigning was followed in the late stages of the century by an "educational" style that sought to downplay partisanship, appeal to independent voters, and educate the mass public; indeed, Cleveland viewed his independence from the Democratic Party in the 1888 election partly as a way for him to be *principled*.[79] Over time, though, these trends would culminate in presidential campaigns that were in general just as likely to revolve around the personality of the candidates as to focus on political issues or party platforms. McGerr concludes, "As politicians and journalists quickly understood, personality was overshadowing partisanship. After the turn of the century, they began to interpret elections as personality contests."[80]

The evidence gleaned from campaign biographies and party nominees' letters of acceptance suggests that in the years after the Civil War, at the presidential level, parties were increasingly discussed in vitriolic terms, independence in politics and journalism became marked, and presidential candidates and presidents began to compete with their parties for the political spotlight. Although this conclusion may seem incongruous with my aim of examining the party constitution and its hold on the nineteenth century, it has not been my intention to avoid the subtlety and complexity of the nineteenth-century political world. Constitutional values remained important in that century, even as partisan values increasingly come to overshadow them; similarly, although these partisan values had a dominant sway over the latter two-thirds of the century, they were likewise challenged, particularly in the post-Civil War period. But beyond merely cataloguing the richness and nuance of the party period, I want to address a weighty theoretical debate regarding the development of "modern" presidential leadership and the role of political parties therein. Jeffrey Tulis has notably argued that the plebiscitary or, in his idiom, "rhetorical" presidency predated the decline of political parties and that one is not looking "deep enough" when one sees the decline of party as leading to the plebiscitary presidency. The evidence assembled here, however, suggests that although the lines of causality are not fully clear, party was in significant decline *before* Teddy Roosevelt and Woodrow Wilson come on the scene. The reason for my disagreement with Tulis's position is that he construes the decline of party rigidly and legally, whereas I focus more on the decline of party in the political culture than on legal reforms and when they came to pass. For Tulis, party decline did not really come about until substantial party reforms were enacted, such as presidential primaries. Because of his stringent criteria for party decline, Tulis can suggest that plebiscitary leadership might even have *caused* the decline of party.[81]

Yet, consonant with revisionist interpretations of the so-called "golden era of parties," my research suggests that party was called into question and delegitimated to a significant extent before Progressive party reforms were enacted in the early twentieth century. In fact, it would seem that the Progressive reforms helped to solidify trends that were already well under way.[82] The writings and actions of journalists, "independent" reformers, political observers, and presidential candidates themselves attest, to quote Schurz again, that there was "a new migration of political forces" at work in the postwar period, and it seems plausible that the plebiscitary presidency followed in the wake of this "migration"—the decline of political parties—instead of the other way around.

A more system-oriented approach, rather than a presidency-centered one, is needed to understand the development of the modern, rhetorical presidency. With the American system of political parties in significant decline at the turn of the century, the office of the presidency was naturally affected in a significant manner. Changes in the presidency were, in an important sense, byproducts of quite marked changes in the political system. As Gerald Gamm and Renee Smith have put it, "Because it led to the development of candidate-centered campaigns, the demise of parties transformed the presidency into a governing institution that rested on direct appeals to the public."[83]

As early as the 1830s, the presidency was in an important sense an office of the people. Although the relationship between the people and the presidency was transacted with party currency and predominantly through elections, there was nevertheless a substantial connection between the two. The people desired to be closer to their national leaders, and parties acted as intermediaries.[84] But parties not only connected the people with their presidents; they kept some distance between the two as well. As a dam regulates the flow of water, so did the parties regulate and control the flow of popular influence on the American presidency. Yet like a weakened dam, enfeebled parties could no longer adequately control the flow of public influence. Thus, it is not surprising that when parties began to decline, there was a concomitant rise in direct relationships between presidential candidates or presidents and the public.

After Jackson became the "tribune of the people" there was no turning back from that relationship. The only question thenceforth was how it would be transacted. For much of the remainder of the nineteenth century, it was conducted through the vehicle of party. Not until parties began losing broad acceptability in the political culture did the original question receive a different answer. The relationship between presidency and people would no longer be transacted primarily by parties but more immediately, through personal appearances and speeches and by a newly liberated, independent press. Freed from the confines of the party system and brought into close contact with the people, the presidential office would come to loom larger on the political landscape.

Until the parties lost their hegemony, then, it was rather difficult for the presidency to move to the center of the political system. With the parties in a diminished state at the end of the century, though, presidents could begin to fill the power vacuum and establish direct and strong relationships with the American people. The office was in all likelihood amenable to plebiscitary presidential leadership under Grover Cleveland and Benjamin Harrison in the 1880s and 1890s. Harrison did not, for the most part, push the presidency in this new direction, but Cleveland certainly did in his second term.

Cleveland's personality was not well suited to exercising presidential power in a strong, plebiscitary manner. Nevertheless, he fashioned a stronger, more personal presidency and did, if somewhat reluctantly, make bold appeals to the people through public letters and the newspapers to augment his power.[85] The party system, though, was still strong enough to constrain Cleveland from arrogating *extensive* powers to himself, or, to put it another way, the reluctant Cleveland was not a worthy adversary, even for an increasingly enfeebled party system. As Silbey explains, however, "After the McKinley-Bryan realignment, voter turnout fell sharply, ticket splitting increased, and the number of strong, consistent partisan voters decreased significantly, in a long, downward slide."[86] With the party system continuing to degenerate, Cleveland's successors would be less reluctant to wield presidential power.

Given the evidence presented here, it should come as no major shock that a recent biographer of McKinley, Lewis Gould, has called him the first modern president. The continuing decline of party, coupled with Republican electoral security as a result of this realignment of the 1890s, gave William McKinley (and then his successor, Teddy Roosevelt) prime opportunities to experiment with the presidency's public stature and power. Not only did McKinley have a keen sense of the importance of press relations to his presidential success, but, as Gould writes, "McKinley's use of what Theodore Roosevelt called the bully pulpit is still one of his least recognized contributions to the emergence of the modern presidency."[87] In light of the declining importance of party the possibilities for direct relationships between the president and the public were there to be realized and exploited, and McKinley took advantage of them much more heartily than had his predecessor, Cleveland.

In fact, it is tempting to mark the presidency of William McKinley as the transition point from the party-period presidency to the modern presidency. Perhaps more important than his sensitivity to press relations and cultivation of the "bully pulpit"—particularly with his winning of a second term—he began to conceptualize the presidential office in plebiscitary terms. Many students of the historical presidency are familiar with McKinley's statement to his secretary, in the aftermath of the Spanish-American War, "I can no longer be called the President of a party; I am now the President of the whole people," and perhaps too much has been made of this private remark to an aide—but it does not appear to have been an isolated, anomalous comment. For instance, in a speech to the Union League Club three weeks after his reelection in 1900, McKinley similarly remarked that he was now the president of the "whole American people." What is more, this transpartisan theme, incipient in McKinley's first inaugural address, was quite explicit in the second. Further, according to Gould, his last speech before his death was to be the keynote speech launching the policies of his second term, demonstrating yet again that McKinley "had never been averse to using the presidency as a bully pulpit."[88]

Yet one must be tentative in labeling McKinley the first modern president, wary of placing too much structure on a process that was somewhat fluid and incremental. The desire for strict political, historical markers, though understandable, is largely misguided. It is more appropriate to view political history as "layered," with succeeding periods mixing and overlapping, thus rendering precise categorization of events and figures often facile.[89] One should see McKinley—or Cleveland or Theodore Roosevelt—as neither a party president nor a modern president but, rather, as a figure in a transitionary period containing elements of both party and plebiscitary cultures. It is this transition, occurring in the later nineteenth and continuing into the twentieth century, that suggests the role of declining political parties in the development of modern presidential leadership and provides a critical basis for my later argument that strengthened parties are necessary for tempering and restraining the modern presidency.

Although there was no sharp break, then, between the party period and the modern period, there was a lengthy transition with movement in largely one direction. As Joel Silbey has said, after 1893 the American nation, if not yet a postpartisan one, "was clearly a postpartisan-dominant one."[90] And the presidency was undoubtedly entering a new phase in this postpartisan-dominant era, a phase in which the party mantra "Principles Rather Than Persons, Measures Rather Than Men" would have less and less relevance.

Chapter Four
The Presidential Mandate
Presidents and Parties in Inaugural Addresses

And now, at the close of this first century of growth, with the inspirations of its history in their hearts, our people have lately reviewed the condition of the nation, passed judgment upon the conduct and opinions of political parties, and have registered their will concerning the future administration of the Government. To interpret and to execute that will in accordance with the Constitution is the paramount duty of the Executive.

James Garfield, Inaugural Address, 1881

Winning elections and governing are two rather different enterprises. The presidential office, at least viewed through the lens of nineteenth-century elections, was a partisan office; the presidency was not immune to the powerful pull of the party constitution. Yet a full examination of presidential leadership and behavior in the party era demands a closer look at political actions and behavior at the governing stage as well.

First, however, I look at the point of transition between candidacy and presidency represented by the inaugural address. Every president gives an inaugural address, and it has usually been seen by him and by observers as his opportunity to expound on his philosophy of government and to discuss what he will do in office. As such, these addresses are an important source for understanding the office of the presidency and especially the roles of party and the people vis-à-vis the presidency. If there is a distinct separation between candidates and officeholders, it may surface in the inaugural statement. One example of this separation might be found in Jefferson's famous (but also ambiguous) comment, "We are all Republicans, we are all Federalists." Some have interpreted this statement to mean that once in office, a president is no longer a partisan but is beholden to the whole people through fidelity to the Constitution.[1] Yet a new president may well see his role as one of redeeming campaign promises and party commitments.

This chapter examines the inaugural addresses of the presidents from Washington through George W. Bush.[2] Although I focus extensively on the party period, I consider all inaugurals, for they represent a consistent source of data across presidential history.[3] That all presidents give inaugural addresses provides a rare opportunity to compare presidents across time and eras.[4] I highlight important differences between the inaugural addresses of the early, constitutional period (before the 1830s), the party period (1830s–1890s), and the plebiscitary period (roughly, 1900–). The earlier presidents saw themselves as constitutional officers with a minimal relationship to the people. The party period tied the president more closely to the people's will, especially as expressed through party. (The brief look at newspaper reception of party-period inaugurals, which ends the chapter, lends considerable support to the notion of the party constitution and presidential party leadership.) With the development of the plebiscitary period, presidents often eschewed both party affiliation (although not entirely) and the role of constrained constitutional officer, envisioning themselves rather as the direct representative of all the people, the leader of the nation. They also began to efface the distinction between the people and the president as the country became bound up inextricably with the person of the president.

Inaugural addresses are sometimes dismissed because of their banality or their stilted form.[5] Nevertheless, they furnish an important perspective on American political history, reflecting to a significant degree, American political culture across time. Particularly, since the addresses afford presidents an opportunity to comment on American politics and the job of the president in the political system, they can be of assistance in tracking changing conceptions of presidential leadership.

Inaugural addresses are normally analyzed in one of two ways. Some scholars seek to identify their permanent and enduring themes.[6] Other scholars turn to inaugural addresses to illustrate the changes over time in the American political system.[7] As I am interested in change over time, I take the latter tack, yet I do not wish to suggest the absence of enduring themes and continuities. As Louis Hartz pointed out so effectively years ago, Americans have always shared a number of fundamental assumptions that are reflected in their politics.[8] Moreover, presidents admittedly use inaugural addresses, in part, to appeal for unity and harmony among the American people. Yet there are important differences amid the continuities.

Among notable analyses of nineteenth-century inaugurals tending to see in them much similarity and continuity, James Ceaser and his colleagues propound what has become the conventional view:

> The character of the Inaugural Address illustrates the general character of presidential popular speech during the period [nineteenth century]. Given on a formal occasion, it tended to follow a pattern which was set by Jefferson's First Inaugural Address in which he delivered an exposition of the principles of the Union and its republican character. Although Jefferson's speech might in one sense be considered a partisan document, in fact he sought to be conciliatory toward his opponents. More important still, he presented his case not as an attempt to win support for the particular policies of a party but rather as an effort to instruct the people in, and fortify their attachment to, true republican principles. The form of inaugural address perfected by Jefferson proved a lasting model throughout the century. . . . [S]ubsequent addresses . . . consistently attempted to show how the actions of the new administrations would conform to constitutional and republican principles.[9]

On this view, then, inaugural addresses in the nineteenth century were primarily used by new presidents to instruct the people in republican doctrine or, in other words, to educate the people in constitutional principle and thereby pay deference to the Constitution; party policies and principles had only a minor—if any—place. Even Jefferson, the first true partisan president, used the inaugural not "as an attempt to win support for the particular policies of a party" but as a means of enlightening the people about republican principles. Leaving aside, for the moment, that Jefferson's understanding of republican principle meshed almost exactly with that of the Democratic-Republican Party and anticipated a new form of address, one may concede that this so-called Jeffersonian model characterizes an important slice of nineteenth-century inaugural addresses. But with the penetration of the presidential office by the popular democracy of political parties, the model was substantially altered.

Ceaser and his colleagues' understanding of the nineteenth-century inaugural address elides the crucial role of political parties in the election of presidents and the changes in the political system wrought by mass suffrage. To be sure, nearly all nineteenth-century presidents mentioned and discussed the Constitution, whereas very few twentieth-century presidents did so.[10] Also, very few nineteenth-century presidents attempted to become the "national voice," as did Woodrow Wilson. Yet these quite important and extensive differences *between* the nineteenth- and twentieth-century inaugural addresses should not blind observers to the seminal changes *within* each century. Clearly, political parties and their principles were quite important to the nineteenth-century inaugural address, and nineteenth-century presidents, via those addresses, acknowledged themselves bound not simply to the Constitution and "republican principles" but to the parties (and the public) that had elected them to the office. Still, parties were initially lambasted, and their acceptance was gradual, as a brief look at the early inaugurals demonstrates.

"No Separate Views nor Party Animosities"

The inaugural addresses of the first six presidents comport well with the picture of nineteenth-century addresses sketched by Ceaser and his colleagues. They embody a "constitutional" conception of the presidency which comprises, particularly, an "independence of the executive" and a healthy distance between the president and the people. The executive, under this model, is beholden to the Constitution, not to public opinion or political parties. Washington set the tone in his first inaugural. As Tulis says, he sought "to praise virtuous men, to display his own character and virtue, and to implore fellow officers of the government to take their guidance from the Constitution and from 'that Almighty Being who rules over the Universe.'"[11] There is no suggestion that he will use public opinion or his affiliation with a political party to guide his conduct in office. In fact, he promises that under his leadership "no separate views nor party animosities, will misdirect the comprehensive and equal eye which ought to watch over this great assemblage of communities and interests." Moreover, he cautions against too rashly employing the amending power granted by the fifth article of the Constitution.[12] Washington's fidelity and deference to the Constitution and his trust in virtuous men rings out in his first inaugural address. His second, a very short document, is also quite clear on this front: Washington is devoted to the Constitution and its protection.[13]

John Adams's inaugural address also fits neatly with the constitutional model. After dilating on the history of the United States and its providential nature, Adams expresses his veneration for the Constitution and its principles.[14] Like Washington, he sees the office of the presidency as being charged with upholding the Constitution, not political parties or the will of the people as expressed at the ballot box. Indeed, Adams admonishes the people to be cautious, because it is plausible that "the Government may be the choice of a party for its own ends, not of the nation or the national good." Departing somewhat from Washington's example but still in line with the constitutional model, he also outlines his political principles or philosophy of government. In addition to respect for the Constitution he stresses, inter alia, the delicate balance of power between the federal and state governments. Adams is articulating his own understanding (as virtuous leader) of republican principle and the Constitution, not, ostensibly, that of any party or public will to which he feels loyalty.[15]

Although Jefferson's inaugurals still largely embody the constitutional model, his case is not as cut-and-dried. Ceaser and his colleagues are right to say that Jefferson, in his first inaugural, was trying to temper his partisanship and that he was much concerned with articulating republican principle. Nevertheless, he does make partisan claims, and his exposition of republican principle is undoubtedly partisan; partisanship has begun to pervade the political system. Jefferson is not merely outlining his own understanding of republican principles but articulating his party's understanding of republican doctrine. What is more, this is a party that had prevailed, as Jefferson put it, in "the contest of opinion through which we have passed."[16] This passage is critical to my analysis, for it appears at odds with the original constitutional model.

The constitutional model holds that presidents, upon election, owe their allegiance to the Constitution, not to public opinion or political parties.[17] Jefferson is implying a much more popular role for the presidency. He feels obligated, at least in part, to the majority that elected him and his party to office; he must redeem the pledges made to the people in the "contest of opinion." To use Jefferson's idiom, the "voice of the nation" has spoken through the election and validated his and his party's political principles. It is not surprising, then, that the political principles he outlines in the address correspond to those of the Democratic-Republican Party, which he led during the election of 1800—though to be sure, Jefferson does make appeals for unity, asking all to "arrange themselves under the will of the law, and unite in common efforts for the common good."[18]

This latter sentiment most likely derived from both practical and philosophical considerations. On the one hand, Jefferson's appeals for unity made good political sense. A triumphant politician in a majority-rule system cannot afford to alienate and offend the losers in a political contest, thereby inviting extensive (and likely excessive) scrutiny and calumny: "Jefferson refused to begin his term with a radical agenda, arguing in part that slender majorities such as his do not lend themselves to political upheavals," writes Michael Riccards.[19] On the other hand, as is well known, Jefferson was suspicious of parties and saw them as useful only for overcoming factionalism: that is, as parties to transcend party. Jefferson envisioned the Democratic-Republicans as a party that would transcend party animosity and unite the nation.[20]

After this unification was completed, however, what role might the presidency fill? On Jefferson's model, the presidency might be the agent of popular change only very briefly and then revert back more regularly to a constitutional clerkship. That Jefferson was really an agent of "the people," moreover, is a suspect claim. Granted, suffrage was expanding around the turn of the century; nevertheless, this expansion was not on a par with that of the 1830s, which necessitated the development of mass political parties to organize the newly enfranchised. The "contest of opinion" to which Jefferson refers encompassed only a fragment of the population in 1800; it was not yet a truly "popular" phenomenon. As Forrest McDonald has put it, "The decision was in the hands of no more than a thousand men, and for practical purposes it turned on the activities of two or three dozen factional leaders."[21] Thus, Jefferson's first inaugural (and second one as well, which was quite consistent with the first) anticipates what is to come but remains bound up with the original model. Although he acknowledges an electoral pull and a loyalty to the partisans who elected him, this electoral pull is rather limited and elitist, and Jefferson also seems ambivalent about the utility and role of political parties. There remains much in his inaugurals that squares with the constitutional model, such as his praise of the Constitution, the Congress, the Court, and virtuous men and his (slightly disingenuous) statement that the executive merely implements the laws impartially.[22]

The inaugurals of James Madison and James Monroe revert to the style of Washington and Adams, in line with the constitutional model. Madison's first praises virtuous men, articulates constitutional principle, and, significantly, does not refer to a "contest of opinion," as Jefferson had done. Rather, Madison, in both his inaugurals, speaks of the station to which he has been elected as a "trust"; in the second he says, "The impressions made on me are strengthened by such an evidence that my faithful endeavors to discharge my arduous duties have been favorably estimated, and by a consideration of the momentous period at which the trust has been renewed."[23]

Although clearly affiliated with the Jeffersonians and the Democratic-Republican Party, Madison did not see his election as necessarily prescriptive in character; he was entrusted by the people to discharge the office as he saw fit; his character, virtue, and ability were what the people placed confidence in, not his political principles or his pledges to act in one way as opposed to another. Madison was more likely than Jefferson, then, to see the presidency as a constitutional office rather than a place of popular leadership, even in Jefferson's constrained sense. Still, Madison's espousal of principles is much more in line with the Democratic-Republican Party than with the nearly moribund Federalist Party.[24] The presidential office was somewhat colored by partisan influence at this time.

Both of James Monroe's inaugurals similarly stress the "trust" to which he has been called.[25] Like Madison, he saw his election not as part of a majority validation of principles or of a political party but as "the expression of their [the people's] good opinion of my conduct in the public service." This language is precisely in line with the constitutional norm that election to office should be based not on pledges to the people but on a candidate's reputation and esteemed public service. Further, Monroe's statement of political principles in both addresses is a rather noncontroversial explication and praise of the American political system, wherein the executive has delimited tasks and pays proper deference to the other branches of government.[26]

Moreover, with statements such as "Discord does not belong to our system" and "Our system will soon attain the highest degree of perfection to which human institutions are capable," Monroe espoused the belief that an Era of Good Feelings free from partisanship had been (or would shortly be) achieved.[27] He saw himself as part and parcel of this era of harmony, believing that a president could help overcome faction and party through his upright behavior, his moderate example, and his devotion to the Constitution. Clearly, in his patronage policies and in his generally moderate course of official action, Monroe endeavored to establish and secure harmony, yet he eschewed "direct or even indirect appeals to the public," writes Ralph Ketcham, to fortify this so-called position of national harmony.[28] The presidency, for Monroe, was a position of national leadership bolstered and legitimated by constitutional provision rather than by popular support.

John Quincy Adams followed a course comparable to that of Madison and, particularly, Monroe; he saw himself as a national leader whose primary source of power was the Constitution: "In unfolding to my countrymen the principles by which I shall be governed in the fulfillment of those duties my first resort will be to that Constitution which I shall swear to the best of my ability to preserve, protect, and defend." Adams, it should be further noted, said nothing of an allegiance to any popular movement or political party. Indeed, he inveighed multiple times in his address against the "baneful weed of party strife" and lauded the United States for the harmony that it was then experiencing—although he was undoubtedly eliding the factionalism that was rampant at the time.[29]

What is interesting about John Quincy Adams, however, and what makes him in Ketcham's term a "paradoxical president," is that although he vilified parties, he also championed an active agenda for the national government, including internal improvements and the establishment of a national university. The paradox is that a president who promotes a major agenda needs support, needs a powerful constituency behind him or at least needs to be in touch with popular sentiment, yet Adams consistently disavowed parties and would not work to build a supportive coalition. He continued to operate according to a set of doctrines and ideas that were increasingly less relevant. A president could no longer—if, indeed, he ever could—expect to be supported simply because of a distinguished record of public service and patriotism or because he *was* the president. "Intentions upright and pure . . . [and] a heart devoted to the welfare of our country" would, unfortunately for Adams, not be sufficient to establish a national agenda.[30] Presidents would increasingly need to be more attuned to public sentiment, especially that expressed through elections.

"The Recent Demonstration of Public Sentiment"

As is well known, the time of Andrew Jackson is generally referred to as Jacksonian Democracy, the emphasis being as much on the latter as on the former term. With the widespread extension of white male suffrage, the popular election of presidential electors, and the concurrent faith in "the people" and popular sovereignty witnessed in the late 1820s and 1830s, one might naturally expect to see new conceptualizations of presidential leadership. Yet the inaugural address was not influenced nearly as strongly as might have been predicted; Jackson's are "bland" and fairly conventional, considering that he saw himself as "tribune of the people."[31] Nevertheless, with Jackson there were important changes, and by the mid-1840s a more complex inaugural form had emerged. The original constitutional model became augmented and to an extent superseded by new concerns: presidential duties, ideas, and principles were more closely connected with political parties, popular sentiment, and the ballot box. Presidents would continue to praise the Constitution and the other branches of government and to relate their principles to republicanism, but their principles and interpretations of the Constitution would be less and less solely their own. Increasingly, they would be admixed with those of the party and the people as expressed through campaigns and elections.

Nineteenth-century inaugurals after Jackson almost without fail pay heed to the public will and the mandate of the recent election.[32] Moreover, most refer to pledges made during the campaign and to party platforms, some going so far as to quote platform planks. These presidents regarded their role not simply as that of an impartial clerk but instead as that of an executive with allegiance to a political party and its popularly validated political principles.

It should be stressed, though, that "party" presidents of the nineteenth century were such within the general purview of the Constitution. That is, although they saw their actions as having a popular basis, they still respected the Constitution and the other branches of government, particularly the Congress—unlike plebiscitary presidents, who often magnify their office at the expense of both the Constitution and Congress.[33] Party presidents considered themselves caught up in the will of the majority and Congress as inextricably bound up with them as part of the government.

The shift to a party presidency can be discerned in two major aspects of inaugural addresses after John Quincy Adams: presidents' increasing references to political parties and popular sentiment as a guide to their actions, and the increasingly partisan coloring of their articulations of republican principle. These changes were not wholesale; nineteenth-century inaugurals after Adams still conformed, to varying degrees, to the constitutional model. Nevertheless, there were significant and fundamental differences in the form and message of inaugural addresses.

Even though the election of Jackson was a watershed event in American politics and the development of the presidency, his inaugural addresses were not vastly dissimilar from those of his predecessors. Quite reserved in his first address, he takes pains to set out his understanding of republican and constitutional principles and calls himself "the instrument of the Federal Constitution." What is more, he pays deference to Congress, hardly implying the clashes that were to come as he staked his claim as "tribune of the people." Yet in line with the more popular addresses of Jefferson are Jackson's expositions of his political principles. In both inaugurals he outlines anti–Clay/Adams and anti–American System principles, such as strict construction of the Constitution and economy in government, which most observers (including Jackson) believed had been validated by his election.[34]

But what ultimately distinguishes Jackson from those who came before him is a striking passage in the first inaugural which indicates the democratic tenor of the times: "The recent demonstration of public sentiment inscribes on the list of Executive duties, in characters too legible to be overlooked, the task of *reform*, which will require particularly the correction of those abuses that have brought the patronage of the Federal Government into conflict with the freedom of elections, and the counteraction of those causes which have disturbed the rightful course of appointment and have placed or continued power in unfaithful or incompetent hands."[35] Whereas the early presidents mainly characterized their relationships with the public as a "trust," Jackson suggests a different relationship, one that harks back to Jefferson's rhetoric in his first inaugural. Just as Jefferson suggested bowing to the majority, Jackson says that public opinion as made manifest in the recent election "inscribes" certain "duties" on the executive, duties related mainly, although not exclusively, to matters of patronage and to placing loyal men in federal government positions. Patronage may seem a trivial issue now, but it was not so in the 1820s; the more popular understanding of the office articulated by Jefferson was reappearing, in even stronger fashion, for whereas Jefferson's popular mandate did not rest on wide and broad suffrage, Jackson's mandate did.[36] The era of popular government may be said to have commenced here, with the executive becoming an important player in the new democratic arrangement.

Van Buren's inaugural address pushed this popular understanding of the presidency even further. To be sure, as in nearly all inaugurals of the nineteenth century, there is plenty of discussion of the Constitution and praise of virtuous men, but there is much more as well. Jackson referred to the "recent demonstration of public sentiment" and how it mandated that he pursue a course of "reform"; Van Buren is even clearer about the relationship between the people and the president and his adherence to Jackson's principles and sentiments. The party system not being firmly established yet, he does not speak of allegiance to a party and its principles; nonetheless, even though public opinion was not being channeled primarily through parties at this time, the address makes manifest the influence of public opinion on the presidency.[37]

The people, on Van Buren's view, did not simply select leaders but also selected the ideas and principles that these leaders were to follow in office:

> Perceiving before my election the deep interest this subject [domestic slavery] was beginning to excite, I believed it a solemn duty fully to make known my sentiments in regard to it. . . . I then declared that if the desire of those of my countrymen who were favorable to my election was gratified "I must go into the Presidential chair the inflexible and uncompromising opponent of every attempt on the part of Congress to abolish slavery in the District of Columbia against the wishes of the slaveholding States, and also with the determination equally decided to resist the slightest interference with it in the States where it exists." . . . The result [of the election] authorizes me to believe that they [these sentiments] have been approved and are confided in by a majority of the people of the United States, including those whom they most immediately affect.

> To enter on this occasion into a further or more minute exposition of my views on the various questions of domestic policy would be as obtrusive as it is probably expected. Before the suffrages of my countrymen were conferred upon me I submitted to them, with great precision, my opinions on all the most prominent of these subjects. Those opinions I shall endeavor to carry out with my utmost ability.[38]

These passages are both intriguing in what Van Buren implies about the popular quality of the office of president. The first one refers to his making his opinions known before the election as a "duty," and he sees the election as having validated those opinions. The second passage draws the connection between the people and the executive office even more sharply. Not wanting to importune the people with excessive discussions of political principles—although he does at one point mention strict construction of the Constitution[39]—Van Buren again cites the opinions that he made known before the election, suggesting that as president, he will honor them. This is a notable change from the founding proscription against selecting leaders on a basis other than their virtue and past public service. Instead of saying that he has been given a "trust" by the people, entailing that he will act as he sees fit once in office, Van Buren stresses the obligation he feels to honor the principles on which he ostensibly campaigned. The executive office was becoming a seat of popular leadership.

The inaugural address of William Henry Harrison, the nation's ninth president, is a very interesting case. The longest ever given, it exhibits all the ironies and paradoxes of the Whigs and their political philosophy. For example, Harrison claims throughout the address that the president should be deferential to Congress because the Congress, not the president, is truly connected with and representative of the people: "It is preposterous to suppose that a thought could for a moment have been entertained that the President, placed at the capital, in the center of the country, could better understand the wants and wishes of the people than their own immediate representatives, who spend a part of every year among them." Yet at the same time, Harrison argues that leaders (including, presumably, himself) must carry out the "pledges and promises" made to the people before the election. As he puts it, responding to opposition attacks that he was simply making empty pledges in the campaign of 1840, "It may be thought that a motive may exist to keep up the delusion under which they [the people] may be supposed to have acted in relation to my principles and opinions." The import of Harrison's statement is unmistakable: he intends to redeem the campaign pledges that he made to the people; he was, after all, a popular leader.[40]

With the pull of party becoming stronger at this time, it is instructive to examine closely Harrison's views of party as expressed in his inaugural. In classic Whig fashion, he was ambivalent. On the one hand, he is critical of party, going so far as to claim that "the spirit of party, assuming to be that of liberty, is harsh, vindictive, and intolerant, and totally reckless as to the character of the allies which it brings to the aid of its cause." And, further, "The reign of an intolerant spirit of party amongst

a free people seldom fails to result in a dangerous accession to the executive power introduced and established amidst unusual professions of
devotion to democracy." On the other hand, toward the end of his dilatory address, he comes to a more moderate understanding of party, re-
marking that parties should be "tempered" and allowing that they may
be necessary "to secure a degree of vigilance sufficient to keep public
functionaries within the bounds of law and duty." But, he adds, "at that
point their usefulness ends."[41]

It appears, then, that Harrison was torn between vilifying parties and
acquiescing in their growing acceptance—standard Whig political philosophy and rhetoric. At the root of this antiparty hostility was the belief
that parties necessarily would tend toward consolidation of power in the
executive branch, as Whigs thought the "Jacksonian" party had done.
Thus, it was with Jackson in mind that Harrison declared, "All the
influence that I possess shall be exerted to prevent the formation at least
of an Executive party in the halls of the legislative body."[42] Presumably,
however, parties that created cooperation between the branches, without domination of one by the other, would be at least palatable to Harrison, and this was likely what he had in mind when he more favorably
cast parties in the address. According to Daniel Walker Howe, that "Harrison summoned a special session of Congress to enact the Whig economic program" and replaced Democratic appointees with Whigs would
seem to lend credence to this view.[43] Thus, for all Harrison's constitutional
rhetoric and spleen regarding parties, his inaugural nevertheless is something of a partisan, popular document and as such diverges from the constitutional model.

The election of 1844 being an archetypal party-period election, James
Polk's inaugural address, not surprisingly, is almost exactly what one
would expect from a "party constitution" president. Tulis has noted its
innovations but contends that it is still quite similar to the constitutional
model—and Polk does say that "a concise enumeration of the principles
which will guide me in the administrative policy of the Government is
not only in accordance with the examples set me by all my predecessors,
but is eminently befitting this occasion."[44] Yet the basis and source of
support of these principles had changed. The early presidents were, in
the main, outlining their individual philosophies of government or those
of an elite party network; Polk was outlining the principles of his (mass)
political party and those on which he and his party campaigned. In a very

real sense he was outlining the political principles of the popular majority that had elected him to office.

Like those of Van Buren and Harrison before him, Polk's inaugural makes reference to his preelection statements and opinions. But since by 1844 the party system was firmly rooted and public opinion largely channeled through parties, presidents' pledges were being identified more clearly with a political party and its philosophy. Polk makes the connection between pledges and promises that he has made and the Democratic Party. A statement toward the end of his inaugural, christens the party period in American politics:

> Although in our country the Chief Magistrate must almost of necessity be chosen by a party and stand pledged to its principles and measures, yet in his official action he should not be the President of a part only, but of the whole people of the United States. While he executes the laws with an impartial hand, shrinks from no proper responsibility, and faithfully carries out in the executive department of the Government *the principles and policy of those who have chosen him,* he should not be unmindful that our fellow-citizens who have differed with him in opinion are entitled to the full and free exercise of their opinions and judgments, and that the rights of all are entitled to respect and regard.[45]

In the first sentence of this passage, Polk makes clear that the trend toward party prominence is nearly inexorable ("almost of necessity") and unabashedly casts his lot with the forces of progress. To be sure, he does take pains to conciliate the losing party in the contest, the Whigs, saying that he will not abridge the rights of his opponents to voice their opinions or use his station to discriminate against them. But he is still firmly an adherent to the principles of "those who have chosen him." Polk is certainly not ambiguous or noncommittal about what those principles are. He recites a litany of political principles, some banal (balancing power between federal and state governments), but others standard Democratic doctrine: strict construction of the Constitution, opposition to a national bank, tariff for revenue only, no assumption of state debts, and the annexation of both Texas and Oregon.[46]

Again, however, I wish to stress that although Polk's address is popular and partisan, it is also constitutional, acknowledging a limit on his powers and paying deference to Congress (unlike presidents after Woodrow Wilson). But Polk was disciplined as an executive by the party system, as were all presidents in the party period. Not until the party system began to erode, especially around the turn of the century, would the executive's relationship with the people cease to be so mediated, allowing the stature and power of the office to grow.

Zachary Taylor, who endeavored quite admirably but ultimately unsuccessfully to be free of party affiliations in his 1848 presidential bid, had given in to the party system by the time the election was in full swing, declaring that he was indeed a "Whig, but not an ultra Whig." A similar defiance mixed with acquiescence characterizes his inaugural address. Taylor praises the Constitution and virtuous men; pledges to "maintain to the extent of my ability the Government in its original purity and to adopt as the basis of my public policy those great republican doctrines which constitute the strength of our national existence." He thus places himself in the stead of patriot king and heir to Washington. What is more, in discussing patronage, he seems to suggest that he will not have party in mind at all when making appointments. Even so, although his address seems prima facie like that of a Washington or a Monroe, it reveals the popular qualities of the presidency. For instance, regarding the way he will execute the office, Taylor says, "I this day renew the declarations I have heretofore made": that is, his previous declarations about "great republican doctrines." Like Harrison and the Whigs in general, Taylor makes the founding norms subject to the ballot box and popular contention. What is more, although laconic in his statement of principles, he does remark that he will recommend to Congress "measures" to "secure encouragement and protection to the great interests of agriculture, commerce, and manufactures, to improve our rivers and harbors, to provide for the speedy extinguishment of the public debt, to enforce a strict accountability of the part of all officers of the Government and the utmost economy in all public expenditures."[47]

This statement is far too similar to Whig doctrine to be coincidental, particularly the statement in the "Resolutions Adopted at Whig Ratification Meeting" in 1848: to wit, that Taylor's administration was to be one "of Prosperity—now more than ever needed to relieve the nation from a burden of debt, and restore industry—agricultural, manufacturing and commercial—to its accustomed and peaceful functions and influences."[48] Improvements too had always been part and parcel of Whig philosophy. That Taylor, as Newton Lott points out, prepared his "address with the help of leading party members" also suggests that he was far more amenable to party influence and connections than some of his public rhetoric would intimate.[49] Thus, even old "Rough and Ready," a reluctant partisan and popular leader, expressed his fidelity, if only mildly, to the Whig principles of those who elected him.

The 1848 election was the last before the Civil War in which the issue of slavery did not play a major role. The most important parts of both Franklin Pierce's and James Buchanan's inaugurals revolved around the issue of slavery. Pierce's does make reference to standard Democratic policies such as support for expansionism and patronage, but the heart of the speech is clearly contained in the passages dealing with slavery. Pierce admonishes that the federal government should be kept in its proper sphere regarding "matters strictly domestic" and then reiterates "briefly my views upon an important subject which has recently agitated the nation to an almost fearful degree." These views, he goes on to say, "were not unknown before the expression of the voice which called me here. My own position upon this subject was clear and unequivocal, upon the record of my words and acts, and it is only recurred here because silence might perhaps be misconstrued." He then stresses that slavery should not be interfered with and that the Compromise of 1850 should be honored, sentiments very much in line with the Democratic platform and his campaign pledges.[50] Noteworthy, again, is this understanding that a candidate should make his views known before the election so that the people have a more direct control of the government. Pierce obviously took his preelection pledges seriously and aimed to carry them through.

The inaugural address of James Buchanan differs little from Pierce's, both animated first and foremost by issues of slavery. Buchanan also relates his election to the popular will. As he rather optimistically and quixotically puts it: "We have recently passed through a Presidential contest in which the passions of our fellow-citizens were excited to the highest degree by questions of deep and vital importance; but when the people proclaimed their will the tempest at once subsided and all was calm. The voice of the majority, speaking in the manner prescribed by the Constitution, was heard, and instant submission followed. Our country could alone have exhibited so grand and striking a spectacle of the capacity of man for self-government."[51] This is hardly in line with the sentiment of the founders. Buchanan's talk of a contest "excited" by "questions of deep and vital importance" rather than "men of great character" is not surprising, of course, for he was very much a proponent of party government and of a "Principles Rather Than Persons" philosophy of politics. Although Buchanan pays lip service to some token Democratic principles and planks (strict construction of the Constitution, states' rights), he comes down squarely with his Democratic Party on the real issues that revolve specifically around slavery. He favors the idea of "popular sovereignty" and fervently hopes that it will put an end to the agitation that abounds in the country.

Perhaps of most interest are Buchanan's viewpoints on parties. A crude analysis might take him as inveighing against them when he laments "the geographical parties to which it [slavery agitation] has given birth, so much dreaded by the Father of his Country."[52] But note the qualifier "geographical." Buchanan, a warm supporter of party for so long, would never condemn *national* parties, but he was clearly frightened by the specter of sectional and geographical conflict manifesting itself in the new Republican Party, which was almost exclusively northern. Even his beloved Democratic Party would not be impermeable to the sectional agitation to which slavery gave rise.

"To Interpret and to Execute That Will in Accordance with the Constitution"

Inaugural addresses after Buchanan, with a few exceptions, continued to reflect the hold of party on the American political system. Lincoln's first inaugural was delivered under very inauspicious conditions: the nation had witnessed the secession of seven states, and there was a sense of impending doom in the air with the election of a Republican president.[53] Lincoln strove admirably to conciliate the secessionists and restore peace and order, but they would have none of it.

What is striking about the first inaugural is the way Lincoln attempts to defuse the situation in an appeal to his preelection pledges and the Republican platform. Almost immediately in the address, he refers to one of his campaign speeches in which he said: "I have no purpose, directly or indirectly, to interfere with the institution of slavery where it exists. I believe I have no lawful right to do so, and I have no inclination to do so. . . . Those who nominated and elected me did so with full knowledge that I had made this and many similar declarations and had never recanted them; and more than this, they placed in the platform for my acceptance, and as a law to themselves and to me, the clear and emphatic resolution which I now read."[54] Lincoln then takes the unprecedented step of excerpting the Republican platform of 1860, which resolved not to touch slavery in the states where it already existed.

Lincoln undoubtedly showed his fidelity to his party and its platform with this gesture. He cast the presidency as a popular office and saw himself as bound, by the dictates of the 1860 election, to the pledges that he and his party had made. Yet Lincoln's case also illustrates one of the major characteristics of the nineteenth-century understanding of the presidency as popular office. Nineteenth-century presidents saw the popular will as bolstering or supporting them in their political principles, but only within constitutional bounds. Public opinion could not and should not be used to contravene the Constitution or expand its grants of power, as in Theodore Roosevelt's "stewardship" sense. As Lincoln put it in the first inaugural: "The Chief Magistrate derives all his authority from the people, and they have conferred none upon him to fix terms for the separation of the States. The people themselves can do this if also they choose, but the Executive as such has nothing to do with it."[55] This sentiment contrasts with that of many twentieth-century addresses, wherein newly elected presidents see themselves as embodiments and leaders of public opinion, paying little or no deference (or even attention) to the Constitution.

Interestingly, Lincoln's second inaugural is more in line with twentieth- than nineteenth-century addresses. Coming near the end of a terribly bloody and extended civil war, it is in an important sense incomparable with other inaugural addresses. Indeed, not only is the context in which it was given incommensurable, but in its content and substance it is sui generis. One is struck by the role that Lincoln creates for himself as president, carving out a place not simply as a popular leader charged with administering the government but as the nation's moral leader.

Lincoln does not specifically call himself the moral leader, but throughout the address he seeks to educate the people and exhort them "to face the deepest truths about themselves."[56] Of course, context has much to do with his casting himself in this manner. Having just been resoundingly reelected at the head of the so-called Union Party, he may rightly have judged his role in protecting the Union as one transcending ordinary, partisan politics. Interestingly, in doing so, his address anticipates the form of inaugural that would come to predominate in the twentieth century (although none would approach Lincoln's elegance).

This form is not a surprise, given the conditions Lincoln faced, but it is far less clear why such addresses seem to be necessary today, even in times of no crisis.[57]

With the noted exception of Lincoln's second, the inaugural addresses of presidents since Van Buren had referred to "pledges" or "declarations" made before the election, and almost all linked the new president to a political party. The inaugurals of Ulysses S. Grant furnish another exception to this general rule. Grant was, of course, the major Civil War hero; moreover, he had had little prior involvement in politics. For both reasons, Grant was seen to be exactly what the country needed after a terrible war and the bitter confrontations between the current president, Andrew Johnson, and Congress.[58]

Such a role was acceptable to Grant. In his letter accepting the Republican nomination in 1868, he hardly casts himself as a warm party supporter, and he carries over this ambivalence, if not indifference, to party in both his inaugural addresses. Neither address says anything about pledges Grant has made regarding issues or the support of a political party. Nor do they mention the Republican Party or any pressing issues that could be associated with it.[59] Grant speaks as distinguished citizen and war patriot, not as the representative of a political party. At least in the rhetoric of his inaugural addresses, he attempts a return to the patriot king notion of leadership that had been attractive to the early presidents.

Grant puts it this way in his first inaugural, saying of the presidency that "I commence its duties untrammeled." In the second, he opens by saying, "It has been my endeavor in the past to maintain all the laws, and, so far as lay in my power, to act for the best interests of the whole people."[60] He does not say simply the "best interests of the people"; rather, he makes sure to stress that he is concerned with the "whole" people and that he is an impartial leader. Through his national stature and his reputation as one "above politics," he hopes to unify the country; he sees his leadership as resting not so much on a popular, partisan mandate as on his heroic and nonpartisan persona.

Interestingly, Grant approximates the earlier model of presidential leadership, at least in his inaugurals, even more than both William Henry Harrison and Zachary Taylor, the only Whig presidents. Their references to previous pledges and declarations indicated the popular bases of their leadership. Grant, to be sure, was nothing if not popular, but his was a different popularity from that which bound leaders to the people around a particular party philosophy and set of principles. Grant, like the early presidents, was not concerned with party popularity; rather, he was concerned with public confidence and support owing to his public service and patriotism, because of which he would be trusted to execute the office of the presidency as he saw fit. Nothing beyond the selection of the leader, other than continued trust in the leader, was demanded of the people.

With the unusual and contested election of Rutherford B. Hayes in 1876, inaugural addresses reverted to their party form. Given that Hayes arguably should not have been elevated to the presidency, he expressed his partisanship and referred to preelection pledges and declarations far more than one might expect. After all, Samuel Tilden had most likely won the election, and in any case, only the Senate was of the same party as Hayes.[61] One would not have been surprised had he appealed wholesale to both Democrats and Republicans for unity under such conditions.

To be sure, there are conciliatory remarks. For instance, Hayes argues that the South must be moved swiftly toward local self-government. This opinion is unquestionably not in line with his party's sentiment, Republicans being more inclined to use the federal government to protect the rights of blacks after the Civil War and being more amenable to federal power in general. Moreover, Hayes insists that "party ties and the prejudice of race will be freely surrendered in behalf of the great purpose" of restoring local government in the South.[62] Hayes is reaching out here, trying to be an impartial leader so as to defuse the contentious feelings surrounding his election. Yet it is surprising how much his inaugural resembles a standard party constitution address. Much of it, interestingly, does not read as if there had been a less-than-decisive election, or as if his Republicans controlled only one chamber of Congress. Instead, in the second paragraph of Hayes's inaugural, he refers to the pledges he made before the election and his intention of following through on them:

> At the outset of the discussions which preceded the recent Presidential election it seemed to me fitting that I should fully make known my sentiments in regard to several of the important questions which then appeared to demand the consideration of the country. Following the example, and in part adopting the language, of one of my predecessors, I wish now,

when every motive for misrepresentation has passed away, to repeat what was said before the election, trusting that my countrymen will candidly weigh and understand it, and they will feel assured that the sentiments declared in accepting the nomination for the Presidency will be the standard of my conduct in the path before me, charged, as I now am, with the grave and difficult task of carrying them out in the practical administration of the Government so far as depends, under the Constitution and laws, on the Chief Executive of the nation.[63]

"One of my predecessors" alludes to Lincoln, who similarly argued, in his first inaugural, that he would consider himself bound by his preelection statements.[64] The passage further affirms that presidential leadership at this time had a popular cast: Hayes believes he has been elected to carry out the principles validated by the election. Still, as he notes, popular leadership is constrained by the Constitution and its prescriptions for executive power.

Hayes's mention of his letter of acceptance of the Republican nomination not only suggests that acceptance letters were taken more seriously over time but also evidences the fealty that Hayes exhibited toward the Republican Party.[65] Indeed, he mentions political parties and the importance of platforms and acceptance letters several more times throughout the message, such as in regard to his views on civil service reform and financial matters. Perhaps most important, he declares: "The President of the United States of necessity owes his election to office to the suffrage and zealous labors of a political party, the members of which cherish with ardor and regard as of essential importance the principles of their party organization; but he should strive to be always mindful of the fact that he serves his party best who serves the country best."[66] This passage reprised Polk's inaugural statement from more than three decades earlier regarding the relationship of parties to the presidency. Certainly, Hayes was trying to be gracious to Democrats, but the main point is clear: a president should do what he can, without injuring the state of the country or violating the Constitution, to serve his party and its principles.

Although Hayes's inaugural represented a return to the party form that had characterized most addresses from Van Buren to the Civil War, his was not unlike Grant's in that it broached few issues of substance. Garfield's inaugural address and Cleveland's first (at least to an extent) would be rather vacuous as well, likely as a result of the very close competitiveness of the parties at the time. Although references to party and popular mandates would persist, the platforms of the parties were so similar between 1876 and 1884 that there would not be much room for controversial party principles in the addresses.

Garfield's inaugural engages in more than the usual litany of banalities, moving from noncontroversial discussions of finance to entirely safe denunciations of Mormons and polygamy. In regard to illiteracy and black enfranchisement, he stresses that "partisanship should be unknown." Yet one finds some partisan issues, albeit muted, in his address, such as his advocacy of "protectionism" and his strong support for federal aid to education efforts.[67] What is more, even though most of the issues he discusses exhibit little bite or party controversy, the speech adheres to the party form: "And now, at the close of this first century of growth, with the inspirations of its history in their hearts, our people have lately reviewed the condition of the nation, passed judgment upon the conduct and opinions of political parties, and have registered their will concerning the future administration of the Government. To interpret and to execute that will in accordance with the Constitution is the paramount duty of the Executive."[68] Although it would be hard to locate a mandate for a clear course of action in Garfield's election or the election of the Republicans, he nonetheless feels bound to understand the president's role within a popular (partisan) political system.

Furthermore, Garfield's description of popular presidential leadership under the party constitution is perhaps the most coherent and straightforward to be found in any of the party-period inaugurals. The president, though bound to the will of his political party and its principles, must interpret that will "in accordance with the Constitution." As I have stressed, the party model of presidential leadership expanded the relationship between the president and people, but that expansion did not come at the expense of the Constitution. Not until the close of the nineteenth century did presidents begin to see themselves as embodiments of the nation and the public and their references to the Constitution, consequently diminish.

Grover Cleveland's inaugural in 1885 furthers the party conception of the presidency and parties, although Cleveland even more than other party presidents strongly expresses his opinion that party considerations should be subservient to the Constitution: "Amid the din of party strife the people's choice was made," but good government "depend[s] upon a proper limitation of purely partisan zeal and effort and a correct appreciation of the time when the heat of the partisan should be merged in the patriotism of the citizen." In administering the office, he says, he will be guided by "a cautious appreciation of those functions which by the Constitution and laws have been especially assigned to the executive branch of the Government." Further, he closes his address by expressing his determination that "merit and competency shall be recognized [for civil service positions] instead of party subserviency or the surrender of honest political belief."[69]

Nevertheless, Cleveland also admonishes citizens to engage in "an ungrudging acquiescence in the popular will," which was, of course, expressed in favor of the Democratic Party. Although Cleveland is no James Polk expressing clearly the ambit of the Democratic creed, his short address still emphasizes unmistakably Democratic issues and stances. Cleveland comes out against having considerable surplus in the Treasury, for the excess revenue would always be too tempting for the federal government—a common Democratic mantra. Relatedly, he criticizes, if a bit obliquely, the high tariff system that would be likely to contribute to excess revenue in the Treasury.[70] This laissez-faire attitude toward business and a distrust of a powerful federal government were standard Democratic principles, and Cleveland is careful to pay them mind; he feels a popular, electoral obligation to do so.

Benjamin Harrison's inaugural address of 1889 fits well with the party understanding of presidential leadership. Harrison is not nearly so sanctimonious as Cleveland about civil service reform and patronage, stating that "honorable party service will certainly not be esteemed by me a disqualification for office, but it will in no case be allowed to serve as a shield of official negligence, incompetency, or delinquency." What is more, he is very straightforward in his political views, clearly siding with Republicans. For instance, he spends a good deal of time defending the idea of a protective tariff, the major issue of the 1888 campaign, as well as the idea of a surplus of revenue in the Treasury. And in a clear jab at the Cleveland administration he is replacing, he recommends that "our pension laws should give more adequate and discriminating relief to the Union soldiers and to their widows and orphans."[71]

Although Harrison clearly positions himself with the Republicans on the issues and principles he discusses, unlike many presidents of the party period he does not explicitly discuss his views about the proper role of the presidency and its relationship to political parties. From his adherence to Republican principles, however, and his statement admonishing the people to "accept an adverse judgment [at the ballot box] with the same respect that we would have demanded of our opponents if the decision had been in our favor," it would seem a reasonable inference that he saw the presidency as a party office. But whether the president should be a "leader" or an "agent" of his party is not clear from the address.[72] Given his many references to the Constitution throughout the address, though, it is at least unlikely that he saw his popular, party role as pushing against or overriding the strictures of the Constitution.

Cleveland's second inaugural address furnishes an intriguing counterpoint to his first and represents the beginning of a transition in presidents' conceptions of the office. In 1893 he casts the presidency in far more personal and popular terms than in 1885, and he seems less obsessed with the Constitution and constraints on executive power. Some of the change in tone may be due to its being a second inaugural,[73] but there is clearly more at work. His opening statement indicates the change markedly: "In obedience to the mandate of my countrymen I am about to dedicate myself to their service under the sanction of a solemn oath. Deeply moved by the expression of confidence and personal attachment which has called me to this service, I am sure my gratitude can make no better return than the pledge I now give before God and these witnesses of unreserved and complete devotion to the interests and welfare of those who have honored me."[74] Cleveland's pledges of devotion to the interests of "those who have honored" him and view of his election in part as the result of "personal attachment" are quite consistent with his campaigns in 1888 and 1892 (particularly 1888) in which, although not actively soliciting the suffrages of the people, he attempted to put the party under his leadership primarily through the tariff issue.[75]

Cleveland sees his election as tied intimately to the tariff question and the Democratic Party, with himself at the head. Although he does mention peripheral issues such as pensions, the tariff dominates his address because the voters have "condemned the injustice of maintaining protection for protection's sake . . . [which] stifles the spirit of true Americanism and stupefies every ennobling trait of American citizenship." Further, "The people of the United States have decreed that on this day the control of their Government in its legislative and executive branches shall be given to a political party pledged in the most positive terms to the accomplishment of tariff reform. They have thus determined in favor of a more just and equitable system of Federal taxation. The agents they have chosen to carry out their purposes are bound by their promises not less than by the command of their masters to devote themselves unremittingly to this service."[76]

But what is the role of the executive in all of this? To be sure, Cleveland would not have been Cleveland had he not made a pitch for keeping the presidency within constitutional bounds—and so he does toward the end of his address. Yet one passage is a striking anticipation of Teddy Roosevelt's "stewardship" theory of the presidency. In reference to maintaining the financial situation of the country, Cleveland says, "So far as the executive branch of the Government can intervene, none of the powers with which it is invested will be withheld when their exercise is deemed necessary to maintain our national credit or avert financial disaster."[77] This is not the Cleveland who, in the rhetoric of his first inaugural, was vigilant about keeping the executive within its proper sphere, seemingly preferring a weak executive to a strong one. Rather, this is a Cleveland imbued by his popular mandate with the sense that he should use the office more expansively to look out for the people's interests through his leadership of the Democratic Party. Here is a president who sees himself as the unequivocal head of the Democratic Party, quite at odds with previous party presidents, who saw themselves perhaps leading but certainly not dominating the party.

William McKinley's two inaugurals further evidence this transition toward a president's more active leadership of party and expanded role in governing. In the first, dominated by financial concerns, he casts himself as the leader of the Republican Party, but he is still careful to be deferential to Congress. The party and its principles having been ratified by the people in the 1896 election, McKinley "earnestly hope[s] and expect[s] that Congress will, at the earliest practicable moment, enact revenue legislation that shall be fair, reasonable, conservative, and just." Furthermore, he announces that he will convene a special session of Congress, an action that "it has been the uniform practice of each President to avoid," to enact "the national verdict of 1896." Although McKinley is simply employing a power granted him by the Constitution, it has, as he mentions, been rarely wielded. But he feels bound by the will of the people in the 1896 election and hence obligated to use his office to enforce that will.[78]

Interestingly, in a passage that anticipates the tenor of his second inaugural, McKinley suggests toward the end of his first address that the will of the people should be binding not simply on the winning party but on the whole of government: "The triumph of the people, whose verdict is carried into effect today, is not the triumph of one section, nor wholly of one party, but of all sections and all the people." Peculiarly, McKinley is suggesting that all should respect the will of the people, not simply the winning party; this would seem to depart somewhat from the sentiment in Polk's address, where he expressly acknowledges a continuing opposition to the Democratic Party even after his election.[79] Extending this theme, McKinley's second inaugural address appears to mark an important break with earlier conceptions of the executive office and its relationship with the public. He reiterates his understanding of party government and the will of the people via elections. Moreover, he clearly accords Congress an important role in governing: "The national verdict of 1896 has for the most part been executed. Whatever remains unfulfilled is a continuing obligation resting with undiminished force upon the Executive and the Congress." Yet later in the address, McKinley intimates that the standard idea of party government may be experiencing a revision. Talking about beginning his second term, McKinley remarks: "I should shrink from the duties this day assumed if I did not feel that in their performance I should have the co-operation of the wise and patriotic men of *all* parties. . . . The national purpose is indicated through a national election. It is the constitutional method of ascertaining the public will. When once it is registered it is a law to us *all*, and faithful observance should follow its decrees."[80]

McKinley seems to be suggesting something more than that a president should be a good party man; rather, he should be a leader of all the people, and partisanship should subside after an election, with everyone acknowledging the public will. His suggestion is quite similar, although with far less rhetorical flourish, to sentiments in Wilson's first inaugural (cited below). Without reading too much into McKinley's words, it seems plausible that he is reconceptualizing the office. Among the possible explanations why leaders began to overshadow their parties in the late nineteenth century, one that I have not yet examined in detail is particularly important in McKinley's case: the increasing involvement of the United States, and the executive, in foreign affairs. McKinley's second address is dominated by discussions of foreign affairs and contains sweeping statements that seem to bind the executive and the nation together:

> There are some national questions in the solution of which patriotism should exclude partisanship. Magnifying their difficulties will not take them off our hands nor facilitate their adjustment. . . . We will be consoled, too, with the fact that opposition has confronted every onward movement of the Republic from its opening hour until now, but without success. The Republic has marched on and on, and its step has exalted freedom and humanity. We are undergoing the same ordeal as did our predecessors nearly a century ago. We are following a course they blazed. They triumphed. Will their successors falter and plead organic impotency in the nation?[81]

These words are a barely concealed attack on those, such as William Jennings Bryan, who had criticized McKinley's financial policies and also "his acquisitions of Cuba, Guam, and the Philippines." What is notable, though, is that McKinley spins the criticism of "obstructionists who despair" as directed not only against himself or his administration but against the Republic and the nation.[82] Such remarks are clearly not those of a president who sees himself as a party leader or constitutional officer only; they are the statements of one who feels an identification of self with the American people and the nation, one who seemingly embodies the nation.

The growing U.S. role in foreign engagements, particularly the Spanish-American War, helped to change the standard perception of the presidency. As Sidney Milkis and Michael Nelson have pointed out, McKinley's international engagements "subdued partisan differences. For the first time since George Washington, the president attained a status above party politics." Charles S. Olcott, a McKinley biographer, saw McKinley's presidency in similar terms: "It was a distinctly new McKinley who faced the cheering crowd before the Capitol on Inauguration Day, March 4, 1901. Four years before, the man who took the oath of office was McKinley the Republican, the triumphant leader of his party. . . . Now it was McKinley the national President, standing before a reunited nation from which sectionalism had been driven away; a President whose judgment had been vindicated and his principles approved, a President returned to power with the confidence and goodwill of the wise and patriotic men of all parties."[83]

Inaugural addresses in the party period of the nineteenth century indicate the signal influence of popular elections and political parties on the presidency. That presidents were associated with and felt an obligation to their parties and their principles suggests that presidents were popular, democratic leaders. Parties, as several presidents noted in their addresses, were conceived as the mechanisms by which the people could exert substantial influence on their government; they were, in essence, organized public opinion. By bowing to the dictates of their parties, presidents were, in a very real sense, contravening the constitutional dictum that the president should be "independent," not only of Congress but of public opinion. To be sure, presidents in the nineteenth century did not see their popular, partisan backing as entitling them to disregard the Constitution; rather, they used their popular support to push the party's agenda through constitutional channels, with due deference to Congress.

True, the development of the presidency qua party office had itself been gradual, not dramatic. By 1844, however, presidents' affiliations with parties, in their electoral and governing manifestations, were a staple of inaugural addresses and continued as such well into the twentieth century, though with Cleveland and McKinley, there were signs that the president's role vis-à-vis the party would soon change substantially.

"Their Leader In Affairs"

Twentieth-century inaugural addresses, contrasting sharply with nineteenth-century addresses in both the constitutional and party periods, evolved after McKinley toward what I call the plebiscitary model.[84] Whereas changes in form were substantial in the addresses of Cleveland and McKinley, Teddy Roosevelt altered it even more significantly in his short address. He makes no references to Congress, political parties, or electoral mandates and no mention of keeping the executive within proper constitutional bounds—in fact, there are no references to the Constitution at all. Furthermore, Roosevelt consistently employs the term "we," seeking to bind his presidency up with the destiny of the nation. As Barbara Hinckley has argued, "The government, as Roosevelt portrays it, is centered in a president who speaks so completely for the nation and the American people that they do not need to be mentioned separately."[85] For example, in discussing the challenges facing him and the United States, T. R. declares, "If we fail, the cause of free self-government throughout the world will rock to its foundations."[86] The notion of the president as leader of "all of the people," rather than merely of a party or of the victorious majority, is made manifest in Roosevelt's address.

In marked contrast to his predecessor's, however, William Howard Taft's inaugural address reverts to the party model of the nineteenth century. As a strict observer of the Constitution, Taft is very much concerned with it and with the proper limits of executive power in his inaugural address. Far less likely than either Roosevelt or the presidents after him to speak in terms of "we" or to bind himself up with the nation, he is quite willing to acknowledge that the government comprised other actors besides the president—particularly Congress.[87] Yet within these constitutional limits, as in the party model of inaugural address, Taft expresses a strong bond with his party and its principles and a good deal of concern with his preelection promises; he makes no fewer than five references to his election pledges and the Republican platform of 1908. Keenly aware of the mandate of the election, Taft also remarks that he will call a special session of Congress "in order that consideration may at once be given to a bill revising the Dingley [Tariff] Act."[88] Although Taft is certainly discarding T. R.'s notion of the executive as "steward of the people," he nevertheless sees the executive as having a popular, partisan base or constituency.

Woodrow Wilson's addresses, not surprisingly, are quite significant in the context of my analysis. In both inaugurals he posits a place for himself and the presidency quite unlike those outlined by previous presidents with the exception of Teddy Roosevelt. Wilson's first message is a little deceiving, for it approximates the party model in important ways: he clearly identifies himself as the executive leader of the Democratic Party and sees his election as a mandate for action. Unlike Polk or Taft, however, Wilson does not relate executive leadership to constitutional boundaries. Rather, he speaks as if his popularity forms the sole basis of his leadership. Moreover, he clearly elevates the executive above its traditional constitutional station; for instance, he makes no mention of Congress as a crucial part of the government.[89]

What is perhaps most remarkable is how intimately Wilson binds himself and the presidency to the American people.[90] Even as leader of the Democratic Party, he views his party's victory differently than previous presidents (except McKinley). Polk, for instance, promised that he would not discriminate against his opponents, but he did not regard his election as uniting "all" behind him. Yet Wilson sees the Democratic victory as a victory not just for a majority of citizens but for the whole of America: "Here muster, not the forces of party, but the forces of humanity. . . . I summon all honest men, all patriotic, all forward-looking men, to my side." This sentiment is even more marked in Wilson's second inaugural address. As in the first, the Constitution and Congress are missing in action—but this time, so are the Democrats and partisans. Instead, he binds up the government almost wholly with the person of Woodrow Wilson, "because the people of the United States have chosen me for this august delegation of power and have by their gracious judgment named me their leader in affairs."[91] Wilson is the plebiscitary leader.

The Republican presidents of the 1920s, Harding, Coolidge, and Hoover, all represent something of a return to the party model form of inaugural address, delineating a more modest role for the presidency and showing more deference to their political parties and Congress. Warren Harding, in marked contrast to the high expectations placed upon more modern presidents, does not assume "that there is to be sole responsibility in the Executive for the America of tomorrow," and Calvin Coolidge pointedly defends political parties and responsible party government: "Since its very outset, it has been found necessary to conduct our Government by means of political parties. . . . There is no salvation in a narrow and bigoted partisanship. But if there is to be responsible party government, the party label must be something more than a mere device for securing office. . . . When the country has bestowed its confidence upon a party by making it a majority in the Congress, it has a right to expect such unity of action as will make the party majority an effective instrument of government." Herbert Hoover further reinforces this party understanding of government and presidential action: "In our form of democracy the expression of the popular will can be effected only through the instrumentality of political parties. . . . It follows that the government both in the executive and the legislative branches must carry out in good faith the platforms upon which the party was intrusted with power."[92]

Yet all three inaugural addresses continue the trends—if somewhat abated—toward identifying the president with the nation and neglecting other actors such as Congress. Moreover, alongside the respect for

Congress and concern with constitutional balance, one can see a decidedly modern characterization of the presidency. A statement from Coolidge's inaugural gives a good sense of how things had changed by the 1920s: "The essence of a republic is representative government. Our Congress represents the people and the States. In all legislative affairs it is the natural collaborator with the President. . . . I welcome its cooperation, and expect to share with it not only the responsibility, but the credit, for our common effort to secure beneficial legislation."[93] Coolidge almost puts the action of legislation with the president who will then "welcome" or solicit congressional involvement in the process. Even under the watch of a conservative Republican, the office of the president was growing in power and importance relative to Congress and other political actors, including parties.

After Hoover, there would be no more reversions to the party model of inaugural address. The modern trends begun with Cleveland, McKinley, T. R., and Wilson continued and grew more dominant. Presidents more and more came to cast the government as "presidential," rarely mentioning Congress and other actors, and to bind themselves ever more closely with the nation and the American people.[94] Perhaps no modern inaugural address better articulates this understanding of the relationship between the president and the people than Jimmy Carter's: "You have given me a great responsibility—to stay close to you, to be worthy of you, and to exemplify what you are. . . . Your strength can compensate for my weakness, and your wisdom can help to minimize my mistakes."[95] Moreover, the Constitution and analyses of the role of the president within the constitutional framework are almost entirely absent from these later addresses.[96] There is little talk about restraints on the presidency and usually little concern with balance in the American political system.

Concomitant with this movement of the presidency to the center of the action is a trend in inaugural addresses toward investing presidency and government with awesome (and likely unattainable) expectations. John F. Kennedy, for instance, says that in the "long history of the world, only a few generations have been granted the role of defending freedom in its hour of maximum danger. I do not shrink from this responsibility—I welcome it." Ronald Reagan asserts that "we have every right to dream heroic dreams. . . . Your dreams, your hopes, your goals are going to be the dreams, the hopes, and the goals of this administration, so help me God." And Bill Clinton in his first inaugural exhorts the nation: "From this joyful mountaintop of celebration, we hear the call to service in the valley. We have heard the trumpets. We have changed the guard. And now, each in our way, and with God's help, we must answer the call."[97]

Perhaps most interesting is the declining role of parties and elections in inaugural addresses since Hoover; from Franklin D. Roosevelt's through to the present, partisan references and talk of elections have substantially declined. As Hinckley has put it, "It could not be known from the presidents' accounts that they were associated with a party or had won an election. Indeed, one would not know how they had come to office, whether through election, monarchical succession, or divine anointing."[98] Because presidents have become so identified with the nation and the American people, because they are thought to embody not only the government but the people, they are loath to cast themselves as partisans, as politicians. Because they are plebiscitary leaders, it is almost tautological for them to spell out the popular electoral connection between president and people; they are so obviously linked to the American people that the relationship need not be explained.

There are, of course, interesting exceptions to these general contours. The first George Bush's address, for instance, departs from the plebiscitary model on several counts: he is willing not only to speak frankly about parties and partisanship but also to champion the virtues of compromise and pay deference to congressional prerogative. What is more, Bush appears to reject an all-encompassing view of the presidency: "A President is neither prince nor pope, and I don't seek a window on men's souls." And in almost direct opposition to the sentiment (quoted above) that Clinton would convey four years later, he says, "Some see leadership as high drama, and the sound of trumpets calling, and sometimes it is that. But I see history as a book with many pages, and each day we fill a page with acts of hopefulness and meaning."[99]

But these sentiments constitute an exception to the general drift of modern inaugural addresses, which routinely invest the presidency with extensive expectations. They downplay (if they mention at all) the role of Congress and other actors in the political system, bind the presidency and the American people intimately together, and tend to neglect (if not vilify) those engines of nineteenth-century American democracy: political parties.

That the presidential office is now more democratic and popular is a truism, on the modern understanding of presidential leadership. From the perspective of the party era, however, the modern addresses would likely seem inconsistent with what nineteenth-century Americans had come to understand as democracy. Democracy, in the party era, did not revolve around one central, pseudomonarchical figure; rather, it involved the interactions of a network of individuals and groups: legislators, executives, party leaders, and the public, across all levels of government.

F. D. R., a main primogenitor of the modern presidency and its leadership assumptions and expectations, seemed to sense that accretion of power in the executive could pose problems for democratic governance. Indeed, he struggles with this antinomy in his first two inaugural addresses, saying in the first: "We do not distrust the future of essential democracy. The people of the United States have not failed. In their need they have registered a mandate that they want direct, vigorous action. They have asked for discipline and direction under leadership. They have made me the present instrument of their wishes. In the spirit of the gift I take it." And in the second inaugural, clearly grasping the potential contradictions between extensive executive (and federal) authority and democratic self-government, he opines: "Four years of new experience have not belied our historic instinct. They hold out the clear hope that government within communities, government within the separate States, and government of the United States can do the things the times require, without yielding its democracy. Our tasks in the last four years did not force democracy to take a holiday."[100] F. D. R.'s successors would expend less (public) effort worrying about the possible problems for democracy posed by their leadership.

"Bound, beyond the Power of Emancipation, to Party Principles and Measures"

Given its departure from the conventional view of nineteenth-century inaugurals, some may be hesitant to accept the interpretation of party-period inaugurals offered here. A look at their newspaper reception, however—that of the *National Intelligencer, Baltimore Sun, New York Tribune,* and *Washington Evening Star*—reveals a strikingly similar understanding of their meaning and function.[101]

Consistent with my analysis of inaugural addresses, newspaper coverage of inaugurals prior to Harrison's in 1841 tends to characterize them as relatively nonpartisan and unremarkable.[102] In 1841, however, the *Sun* and the *Intelligencer*—the two of the four papers which had begun publication by this time—filter Harrison's inaugural through the lens of party. The Democratic *Sun* chooses to emphasize that "party spirit receives no favor at his hands, but on the contrary, [is] very decidedly condemned." The Whig *Intelligencer,* however, sees the inaugural event as "the consummation of the great political contest which terminated in the election of Gen. Harrison" and describes his address as an "authoritative enunciation" of Whig principles. What is more, the *Intelligencer* later in the week exhorts Whigs in the western states to vote for Whig congressmen (House elections were not at this time uniform, many states electing members in odd years and in months other than November) who will "assist the President to carry out their will." The president is certainly a party leader to the *Intelligencer.*[103]

By 1845 there is less disagreement among the papers, which now include the *New York Tribune.* The *Sun,* though emphasizing the independent or even antiparty aspects of Polk's address, also notes its "strict constructionist" perspective—hardly a nonpartisan position—and the *Intelligencer* and *Tribune* both stress its partisan nature. The *Intelligencer* sees through the supposedly "independent" passages to assert that the address shows Polk "bound, beyond the power of emancipation, to party principles and measures." The Whig *Tribune* is nearly as harsh: Polk is a "small man for President, and is capable of doing very mean and bad things for his party." It should come as no surprise that the *Tribune* editors will do "all in our power to resist and defeat the bad measures he will persist in forcing on the Country."[104]

Reporting the inauguration of Taylor—that "Whig but not an ultra Whig"—newspaper coverage is accordingly ambiguous. The *Sun* philosophizes that government will be "immediately subject in a certain extent to the influences, prejudices and purposes of new minds." The *Intelligencer,* however, opines that the "voice of party and of faction will be hushed by the loud acclaim of the people wherever this address is read." The *Richmond Whig,* prominently quoted in the *Intelligencer* of the same day, lauds Taylor's address and contrasts it with recent inaugurals that were "better suited [for] the editorial columns of a party newspaper than the mouth of a President elect." Yet many other Whig papers, as quoted in the *Intelligencer,* saw the inaugural as a decidedly Whig document which should, as the *Virginia Herald* put it, "give assurance to every Whig that he has not been mistaken in his man."[105]

By 1853, with the *Evening Star* having joined the ranks, all four papers are established. Pierce's rather unexceptional inaugural in 1853 does not provoke much examination or analysis from either the *Sun* or the *Star.*[106] The Whig *Intelligencer* and *Tribune* are quite critical, however, the latter arguing that "we belong to that large portion of the American People to whom he [Pierce] (in common parlance) 'owes nothing.'"[107] Buchanan's inaugural of 1857 "breathes an emphatic Democratic spirit," as the *Star* phrases it.[108] Yet the *Intelligencer,* curiously, finds little in the inaugural to criticize, the editor incredulously reports. The *Tribune,* now firmly in the Republican camp with the demise of the Whigs, sees things a bit differently: "Mr. Buchanan and many other politicians have turned traitors to democracy, have been ready for the sake of Presidencies and other offices to betray liberty." Most specifically, the *Tribune* objects to the Democratic policy of "popular sovereignty" (which Buchanan undoubtedly upholds in the inaugural): "Vainly did we point to the Cincinnati Democratic Platform as artfully embodying the very doctrine of Territorial pupilage and wardship which it was vaunted as denying."[109] Here is not only the connection of newly elected presidents to principles and parties but also the importance of party platforms to presidential action.

Lincoln's first inaugural is viewed almost universally as a party document. The *Star* sees that the inaugural has "utterly exploded party here (as it must to a great extent everywhere else) so far as the duty of standing by the Union is concerned," but the *Tribune* lauds Lincoln, for he "has successfully resisted the pressure upon him to recede from the Republican position on which the party won its victory, and, in his Inaugural, stands firm." The *Intelligencer* notes also Lincoln's affiliation with the Republican Party and his fidelity to election and partisan pledges. The *Sun* stridently criticizes his "black republicanism" and rather breathlessly observes that "for the first time in the history of the country, we are told in the inaugural of a President, not of his constitutional duties as explained by the constitution and decisions of the Supreme Court, but of his duties as laid down by a party creed, and expounded by party leaders."[110] The *Sun* was right to identify the precedent in Lincoln's inaugural, yet it is certainly also eliding the partisan qualities of inaugurals since Jackson. Rather than such a departure from past practice, Lincoln's action was a sign or confirmation of the firm establishment of parties by 1861.

Not surprisingly, Lincoln's second and Grant's two inaugurals are more characterized as nonpartisan and independent addresses. Lincoln's second, unique among inaugurals in seeking to rally a weary people during the waning days of a bloody civil war, is dismissed only by the *Sun;* the other three newspapers strongly praise it. The *Intelligencer* approximates most closely what became the historical judgment: speaking of the famous concluding paragraph, the editors say that the words "are equally distinguished for patriotism, statesmanship, and benevolence, and deserve to be printed in gold."[111] Grant's first and second inaugurals similarly meet with talk of independence and nonpartisanship. The *Star* remarks of the first that it "seems to have given satisfaction to men of all parties," and the *Sun* finds it "encouraging to hear him declare at the outset that he commences the duties of his office untrammeled."[112] Republican papers are not nearly as thrilled with his seeming independence, the *Tribune* grumbling that Grant "tells us what *he* understands to be the meaning of the Republican party in electing him to the Presidential office." Similarly, the *Intelligencer,* which would cease publication before Grant's second inaugural, urges him to maintain his fidelity to the party and the Chicago platform of 1868 because "on this platform General Grant stepped, and the Republican party triumphed."[113] Coverage of the second inaugural is comparable, with Grant's independence assuming primary attention amid some comments linking him to the Republican party and its principles and ideas.[114]

With Hayes's inaugural in 1877, there is no such ambivalence. The *Star* notes Hayes's "promises" made before the election; both the *Sun* and the *Tribune* show the strong relationship of the inaugural to Hayes's letter accepting the Republican nomination in 1876, the *Tribune* matter-of-factly opining beforehand, "It goes without saying that his address will be in entire harmony with his letter of acceptance"—as, indeed, it was.[115] Garfield's rather bland and banal inaugural is treated accordingly by the *Sun* and the *Star,* neither seeing much of controversy or partisan opinion in it. The *Tribune,* however, finds it a good Republican document; especially with regard to racial issues, his "statement of the case is as strong as the most uncompromising and stalwart Republican could desire."[116]

The *Sun* sees in Cleveland's first inaugural, in 1885, decided evidence of a resurgence of parties and party principles, and the *Star* concurs that "the changes in men and in principles of government will be great." The *Tribune* and the *Star* also perceptively foresee the possible clashes to come between the sometimes independent Cleveland and his Democratic Party. The *Tribune* asks, "Are we to believe that on such and so many vital matters President Cleveland will have the courage and manliness and the capacity to confront and resist the prevailing tendencies of his party?"[117] Harrison's address reveals no such tension with his party. Notwithstanding the *Sun's* self-serving hope that "the office belongs to an individual not a party," the *Tribune* more accurately reports that the inaugural "speaks unhesitatingly and without compromise for those whose convictions have prevailed in the late election, but speaks for them only as they sincerely seek the welfare of the Republic."[118] Cleveland's second inaugural is perhaps even more strongly characterized as a party document and as part of a party movement, but yet again the tensions between Cleveland and his party are evident. The *Tribune* notes disparagingly that Cleveland refers to the Democratic Party as "my party," and the *Sun* remarks that "it will be a Cleveland administration in a much more marked and decided sense even than that of four years ago."[119] Although there is no doubt that Cleveland is a Democrat, there is some uneasiness as to his dominance of the party; the modern presidency is knocking at the door.

Coverage of McKinley's inaugurals evidences the same trends in presidential leadership and presidential importance. Parties are still seen as important players.[120] But his second address especially is characterized as transcending partisanship somewhat and seeking a personal relationship with the American people. The second inaugural shows "no note of party triumph, no exploitation of party purpose," says the *Star;* and in it, reports the *Tribune*, McKinley "speaks directly to the people themselves . . . with a personal assurance and more than ordinary authority."[121] Now certainly McKinley's reelection and assumption of a second term had something to do with this more personal relationship with the people— as already pointed out, second inaugurals tended to be less partisan and principle-laden—yet we also see the beginnings of the modern presidency, developments that would be advanced and more firmly established by Theodore Roosevelt and Woodrow Wilson, as newspaper coverage of their inaugurals also clearly reveals.[122]

Newspaper coverage of party period inaugurals, then, strongly supports my interpretation of those inaugurals. The papers do highlight, at times, antiparty sentiments and claims to independence on the part of presidents; moreover, they do spend some ink extolling the unifying and harmonizing qualities of inaugural addresses. But they also bring into sharp relief the importance of parties to the nineteenth-century political world and presidential leadership as articulated in the inaugural addresses. Presidents were tied almost inextricably ("bound, beyond the power of emancipation," as the *Intelligencer* put it) to political parties, and these parties created a presidency that was a seat of popular leadership.

Inaugural messages provide considerable evidence of the pull of party on the nineteenth-century presidency. Party-period presidents, while maintaining a deferential, balanced constitutional perspective, cast the presidency in partisan and popular terms. Their addresses were responsive to the public will and committed to the principles of the parties that elected them—much at odds both with founding doctrine and early inaugural messages and with modern inaugural messages. The question to be examined next is whether actual governing *practice* in the party period corresponded to the *theory* of governance laid out in the inaugural messages.

Chapter Five

Party-in-Government I
James Polk and Zachary Taylor

The people, by the Constitution, have commanded the President, as much as they have commanded the legislative branch of Government, to execute their will. . . . If it be said that the Representatives in the popular branch of Congress are chosen directly by the people, it is answered, the people elect the President. If both Houses represent the States and the people, so does the President.

James Polk, Fourth Annual Message

Did nineteenth-century presidents work actively and consistently with their parties once they were elevated to the presidency? If not playing the part of active party leaders, did they at least play the more passive, acquiescing role of party agents? Or, once in office, did they largely eschew or downplay party considerations, assuming the mantle of constitutional officer rather than partisan? These are the outstanding questions of this book. The previous chapters have shown that most nineteenth-century presidential candidates were closely affiliated with their parties; that their views and political opinions, almost always in consonance with those of their party, were made known during the elections and formed an important basis for the campaigns; and that these presidents, once elevated to office, paid deference to in their inaugural messages and pledged to act on behalf of the party and its principles. What is more, this was not partisan leadership for the sake of mere party gain; rather, candidates were well attuned to the democratic, popular quality of parties and party leadership.

But for the democratic nature of party leadership to be fully realized, the relationship between the people and the party president needs to be consummated; that is, once in office, a president must take actions consistent with his party. Promising to act as a partisan in the campaign and inaugural message is all well and good, but it is not the same thing as acting with the party in an official capacity. It would be a hollow victory for the people if parties and candidates had little regard for redeeming their campaign pledges once elected. Similarly, if the prime rewards the people received in return for party votes were patronage positions and government contracts, the party platforms and policies espoused therein would seem to have been ornamentation to camouflage a crass instrumentalism more than pledges or visions attuned to the country's best interests.

To determine whether party presidents acted with their parties to promote substantive party positions and policies, I analyze their rhetoric and conduct. I also probe the extent of their aggressiveness in promoting the party agenda, establishing an agent-leader continuum of party leadership. To do so, I employ the case study method. A sample of five well-selected presidencies allows in-depth treatment and affords a substantial base from which to generalize about nineteenth-century presidential behavior in the partisan era.

The five presidents I examine are James Polk and Zachary Taylor in this chapter and U. S. Grant, Benjamin Harrison, and Grover Cleveland in the next. The following criteria governed the selections: (1) the party period must be represented across time; (2) the major parties within the period must be represented; and (3) the presidents should be ones elected by the people in a decisive presidential election. I did not wish to focus on presidents who ascended to the office because of the death of the incumbent or through a controversial election, such as that of Hayes in 1876. The party view holds that the people exert control over their leaders primarily through elections. If a president assumes the office after serving as a relatively obscure vice president or after a disputed election, his electoral ties to the people will be less than clear and strong. The party view must at least be given a fair chance. (For discussion of these selections and the omission of major leaders such as Jackson and Lincoln, see Appendix 2.)

To analyze presidential conduct, I first examined the recommendations for legislation that each president made to Congress, gauging how aggressively they pushed their party agendas, at least in a formal sense.[1] Comparing such requests with his party's platform allows one to judge whether a president felt bound by the platform. Numerous presidential recommendations in State of the Union and special messages in consonance with the party platform imply an aggressive leadership style; very few such requests imply minimal and passive party leadership.[2]

But comparing presidential requests with party platforms is only a start, for platform planks may be such that a presidential recommendation for congressional action would not be the most likely route to honoring them. For instance, the Democratic platform of 1844 was in many ways a negative document, pledging the party *not* to use the government for various reasons. One plank inveighed against allowing the federal government to conduct internal improvements. Polk, to honor this pledge, would not recommend that Congress not enact internal improvements legislation; rather, he would either veto bills for internal improvements or inveigh against them in annual messages or some other format.

For this reason, then, I looked beyond presidents' recommendations to full texts of their annual messages and also to major veto messages, documents that form the second major thrust of the case studies. Annual messages can be used to rally the party and assume leadership without necessarily requesting particular legislation or recommending a course of positive action. For example, a president may denounce certain policies and principles or articulate party positions. Moreover, a major veto, a negative action, can be leveled to sustain and uphold a party position or platform plank. Again, the president here may be seen as assuming the leadership of his party, depending on the tenor of the message.

The third and final thrust of the case studies goes beyond presidents' formal messages and delves into less obvious channels of party leadership, the two main ones being their face-to-face lobbying of congressmen and public lobbying through the newspapers. To determine these, I relied on secondary sources: for whether presidents engaged in personal lobbying of members of Congress, primarily presidential biographies and studies of the individual presidencies; for whether presidents used the newspapers to push the party agenda, several thorough studies of presidency-press relations.[3]

The newspaper analysis is particularly interesting, for it touches on a connection between the people and president beyond the electoral stage, the primary nexus I have been pursuing. Of course, since newspapers were largely partisan until the 1880s, this connection was still established primarily along partisan lines.[4] Through the party press the president would not be trying to lure the *whole* people to his side so much as trying to marshal party solidarity and unity. Nevertheless, this behavior was clearly a kind of popular appeal, for presidents wanted to rally support throughout the country for themselves and their party. In any case, the important point is that presidents turned to newspapers in their efforts to lead and, they hoped, unify the party.[5]

James K. Polk: Molding Partisan Opinion

Some historians but few political scientists have understood the unconventional character of James Polk's presidency, which in certain signal respects stands in stark contrast to those of most of his predecessors.[6] The most important difference for my purposes is that Polk was an unabashed party leader as president.

Comparing Polk's presidential requests to the Twenty-ninth and Thirtieth Congresses with the Democratic platform of 1844 yields some interesting findings. The platform outlined nine major points or planks: (1) no internal improvements by the federal government; (2) no assumption of state debts by the federal government; (3) rescission of the protective tariff; (4) establishment of a constitutional treasury (anti–U.S. Bank); (5) no interference by Congress with slavery; (6) new public lands policy; (7) defense of presidential veto power; (8) support for U.S. title to the Oregon Territory; and (9) annexation of Texas and cession of lands.[7]

During the Twenty-ninth Congress, Polk spoke to five of those nine planks in annual and special messages, going so far as to quote one of them ("constitutional treasury") directly in his first annual message: four requests dealt with the issue of tariff duties, one addressed the constitutional treasury policy, five concerned public lands policies, eighteen concerned action on the Oregon Territory, and three pertained to annexing Texas or acquiring lands from Mexico. During the thirtieth Congress, Polk made requests relating to only four of the nine planks: one to keep slavery out of discussions about acquiring new lands, four regarding public lands policies, six regarding the settlement of the Oregon Territory and two about purchasing or organizing territories from Mexico.[8]

It would seem, on the face of it, that Polk was not a very strong party president. After all, he neglected four of the planks during the Twenty-ninth Congress and five during the Thirtieth. If frequency of request gauges aggressiveness in pushing party planks, Polk ostensibly "championed" only the tariff, public lands policies, and issues of the Oregon Territory. Moreover, he completely neglected to make requests to the Thirtieth Congress about the tariff and the constitutional treasury, two putatively crucial Democratic policies. Thus, Polk would appear to be only modestly a party president, one concerned with only certain policies of the Democratic Party—most important, acquisition of new territories and reform of public lands policy.

A more textured look at Polk's policy advocacy, however, reveals strong party leadership beyond formal requests, which are necessary but not sufficient to understanding his party leadership. Other factors clearly need to be taken into account: the success of some of his major measures in the first session of the Twenty-ninth Congress, the "negative" nature of the Democratic platform of 1844, Polk's major vetoes of internal improvements bills, and the strong rhetoric of his annual messages.

Before the first session of the Twenty-ninth Congress adjourned, Polk had won passage of three major Democratic policies: the acquisition of the Oregon Territory, the reduction of the protective tariff, and the creation of the constitutional treasury. The Oregon Territory and its organization would continue to be issues for the Polk administration, but the tariff and treasury laws, once passed, were in need of no more positive attention from the president—which explains the absence of "requests" for action on these planks after Polk's first annual message. Even so, Polk did not neglect those issues in his later messages. There was no need for further congressional action, but there was call, on Polk's view, at least, for exhortations on the efficacy of these measures and the need to maintain them. In his second message, for example, Polk says of the tariff law just taking effect, "The favored classes who [benefited] under the unequal and unjust system which has been repealed . . . will have no reason to complain if they shall be required to bear their just proportion of the taxes necessary for the support of the Government."[9] Surely this is not a president who is no longer concerned with his pledges and Democratic policies. Rather, it is a president who continues to stoke the partisan fires in his messages to Congress, doing more than just "recommending" measures. Polk is assuming the leadership of the Democratic Party through his continuing advocacy of Democratic principles and policies, even after they have been enacted into law.

The Democratic platform of 1844 was in part a negative document:

four of the nine planks were not calls to action but calls for resisting certain federal action. Polk was pledged to defend against federal funding of internal improvements, assuming the debts of the states, interfering with slavery in the states and territories, and restricting the president's veto power. These planks did not require requests for congressional action. As Charles Sellers has said of Polk's first annual message, "On the subject of internal improvements Polk said—nothing. No political genius was required to understand his implicit recommendation that in this area Congress should do—nothing."[10] To be sure, one of these planks could have been converted into a request: Polk's fourth annual message recommends that Congress either extend the Missouri Compromise line through the new territory, keep out of the issue of slavery in the territories, or leave it to the Supreme Court to decide the issue.[11] This language is very much in accord with the Democratic plank to prevent meddling by Congress with the institution of slavery and to stave off any agitation on that issue—but this is the exception. Generally, the four negative planks did not require Polk to request congressional action.

Upholding one such plank, however, did require more than reticence on Polk's part: he wielded his veto twice to uphold Democratic opposition to the federal government's conducting internal improvements and accompanied the vetoes with messages staking out the typical, orthodox Democratic stance on the subject. Polk had, of course, pledged to uphold the platform of 1844, and any internal improvements bill was clearly in violation of the platform. So when Whigs, joined by enough western Democrats, were able to push through legislation providing for internal improvements largely in western states, signing the bill would have meant abandoning his pledges and his Jacksonian principles.[12] He did not disappoint.

In his first veto of internal improvements (August 1846), Polk argues that internal improvements are neither constitutional nor wise policy for the benefit and good of the country. Speaking as a good Democrat, he avers that "the Constitution has not, in my judgment, conferred upon the Federal Government the power to construct works of internal improvement within the States, or to appropriate money from the Treasury for that purpose." Moreover, "the practical evils which must flow from the exercise on the part of the Federal Government of the powers asserted in this bill impress my mind with a grave sense of my duty to avert them from the country as far as my constitutional action may enable me to do so." Polk then goes on to enumerate the classic Jacksonian objections, such as that internal improvements would lead to a plundering of the public treasury.[13] This standard Democratic doctrine is found, in very similar form, in the Democratic platform of 1844: "The Constitution does not confer upon the General Government the power to commence or carry on a general system of internal improvements."[14]

Polk's veto messages allowed him to preserve the party standard and redeem his party pledges of 1844. But none of this is to suggest that Polk did not see his duty as protecting and upholding the Constitution as well; rather, it is another instance of the lines between a "constitutional" and a "party" presidency becoming blurred or perhaps overlapping. Certainly, one might argue that Polk's vetoes of internal improvements legislation were simply the actions of a constitutional clerk, charged with protecting the Constitution from violation. But the story does not end here. It hardly seems mere coincidence that Polk's second internal improvements veto message, he said, "had been violently assailed by the Whig party." Rather, Polk should be seen as redeeming his pledges made in the 1844 campaign and rallying Democrats to the party standard. He had affirmed the Democratic platform and Democratic doctrine in accepting the nomination of the party, and his inaugural address clearly states it as a president's duty to uphold "the principles and policy of those who had elected him." The vetoes, then, reveal a president upholding the principles of "those who had elected him"—Democrats. Polk himself adds credence to this position in his fourth annual message: the president is "bound to discharge [the veto] as well by his obligations to the people who have clothed him with his exalted trust as by his oath of office, which he may not disregard."[15]

Perhaps Polk's annual messages best encapsulate his strong party leadership. Charles Sellers has argued that "none of [Polk's] predecessors had exploited very fully the great potentialities of the annual message as an instrument of legislative initiative." Yet the potential was there. The public was eager to hear what presidents had to say; their annual messages were not simply routine communications directed primarily to Congress. Sellers has described the reaction that met Polk's first message:

> As the clerk in each house began reading the president's recommendations, a locomotive waiting with steam already up was given the signal to start at top speed with copies for the impatient crowds assembled on the streets of downtown Baltimore. Simultaneously word that the reading had

begun was flashed by the new telegraph to Baltimore, where a carefully guarded bundle of advance copies was placed aboard another waiting locomotive bound for Philadelphia. The clerks finished their reading in Washington at four; an hour and twenty-five minutes later the message was being read at the Philadelphia post office, to shouts of "Hurra! Jackson is alive again." New York had copies by 10 p.m., and within another twenty-four hours the president's words had reached Portland, Maine.[16]

Polk did exploit the hoopla surrounding annual messages to direct attention to certain legislative initiatives, especially those that were positive planks of the Democratic platform of 1844. And he was disturbed when Congress delayed action on some of his recommendations. As his administration's newspaper, the *Washington Union,* put it, "Why is this President's [first annual] message permitted to stand before the country a monument of Executive duty done in obedience to the popular mandate, and of Congressional duty *at a stand,* in the very first stage of performance?"[17]

Polk was perhaps one of the first presidents to attempt to lead forcefully and to unify his party through the annual message, to position himself as the mouthpiece of his fellow partisans. He can be seen as offering exhortations (quite successfully at times, it appears) to fellow Democrats in all four of his annual messages. For example, writes Sellers, "a flood of enthusiastic congratulations [poured] in from Democratic leaders of every faction in every part of the country" in response to the first message. Moreover, Polk notes in his diary "that there was universal approval among all the Democratic members [of Congress] and that the Whigs generally had but little to say on the subject." Further, Polk was not appealing just to Democratic leaders. He was concerned that his final message "will be so long that it will not be read by the mass of people, and by none but the politicians."[18]

Although Polk aspired to party leadership in all four annual messages, his fourth and final one was most special, a fitting epitaph to a truly extraordinary and innovative presidency. When he sent that last message to Congress in December 1848, he knew that Zachary Taylor had been elected president and that the Whigs had come close to taking control of both the House and the Senate.[19] The Democrats were certainly in need of leadership that would harmonize the party, put it back in touch with its traditions, and help it to get past the vexing slavery controversies. Polk had been apprehensive for some time about the effect that slavery agitation would have on the Democratic Party and the Union: on January 4, 1847, he worried in his diary that the agitation "will be attended by terrible consequences to the country, and cannot fail to destroy the Democratic party, if it does not ultimately threaten the Union itself." In the same entry, he resolved to rectify the situation: "I will do all I can to correct it; I will do my duty and leave the rest to God and my country."[20]

Polk's final message seems to be an example of his doing his "duty." To help ease the sectional tensions bubbling to the surface, he suggests several courses of action regarding the organization of the territories. Although he acknowledges that practically speaking, there can be no slavery in territories where climate will not permit its existence, he suggests that the people of each territory should decide the question for themselves, consistent with the Democratic principle of "popular sovereignty" that Lewis Cass had campaigned on in the 1848 election. Or, Polk further suggests, perhaps the Missouri Compromise line should be extended to the Pacific Ocean; he hoped that the nation might "cheerfully and patriotically acquiesce in it, and peace and harmony would again fill our borders." If not, Polk adds, it would be desirable for the judicial branch to resolve the question, and he hoped that the nation would then come together in harmony behind the Court's decision.[21]

With the slavery controversy clearly on Polk's mind, he is worried that sectionalism will rend asunder not just his Democratic party but also his Union. These overt suggestions for addressing the controversy, though, are not as interesting as his less explicit but perhaps more passionate appeal for Union: his rallying of Democrats to the traditional party standards. The Democrats and Whigs had, for over a decade, successfully kept slavery out of national politics through their competition over the economy, the scope of government and executive power, and the U.S. Bank. By rallying Democrats to the old standards, Polk hoped to revive the party and, in the process, also protect his precious Union.

At nearly the halfway point of his final message, Polk launches into a lengthy denunciation of that most hated project of Democrats: the American System. He vigorously lambasts its major provisions—the protective tariff, the U.S. Bank, and the federal funding of internal improvements—saying that it was the "tendency, if not the ultimate design, of the system to build up an aristocracy of wealth, to control the masses of society, and to monopolize the political power of the country." His words recall the Democratic campaign and platform of 1844. Indeed, Polk is in a sense campaigning in this fourth annual message: he is campaigning for the support of the Democracy behind its old standards and away from the sectionalism of current times.[22]

Polk was seeking a position for himself as leader and unifier of the Democratic Party for one last time. Although soon to retire, he was nevertheless aspiring to the leadership of his party and, through his party, to a position of popular leadership much at odds with the original constitutional view of presidential leadership. And Polk's appeal for party unity appears to have been effective. On his view, "The Democratic members [of Congress] all express their satisfaction at my message. . . . The Whig newspapers, so far as I have seen them, are very abusive of it . . . [but] Democratic papers generally speak favorably of it."[23]

Polk's fourth annual message lends credence to the idea that he conceived of the presidency as a seat of popular leadership. He was primarily referring to and justifying his major vetoes when he laid out his understanding of presidential leadership. He not only justifies his vetoes by appeal to the old saw that presidents should veto legislation they believe to be unconstitutional; he goes farther to say that he is obliged to veto legislation if a veto would be in accord with the "will of the people."[24] The founders, of course, did not see the veto as executing the "will of the people" in any direct sense. In fact, they likely saw it as a way of checking the immediate will of the people; it might be in the people's interest in the long term and in an extended sense but not in a direct and immediate sense. Polk, however, ties the veto much more closely to the popular will.

Polk expands upon and clarifies the Jacksonian idea of the president as tribune of the people and the veto as a major means of fulfilling this station: "In the exercise of the power of the veto the President is responsible not only to an enlightened public opinion, but to the people of the whole Union, who elected him, as the representatives in the legislative branches who differ with him in opinion are responsible to the people of particular States or districts, who compose their respective constituencies." The Congress is no longer the only branch that represents the people. The presidency is now also the "people's branch": "If it be said that the Representatives in the popular branch of Congress are chosen directly by the people, it is answered, the people elect the President. If both Houses represent the States and the people, so does the President. The President represents in the executive department the whole people of the United States, as each member of the legislative department represents portions of them."[25] This declaration is quite consistent with the understanding of the office of the presidency in Polk's inaugural address. The people had elevated him to office to implement their will and policies; the presidency was a seat of popular leadership, primarily channeled through parties and elections.[26]

Beyond taking the initiative through formal requests, messages, and actions, Polk was also quite active in leading the Democratic Party through informal channels. Particularly, by personally lobbying congressmen and using his administration newspaper to unify and harmonize the party, Polk sought support for his administration's measures. He was clearly not an adherent of the Whig doctrine that the president should defer to Congress and simply approve its will in most circumstances. Beyond using the formal messages to unify the party and to prod Congress to support his policies, as Charles Sellers has put it, he "skillfully utilized all the tactics for executive leadership of Congress that were eventually to become standard operating techniques of the presidency."[27]

Polk's first strategic move was his selection of a cabinet. Not only did he want to assure that the major geographic regions of the country were represented, but he also wanted to make sure that the major factions and leaders of the Democratic Party were given their just rewards in the form of cabinet posts (Polk operated in a similar manner when it came to dispensing patronage). For instance, he nominated James Buchanan, a major figure within the Democratic Party (and a future president), to head the Department of State. By nominating major party leaders and conciliating the major factions within the party, Polk took an important step toward guaranteeing his own influence with his partisans in Congress. Indeed, cabinet members played an important role in Polk's relationship with Congress.[28]

Another major tactic in Polk's arsenal for dealing with Congress was personal lobbying of members, either by the president himself or by his cabinet members. For instance, Polk, "utilized his cabinet members to lobby the House members in behalf of the Crittenden resolution [a "notice resolution" to the British regarding the Oregon Territory] that had been embraced by the Senate." Likewise, in the battle over the tariff bill of 1846, Polk not only deployed his cabinet and partisan senators to persuade their equivocal colleagues, but he himself urged recalcitrant sena-

tors to support the bill. In particular, he met with the Democratic senator William Haywood numerous times over the course of a week during
the tariff battle, entreating the senator to come on board and support the
policy. Haywood would resign his seat before the final vote took place,
but the "party stayed remarkably cohesive" in the Senate, according to
Sellers, in no small part because of the efforts of Polk and his group of
lobbyists.[29]

At times during the Mexican War, though, the party's loss of cohesion
was troubling. Polk's diary notes Democratic defections on certain administration policies: "I have a nominal majority of Democrats in both
Houses of Congress, but am in truth in a minority in each House." Additionally, "The people elected a majority of both Houses to sustain
my policy, but their Representatives do not do so." Factions within the
Democratic Party were at odds, largely, Polk thought, because of their
jockeying for the next presidential election. But he was determined to
whip these apostates into shape. His plan was not only to push his
cabinet to rally recalcitrant Democrats but also to "send a Measure to
Congress, and make an earnest appeal through them to the country, to
come to the support of the Executive in a vigorous prosecution of the
War against Mexico." He later avers that "if I am not sustained by
Congress I will fearlessly appeal to the people."[30]

How did Polk and his cabinet go about persuading members of
Congress? It is well known that presidents today can do various favors
for senators and congressmen to earn their support: offer rides on Air
Force One, make campaign appearances, contribute party funds, and so
forth. Polk did not have quite the bargaining chips of modern presidents,
but he did have tools of persuasion, often threatening to withhold patronage from Democratic members of Congress who were opposing his
policies. His irritation at a New York faction of the party prompted this
diary entry: "This faction shall hereafter receive no favours at my hands
if I know it."[31] And Senator Thomas Rusk of Texas noted, "I think I was
set down at first as being friendly with [Senator John] Calhoun [a Democratic rival of Polk's], and the consequence is that I have not been able
to procure from him [the president] a single appointment."[32]

In another case, Polk wielded not the threat of withheld patronage but
the threat of political ruination to bring about a congressman's compli-
ance. He told Congressman Andrew Johnson in no uncertain terms that
he had the power to ruin him politically in the eyes of his constituents and

that he would do so if Johnson persisted in his opposition to the administration's policies. Clearly, Polk and his cabinet members were quite active in personally lobbying members of Congress to support the administration's policies. Although the president generally did not get directly involved unless necessary, "when crucial votes were pending, the whole force of high administration officials was dispatched to the Capitol to keep wavering congressmen in line," and Polk was not above calling on some directly.[33]

Personal and proxy lobbying of Congress, though, was not the full ambit of Polk's informal means of persuasion. In fact, as his threat to Andrew Johnson reveals, he knew the value of public opinion in pressuring obstinate congressmen. Consequently, a major concern through the whole of his administration was to maintain close control over the major party news organ in Washington.

The story of Polk's establishment of his own administration newspaper in 1845 is an oft-told tale.[34] Although Andrew Jackson persistently entreated him to retain the *Globe* as the administration organ in Washington, Polk realized by late 1844 that he wanted a newspaper that would be beholden first and foremost to his administration and not to factions or other personalities within the Democratic Party: "As to the press which may be regarded as the Government organ, one thing is settled in my mind. It must have no connection with, nor be under the influence or control of any clique or portion of the party which is making war upon any other portion of the party—with a view to the succession and not with a view to the success of my administration." The *Globe* had alienated too many within the Democratic Party over the years to be effective in building party harmony. Polk wanted an editor of his own choosing so that, as he put it, "the whole party would be United, and I would have a bright prospect of having a successful administration."[35] Over Jackson's objections, then, he established the *Union* as the administration's organ, the preeminent Democratic newspaper in Washington and the nation.

Although newspapers in general were quite important for publicizing presidents' messages to an eager public, the role of the *Union* was not simply to convey his public messages; Democratic and Whig newspapers both engaged in this general task. Rather, the *Union*, to a great extent under the direction of Polk himself, actively tried to whip up support among members of Congress and the public for the president's programs. Without this new organ and, most important, a new editor, said Polk, "the Democratic party who elected me cannot be kept united three months. If Majr [*sic*] Donelson would take charge of the Editorial Department—all sections of the party would be at once reunited and satisfied."[36]

Polk's speculations about the necessity of a new administration organ suggest the function of the Washington party newspaper at that time. The *Union* sat at the head of a vast nexus of party newspapers nationwide; it was, says Sellers, "the source from which the Democratic press throughout the country would take its cues."[37] If the administration newspaper espoused viewpoints or supported policies at odds with those of many Democratic leaders and groups (and their presses) throughout the country, support for the administration would not last very long. If it espoused policies and ideas consonant with most groups within the party, however, it could count on support from the multitude of partisan presses and thereby on support for administration policies and recommendations.

Most writers have agreed that Thomas Ritchie, editor of the *Washington Union,* was very much acting at the behest of President Polk.[38] "The first issue staked out the paper's stance. In so doing, the *Union* reiterated ideas that were contained in [a] prospectus that Ritchie had earlier written for Polk's inspection." Moreover, Polk himself occasionally picked up the pen to craft an editorial.[39] Through Ritchie and the newspaper, he attempted to unite and lead the party that had elected him in 1844. It would be Ritchie's role to push the administration's policies and rally Democrats behind them. There are numerous instances of the *Union* and Ritchie's hard work to ensure the success of Polk's policies. A prominent one is Polk's use of the *Union* to back his view that the Oregon treaty between the United States and Britain should be abrogated. He would reveal this sentiment in his annual message of 1845 but wanted to build support for it through the press before the release of his message.[40] Another instance is the *Union*'s untiring support of tariff reduction, a major policy of the platform of 1844 and one of the aims Polk avowed in his inaugural address. One critic of tariff reduction complained, "Who mounted this editor with *lash in hand,* and *free-trade spurs on his heels,* to *goad our flanks,* and drive us up to the work of repeal?"[41]

And these were by no means isolated examples. According to Sellers, "Polk relied heavily on Ritchie's *Washington Union* to marshal the public opinion that was his ultimate weapon against recalcitrant Democrats."[42] When, faced with Democratic congressmen who opposed him, Polk resolved that he would "fearlessly appeal to the people," he most likely had in mind appeals both through his messages and in the *Union*. Nor was he above using the *Union* to launch personal attacks on obstreperous Democratic members of Congress.[43]

Mel Laracey has suggested that presidents' (especially Polk's) use of the newspapers in the nineteenth century can be seen as instances of "going public."[44] As Samuel Kernell has outlined the concept, it is "a class of activities that presidents engage in as they promote themselves and their policies before the American public. . . . [T]he ultimate object of the president's designs is not the American voter, but fellow politicians in Washington." Polk did indeed use his newspaper to communicate with the American public in order to influence politicians in Washington.

Still, one must be careful to distinguish what Polk was doing from modern presidents' appeals to the public. Unquestionably, he used the *Union* to drum up support for his policies, but the support he was after was of a different kind from that which modern presidents seek. Kernell has identified two ways in which modern presidents go public. First, they may approach a national audience, seeking to appeal to a generally indiscriminate and all-inclusive public to marshal support for their programs and thereby pressure members of Congress to go along with them. Second, modern presidents increasingly appeal to smaller, less than national audiences on behalf of their programs, attempting to win the support of select interest groups so as to assemble or firm up a policy coalition and thus gain influence with Congress. Modern presidents engage in these behaviors particularly because partisanship is waning and they are often faced with Congresses controlled by the opposite party.[45] Often, presidents cannot simply reach out to their partisans (even if they control Congress) but must seek out some vague and independent "public" or numerous individual interest groups to gain congressional support.

Polk's behavior, however, squares with neither of those scenarios. He was appealing neither to an indiscriminate public nor to various interest groups. Rather, he was appealing to Democrats in the populace to support his policies and conform to the party standard that he had been elected to carry out. To be sure, he was all the while hoping that Whigs would jump ship and support his Democratic administration. But one must remember the partisan nature of the newspaper universe at the time. Whig newspapers in Washington were not likely to respond to Polk's appeals in an unprejudiced manner or pass them along to other Whig papers without criticism and vitriol. For the most part, then, Polk used the *Union* to promote party solidarity and appeal to Democrats both in the population and in Congress to support his Democratic policies. In other words, as James Pollard has nicely put it, he used the press as a "moulder of *partisan* opinion."[46]

Even if Polk was attempting to rally only partisans, his behavior highlights the limitations of the "going public" concept as outlined by Kernell. Kernell argues that going public was not prominent in eras of unified party control of government because "if the governing party's leaders were to allow internal disagreements to erupt into public discord, they would be flirting with defeat in the next election."[47] Polk's use of the *Union* (and even his formal messages) to rally partisans, however, suggests that presidents have sought out and utilized public support even when their party was in control of both houses of Congress, that public sentiment has perhaps always been a potential (and sometimes actualized) resource for presidential leadership, even though the public was conceived of in a much more partisan manner during periods of unified party control.

Polk's use of the press also further illustrates the "popular" nature of the presidency in the party era. It shows that campaigning for partisan support did not need to cease once a president was in office, that it occurred also between elections. A president could try to shape and mold public opinion in support of his policies, but, again, it is important to note that the "public opinion" Polk hoped to rally and shape was chiefly that of his partisans, and he sought to shape this opinion through a newspaper that, after all, was hardly independent.

In sum, James Polk's presidency was consistent with the dictates of the party constitution; in fact, he appears to have been an archetypal party president. He campaigned as a strong representative of the Democratic Party and its principles (signified most prominently by its 1844 platform) and, once in office, outlined his intention to maintain fidelity to his party and its pledges to the people. And he clearly consummated the relationship that was initiated with his nomination and then election; that is, he worked tirelessly throughout his term to promote his party's policies and to maintain the unity of the party.

That Polk was in the difficult position of trying to lead a coalitional and factional Democratic Party and that he was ultimately unsuccessful in holding his party together (it lost the election of 1848) need not detract from his identity as a quintessential party president.[48] Success in party leadership is important but can be a red herring; a president who tries to lead his party and succeeds and one who tries and fails are nevertheless both aspiring to party leadership. After all, William Clinton was considered a strong "public" or rhetorical president even though his public appeals had a mixed impact on Congress. Similarly, regardless of Polk's success or failure as a party leader, he considered this role integral to his presidency. Through his formal requests, annual messages, and major vetoes, he sought an unequivocal position of party leadership. He also utilized the informal techniques of personal, proxy, and newspaper lobbying to push his agenda and cultivate the support of partisans in Congress and the broad public. He was, then, more a party "leader" than an "agent" (I return to this leadership typology below). Although his relationship with the public was largely conducted through party channels, the presidency, under Polk, was undoubtedly a seat of popular leadership.

Zachary Taylor: A "Whig but Not an Ultra Whig"

Zachary Taylor was not a partisan in the mold of James Knox Polk. During the 1848 campaign and in his inaugural address, he did not play up his party affiliation. He was unable, however, to extricate himself completely from the party system that had gained so great a hold on the American political system by the late 1840s. Taylor, after all, had been forced to declare that he was a "Whig but not an ultra Whig" in the course of the campaign, and his inaugural address did exhibit important signs of the influence of Whig Party philosophy. But his short term in office (from March 1849 until his death in July 1850) was characterized by this give-and-take between his desired stance of statesman and his acquiescence in the role of party leader.

Although the Whigs did not adopt a formal platform in 1848, their "resolutions" praised Taylor (and Henry Clay) and made vague references to "Whig principles."[49] The main reason the Whigs did not adopt a strong platform in 1848 was that the issues of expansionism and slavery in the territories so deeply divided them.[50] Yet it is clear that most

Whigs, in 1848, were still beholden to the principles of the American System, outlined by Daniel Walker Howe as "purposeful intervention by the federal government in the form of tariffs to protect domestic industry, subsidies for internal improvements, and a national bank to regulate and make tax revenues available for private investment."[51] Though divided on issues of slavery, they were still cohesive on these economic issues, the heart of the Whig program for over a decade. It is this economic program, best encapsulated in the Whig platform of 1844, that provides the benchmark against which to compare Taylor's recommendations and pronouncements. The major provisions of that earlier platform were (1) a well-regulated currency—that is, a national banking system; (2) tariff for revenue and protection of industry; (3) "distribution of the proceeds of the sales of the public lands" for the development and support of internal improvements in the states; (4) a single term for the presidency; and (5) a "reform of executive usurpations." From these major provisions one can extrapolate a faith in the general government (particularly Congress) as the main tenet of the Whig creed.[52]

Since Taylor occupied the White House for only a little over one year, he made a limited number of formal recommendations to Congress.[53] His first annual message provides the bulk of those recommendations (some special requests regarding treaties fall outside of the scope of this study).[54] Unlike Polk, Taylor did not wield the veto during his term, so there are no veto messages to examine. A further distinction from Polk is that Taylor's Whigs had a positive political philosophy compared with the Democrats' negative one. We thereby can place due emphasis on Taylor's recommendations and requests, his active suggestions; and we need not be so sensitive to the possibilities that Taylor's inaction or reticence on certain matters implied or upheld a Whig policy stand.

Many of the recommendations to Congress in Taylor's first annual message are clearly not of a partisan character: for instance, surveying newly acquired lands, revising grades in the army, and paying for the congressional frank through treasury funds, as well as nonpartisan recommendations regarding foreign relations.[55] Yet the campaign of 1848 and even Taylor's 1849 inaugural indicated that "the institution of party itself," writes Michael Heale, "was now too firmly entrenched in the American polity to be bypassed, and the general was obliged to make his tortuous accommodation to it."[56] Try as he might to be a nonpartisan leader, Taylor nonetheless demonstrates his fidelity to the Whig Party through several recommendations regarding domestic policy in the annual message.[57] First, he suggests dealing with the tariff—in typical Whig fashion: "I recommend a revision of the existing tariff and its adjustment on a basis which may augment the revenue. I do not doubt the right or duty of Congress to encourage domestic industry, which is the great source of national as well as individual wealth and prosperity."[58] Democrats, most particularly James Polk, *had* doubted "the duty of Congress to encourage domestic industry." "Incidental" protection, as Polk had put it, was deemed allowable, but certainly the government should not, on the Democratic view, go out of its way to "encourage domestic industry." Polk's monumental fourth annual message the previous year had taken pains to inveigh precisely against such a course of action. Yet here was Taylor, the reluctant partisan, urging traditional Whig economic policy.

Taylor's embrace of Whig principles does not end with the tariff. Although he devotes only a short passage to it, Taylor expresses the Whig suspicion of Polk's constitutional treasury ("subtreasury") system: "The question of the continuance of the subtreasury system is respectfully submitted to the wisdom of Congress. If continued, important modifications of it appear to be indispensable."[59] One of the major goals (and successes) of the Polk administration had been the establishment of the constitutional treasury system as a direct alternative to a national banking scheme. It had, in fact, been a major plank in the Democratic platform of 1844, and its passage had been lauded in the 1848 Democratic platform. It seems doubtful that Taylor would ask Congress to question its continuance out of a disinterested concern for national policy rather than a concern for gratifying his Whig constituency.

Also consistent with the Whig philosophy of federal encouragement of commerce and industry is Taylor's recommendation for establishing an "agricultural bureau, to be connected with the Department of the Interior," because very little aid has been given to agriculture and "this aid is, in my opinion, wholly inadequate."[60] Even though Democrats always saw themselves as the party of the workingman and farmer, they would not ask the federal government to encourage agriculture. The Whigs, by contrast, were not nearly as fearful of using the "General Government" to promote prosperity and commerce—as evidenced further by Taylor's suggestion to Congress to consider the feasibility of a transcontinental railroad.[61]

The Whigs' faith in the federal government was perhaps most apparent in their long-standing support of federally funded internal improvements projects, which were despised by Democrats. It should come as no surprise, then, that even the reluctant Whig, Zachary Taylor, came out in favor of internal improvements in his annual message: "I recommend early appropriations for continuing the river and harbor improvements which have been already begun, and also for the construction of those for which estimates have been made, as well as for examinations and estimates preparatory to the commencement of such others as the wants of the country, and especially the advance of our population over new districts and the extension of commerce, may render necessary."[62] Had James Polk lived to read these words (he died only three months after leaving office), he unquestionably would have found them unpalatable. Had he not just one year earlier, in his last annual message, inveighed against the dreaded American System, with its call for an activist federal government? Taylor's nonchalant attitude regarding the acceptability and desirability of internal improvements is certainly consistent with Whig policy and principles.

Also of note is Taylor's pledge, at the close of his message, that "the qualified veto will never be exercised by me except in the cases contemplated by the fathers of the Republic."[63] This pledge is clearly relevant to Taylor's role as Whig Party leader, but it is paradoxical. On the one hand, it expresses a more "constitutional" understanding of the office whereby the executive uses the veto not to influence policy but only to prevent unconstitutional or hasty legislation. On the other hand, since the idea of a limited executive was fundamental Whig doctrine, the pledge is consistent with party doctrine and with Taylor's campaign promises. Thus, he was in the peculiar position of having a popular and partisan mandate of sorts *not* to use the office of the presidency in the actively popular manner of Polk and Jackson.

In the most important and notable piece of Taylor's annual message, he addressed the admission of California and New Mexico Territories to statehood, which neither Whigs nor Democrats had talked much about in the 1848 campaign. Indeed, both parties had been experiencing internal sectional dissension since the acquisition of the lands from Mexico. Taylor recommends that the territories be admitted without reference to whether they are "free" or "slave" and urges, "We should abstain from the introduction of those exciting topics of a sectional character which have hitherto produced painful apprehensions in the public mind."[64] Slavery was the "exciting" issue that threatened to tear apart both parties unless something was done to mute differences between North and South. Taylor hoped that admitting the new states without reference to it would make slavery a state issue, and few were willing to deny that Congress had no right to meddle with "domestic institutions" in the states, particularly not southerners. Even if a state would decide to prohibit slavery, southerners, being advocates of states' rights, could not help but support that state's right to do so. Moreover, Taylor knew that slavery, not really viable or popular in those territories, would have little chance of being established there. This was, in Elbert Smith's words, "an appeal by a slaveholding president to his fellow slaveholders to face reality and avoid stirring up unnecessary animosities against themselves in a struggle already settled by geography, climate, existing law and customs, and the will of a large population already in California and New Mexico."[65]

Yet probably no amount of commonsense appeal by the president could have assuaged the fear of southerners that northerners were intent on eventually ridding not just the territories of slavery but their states as well. Taylor stuck to his rather sensible proposals concerning the admission of California and New Mexico but was not able to muster support for them before he died in July 1850. It was left to Henry Clay and then Stephen Douglas to effect what would be called the Compromise of 1850, which muted sectional differences until they were reopened by the very same Douglas in 1854 with the Kansas-Nebraska Act.[66] But although the controversy surrounding slavery in the territories engulfed the Taylor administration (and that of his successor, Millard Fillmore), it does not belie Taylor's proclivity for acting with his party and according to its principles: since slavery split the parties along sectional lines, it was not primarily a party issue.[67] Otherwise, the issues that Taylor's annual message addressed are quite consistent with Whig philosophy, even from this president who would have preferred to be only an independent statesman.

Comparing Taylor's recommendations for legislation and statements of his executive policy in his first annual message with the Whig principles outlined above, one finds much overlap. Of the six major Whig tenets—support for a national bank, the tariff, internal improvements, a single term for the president, and a "constitutional" executive plus a general support for the federal government in political affairs—Taylor can be said to have spoken to, if not vigorously championed, five. He did not exhort his partisans to follow his recommendations, but he did recommend important party policies. He questioned the constitutional treasury (the Democratic banking system), supported a tariff for protection, advocated internal improvements, declared his distrust of executive usurpations, and expressed his support for such federal activities as an "agricultural bureau" and a transcontinental railroad. Indeed, Whig luminary Daniel Webster referred to Taylor's message as a "good Whig document."[68] It stands to reason, further, that had Taylor lived and been successful in resolving the slavery difficulties, he would have continued a moderate leadership of the Whig Party according to its traditional economic philosophy. As Elbert Smith has put it, "Taylor and his cabinet members were united in their hopes that the slavery quarrel could be muted, that Southern and Northern Whigs could be reunited to promote the original goals of the Whig party, and that they could win the White House again in 1852."[69]

In Taylor's annual message and its requests of Congress, one can see that Taylor was, in part, fulfilling the role of Whig partisan. But between the categories of "agent" and "leader," Taylor seems more the former than the latter. It is no shock that he did not use his annual message in the demonstrative, partisan manner of his predecessor, James Polk, that he did not make numerous or hortatory recommendations to Congress. After all, an important part of Taylor's campaign in 1848 had been his pledge to return the executive office to its proper, limited scope and, moreover, not to be the president of a mere party. What is surprising about Taylor's message to Congress, given this background, is how much it does traffic in Whig philosophy and recommendations. The independent leader, of necessity, had to make room for the party leader.

That this was so, can be seen further in Taylor's less formal dealings with Congress regarding domestic affairs. He was certainly out of his element when he assumed office in 1849; he was an anachronism, wanting to be a nonpartisan president in an era that was extremely partisan. As Jack Bauer has written, "Zachary Taylor, the outsider, arrived in Washington with an especially naive assumption that good intentions and a genuine dedication to the common good would triumph."[70] What is more, Taylor did embrace the Whig tenet that a president should be deferential to and not actively lobby Congress. Initially, therefore, he did not see it as his job to be a dominant executive wielding power to persuade others (particularly Congress) to do his bidding; rather, he would make limited recommendations which Congress, by force of argument, would accept or reject.

Yet upon assuming office, Taylor found himself taking actions quite out of line with this philosophy. He assembled a cabinet composed entirely of Whigs—not the action of a leader "above party." Indeed, Democrats "caviled because the Cabinet was exclusively Whig," believing that Taylor had promised otherwise. Moreover, he also abandoned the sentiment conveyed in his inaugural that he would dole out patronage in a nonpartisan manner; soon he (or more precisely, his cabinet, to whom he delegated much of the patronage business) was engaging in that very Jacksonian action: distributing the spoils of office to his supporters. Furthermore, Taylor was persuaded by Senator William Seward to establish an "administration organ" in Washington to support his policies. As Holman Hamilton has phrased it, Seward clearly impressed upon Taylor the "need of a Washington newspaper, handing down the party line to Whig dailies and weeklies across the land."[71]

Taylor's choice of a partisan cabinet, his wielding of patronage, and his institution of an administration newspaper clearly suggest that the party system had a significant pull on him. He and the Whigs had inveighed against the tyranny of the Jacksonian executive, but here was the Whig executive arming himself with some of the key tools that Jackson and, especially, Polk had used to persuade Congress to pass their favored policies.[72] But the party system could push Taylor only so far; he truly was an outsider who did not, at least at first, clearly understand the system in which he found himself. For instance, his cabinet selections betrayed a lack of understanding of both Washington politics and party politics: although he selected only Whigs, none were men who had much favor with members of Congress. This fact was quite detrimental, because if none of the cabinet members possessed the confidence of at least some Whig congressmen, relationships between the executive and legislative branches would be (and were) less than felicitous. Considering Taylor's delegation style of administrative leadership and his own outsider status, cabinet members with congressional influence were at a premium.[73]

The cabinet was further deficient, writes Hamilton, because "no Clay or Webster intimate was included."[74] Clay and Webster were the two dominant Whig leaders of the time, yet neither they nor any of their confidants were appointed to the cabinet. This seems a major blunder if

Taylor wanted harmonious relations with Whigs in Congress. And, in fact, his dealings with Congress were never easy or harmonious. His cabinet was not well liked, and by 1850 the Taylor administration and Henry Clay had completely broken off civil relations. Clay commented matter-of-factly in 1850: "I have never before seen such an Administration. There is very little co-operation or concord between the two ends of the avenue. There is not, I believe, a prominent Whig in either House that has any confidential intercourse with the Executive."[75]

Although Taylor's dispensing of patronage was somewhat successful in promoting party unity and drawing support to the administration, his Washington newspaper was, like his choice of a cabinet, to an important extent a failure. Taylor's establishment of the *Republic* as the administration organ offers further evidence of the pull of the partisan political system of the time. Its editors put their relationship to the administration in this context: "If the time should come, when we should differ with the President in our views of public measures as to render it irksome to us to remain under formal obligation to him, we shall then resign the appointment which we enjoy by his selection."[76] To put it less euphemistically, the editors of the *Republic* would do the president's bidding or they would quit their jobs (which, in fact, they did in May 1850). Here again, Taylor showed himself a political neophyte not truly attuned to the new political system.

Taylor's *Republic* was only one of three major Whig newspapers in Washington, the *National Intelligencer* and the *Whig* being the other two. Not only was it problematic to have three voices speaking for the national Whig Party, but the *Intelligencer* was beholden to Henry Clay and Daniel Webster much more than to the Taylor administration.[77] Polk's determination to set up one newspaper in Washington that would speak for the Democratic Party had paid off, and he established the *Union* as the mouthpiece of the party. Taylor was neither as politically savvy nor as fortunate as Polk. He probably had no real chance to consolidate the major Whig organs under his control, but there is no evidence that he even considered doing so. If, at the very least, he had reached out more effectively to Webster and Clay, the prospect of discord among the Whigs and their major papers would have been lessened.[78]

The *Republic* did what it could to cultivate support for the Taylor administration. For instance, the paper came to the defense of Taylor's proposed solution to the slavery difficulties when the plan was assailed by

William Seward and, later, Henry Clay. It branded Seward's speech against the president's suggestion "a lawbreaking, Constitution defying, disunion doctrine" that contravened "Whig teaching as understood and practiced everywhere."[79] And Clay's speech prompted a "five-column editorial" in the *Republic* vilifying Clay and praising the president's plan.[80] The *Republic* could only do so much, but it did do the president's bidding and attempt to cultivate support for the administration among Washington leaders and the general public. It was exceptionally vigorous in promoting Taylor's proposal for the admission of California and New Mexico. Again, then, like Polk's *Union,* Taylor's *Republic* can be seen as seeking to cultivate party support rather than broad and indiscriminate public support. To paraphrase Pollard again, the *Republic* helped Taylor to "mold partisan opinion."

It bears mentioning, finally, that Taylor actually toured the Northeast: "Although the term had yet to be invented," Pollard has said, "Taylor took a mild swing around the circle in the summer of 1849."[81] Interestingly, this trip was not simply ceremonial in function but quite political, leading some to believe that the president was trying to influence state elections in Ohio and Pennsylvania or to rally Whigs of the Northeast around his opposition to the extension of slavery in the territories and his support of protectionism. Taylor not only made a tariff speech in Pennsylvania but gave a talk to a delegation of free-soil Whigs in Ohio which disturbed many southerners with its antislavery tone.[82] Tulis makes much of Taylor's biographer's comment that the president went "to see that section of the country, its people, and its need, that he went to see, *not* to be seen, and had no desire for public receptions."[83] Whatever his professed intentions, however, here was a supposedly nonpartisan executive being received by Whig delegations, making very political speeches at crucial election times in Pennsylvania and Ohio, and forcing speculation that he was attempting to solidify his partisan base.

It is intriguing, moreover, that Taylor's biographers have identified no great uproar regarding those speeches. He was not lambasted, as Van Buren had been, for making partisan speeches or being received by wholly partisan delegations. As might be expected, Democratic papers criticized the journey as Whig papers largely lauded it, but apparently there was no sustained criticism by either Democrats or Whigs about the permissibility of Taylor's trip or his partisan remarks. Democratic newspapers, rather, criticized (or, better, satirized) the trip because Taylor was not a good speaker and because, not surprisingly, they disagreed with what he was saying.[84] In any event, that Taylor would take such a trip is not shocking (other presidents had taken tours), but the partisan nature of his speeches and their timing raise interesting questions about the nature and conventions of the presidential office at mid-nineteenth century. Most important, the trip suggests that the office had become partisanized as well as popularized as a matter of convention.

The catchphrase of Taylor's 1848 campaign, "a Whig but not an ultra Whig," seems to embody best his conduct in office: however reluctantly and incompetently, he did act with his Whig Party to a significant degree. In his first and only annual message to Congress he espoused Whig principles and made recommendations consistent with these principles. Furthermore, in his less formal dealings with Congress, he showed himself to be decidedly, if reluctantly, ensconced in the party system of the late 1840s. Contrary to what many thought he might do, this putative "national" leader selected a cabinet that contained only Whigs, doled out patronage according to party affiliation, and established a partisan newspaper to champion his administration and cultivate support for it. In short, though Taylor was hardly the partisan that Polk was, he took many of the same steps. By the time he assumed office, a president could no longer be a strictly nonpartisan leader; the presidency had become a partisan office. Milkis and Nelson appear to have it right when they say that by 1840 "it no longer was possible for the presidency to be restored to its late Jeffersonian status, however inept a particular president might be."[85] Taylor was, to be sure, a party agent rather than a party leader; nonetheless, he was a partisan president.

In fact, the agency model was probably the only option for Whigs, strong party "leadership" being too close to their bête noire, Jacksonianism. The major Whig leaders of the time certainly seemed to espouse a party-agent understanding of presidential leadership: Seward, a prominent Whig, was the one who suggested that Taylor establish an administration newspaper to give out the party line to newspapers across the country; Clay criticized the administration because neither cabinet members nor the president had established any close ties with Whigs in the Congress; and other Whigs were quick to criticize the administration's lack of intercourse with and lobbying of Whig members of Congress.[86] And former Whig Congressman Abraham Lincoln even went so far as to criticize Taylor for not playing a bigger role in the distribution of patronage and thereby preserving, at least to an extent, the Jacksonian presidency.[87] Of course, Whigs did not expect their president to dominate the political scene as Jackson and Polk had done, but they did expect their president to support Whig policies and to establish a working and harmonious relationship with Whigs in Congress. They expected him to be a party player, if a deferential one.[88]

The subtlety needed, though, for a party-agent style of leadership was largely lost on Taylor. He was definitely expressing good Whig principles when he decried executive usurpation in his campaign letters and inaugural address, but he was unable to grasp fully (or quickly enough) that the president could play an important party role and still not be overpowering and domineering. Interestingly, Taylor did gradually accommodate himself to a stronger role for the presidency than his avowed hands-off, nonpartisan ideal would have allowed. In fact, before he died, he had replaced his intractable editor at the *Republic* with a more supportive one and had resolved to dismiss several cabinet members in order to construct a more workable and stronger cabinet.[89] He had begun to adapt himself to a partisan political reality in which the president had a greater role to play (perhaps too great for some Whigs) than that of severely constrained, nonpartisan figurehead. At the time of his death, writes Bauer, Taylor "had passed from his initial naïve belief in a nonpolitical chief executive to at least the glimmering of a recognition for the necessity of political leadership in the White House [and] the prospects for a strong, positive administration appeared promising."[90]

Chapter Six

Party-in-Government II
U. S. Grant, Benjamin Harrison, and Grover Cleveland

The President should touch elbows with Congress. He should have no policy distinct from that of his party; and this is better represented in Congress rather than in the Executive.

Senator John Sherman to President-elect Benjamin Harrison, 1888

In 1868, with the great Civil War and the bitter feud between Congress and President Andrew Johnson behind them, the American people elected as president the war hero Ulysses S. Grant. Many believed that Grant would provide exactly the leadership the United States needed: patriotic, firm, and nonpartisan. To be sure, Grant's letter accepting the Republican nomination and his inaugural address both indicated that he considered himself above party and aspired to a role of patriotic statesmanship. As Henry Adams put it, upon his election "the new President had unbounded popular confidence. He was tied to no party. He was under no pledges."[1] One commentator even went so far as to opine that Grant would ultimately rank with Presidents Washington and Lincoln as a "political trinity."[2]

Ulysses S. Grant: "Plaything of the Legislature"

Yet Grant did not come close to meeting these great expectations. In fact, he was assailed from all corners and has come to be seen, almost unanimously, as one of the worst presidents in American history. Much of the scorn heaped upon him derived from the numerous scandals that emanated from or touched his administration. Grant was likely at least partly to blame for these scandals, considering what Louis Coolidge called his inveterate "weakness for unworthy friends." But he has been lambasted equally because of his putative poor performance of the duties of the office. According to Ari Hoogenboom, "Grant's attitude that the presidency was a reward—a semi-retirement to be enjoyed—when coupled with his political ignorance, created a weak and passive president who was easily influenced and manipulated by friends, congressmen, and cabinet members."[3]

Although Grant's failure to meet expectations is important to my analysis, I am most concerned with his relationship with his party—which, indeed, was in some ways at the root of many jaundiced views of his administration—and his conception of the connections between the presidency, parties, and the people. As with the previous cases, I analyze Grant's first term along three main fronts: his pushing of legislation by means of formal requests and recommendations, his party leadership through annual and veto messages (although his few first-term vetoes were only of pension claims bills), and his personal and newspaper lobbying of Congress and the public for support.[4]

The 1868 election was not notable for sharp distinctions between the parties. There were, of course, important points of contention, but there were also obfuscation and banality in large doses. The twelve official planks of the Republican platform of 1868 can be condensed to eight that would seem to require action on the part of government and president: (1) continued strong support of the Republican Reconstruction program (entailing black suffrage); (2) no repudiation of national debt and a return to specie payments (to help improve the credit of the United States); (3) equalization and reduction of taxation; (4) administration of government with strict economy; (5) protection of naturalized citizens residing abroad; (6) encouragement of foreign immigration; (7) granting of amnesty to southerners, but not full and complete amnesty; and (8) strong support of pensions for war veterans.[5]

Although the Democratic platform included several of the same planks—such as protection of naturalized citizens and economy in government—there were nonetheless disagreements between the two parties, particularly regarding the role of the federal government in dealing with Reconstruction and amnesty. Of lesser importance but still notable was the conflict over economic policy and the return to specie payments, with Republicans favoring specie and Democrats favoring the continuance of greenbacks.

Grant's requests of legislation to the Forty-first Congress show some fidelity to the Republican platform of 1868, though his first annual message contains only three general areas corresponding to the platform: Reconstruction (including the question of amnesty), specie payments, and reduction of taxation (internal and import taxes).[6] (His second annual address does not treat either Reconstruction or the reduction of taxation but does continue to push the issue of a return to specie.) In judging their significance, one must consider the vagueness and noncontroversial nature of much of the platform; its only really controversial provisions revolved around the continuance of Republican Reconstruction, amnesty for former confederates, and a return to specie payments.[7] That Grant treats these in his recommendations to the Forty-first Congress should be seen as noteworthy.

The first annual message urges Congress to compel Georgia to reinstall the legislature that had been questionably unseated by anti-Reconstruction forces, but it also recommends Virginia's readmission to statehood because the "legislature met and did all required . . . by all the reconstruction acts of Congress, and abstained from all doubtful authority."[8] Although Grant wanted to pursue a more moderate and conciliatory course on Reconstruction, he was pressured by Republican leaders into taking a more radical stance toward the problems of the South. As George Mayer tells it, "The gradual drift of the President toward a repressive policy in the South reflected his increasing dependence on radical Republicans for support and advice."[9]

Yet even as he was faithfully upholding and championing Reconstruction measures, he was still disappointing many congressional Republicans. If the Radicals had forced his hand when it came to the Georgia legislature, he was still too conciliatory for them on the readmission of states. In fact, according to Allan Nevins, "Congress refused representations to Virginia, Mississippi, and Texas until they met certain harsh 'fundamental conditions.'"[10] Later, moreover, Grant issued a request (in the form of a special message) to Congress regarding amnesty of former confederates. He notes that he allowed a recent amnesty bill to become law without his signature because he thought it too harsh and recommends that Congress pass a more conciliatory bill—which it did not do.[11] Clearly, Grant did not go out of his way in dealing with the Forty-first Congress to embody the strong statements on Reconstruction that were outlined in the platform of 1868; nevertheless, he did exhibit moderate party loyalty.

It should also be noted that Grant did not use the recommendations in his messages to provide the strongly popular and partisan leadership of James Polk. Whereas Polk spoke of the tariff in highly moral and inflammatory terms, clearly to rally partisans, there is nothing of this feeling or sentiment in Grant's recommendations on Reconstruction; they are simply recommendations. While he might have tried to rally support for either a radical or a conciliatory approach to the "Southern problem," he merely issued requests and reports; he did not see the presidency as a place of strong leadership, either partisan or independent.

Grant did seem more committed, though, to the issues surrounding the maintenance of the public credit; particularly the resumption of specie payments receives strong backing in his recommendations to the Forty-first Congress. Before Grant's election there had been much political controversy surrounding the question of returning to specie. Many Democrats had begun to favor the issuance of greenbacks to deal with the problem of public credit, yet Republicans remained firm in their support of a return to specie in the 1868 platform.[12] And Grant follows Republican sentiment in his first annual message: "It is a duty, and one of the highest duties, of Government to secure to the citizens a medium of exchange of fixed, unvarying value. This implies a return to a specie basis, and no substitute for it can be devised." In his second annual message he opines that "the evils of a depreciated and fluctuating currency are so great that . . . Congress should look to a policy which would place our currency at par with gold at no distant day."[13]

In the case of specie payment, Grant is not only going along with the Republican Party but also taking at least a moderate position of leadership. He treats the issue in moral terms and conveys a sense that he is resolutely behind a return to a firm basis for the currency. Although Congress would not actually pass a piece of legislation mandating a return to specie until 1875, which Grant promptly signed, he kept the issue alive throughout both his terms in office.[14]

Grant, then, does express some fidelity to the Republican platform of 1868 in his recommendations to the Forty-first Congress. Further, even though not "recommendations" per se, his first and second annual messages do express support of two platform items: protection of naturalized citizens abroad, and liberal provision of pensions.[15] Furthermore, on the tariff, a traditional Republican issue that did not find expression in the 1868 platform, Grant acknowledged support of the conventional Republican position: protection.[16]

Still, one must be careful not to overestimate the extent and intensity of Grant's allegiance to the Republican Party and its principles. Toward the Forty-first Congress he conducted himself more as a Republican than a Democrat; he took positions in his messages that were supportive of Republican policies. Yet though he was neither simply an independent statesman nor merely a constitutional clerk, it is a strain to call Grant a party *leader*. He can be called a party *agent* or party *instrument* but certainly not a leader in the sense of strongly persuading and giving direction to Congress. Grant was much like Taylor in recommending and supporting policies consistent with his party without making many recommendations or making them very strongly. During both of Grant's terms, says William McFeely, "there was no sense that the Republican president was building a party and a government with a coherent and wide-ranging philosophy."[17]

Interestingly, perhaps Grant's most important—but not formal—request to the Forty-first Congress was one that revolved around questions of institutions more than parties. It was well known that Grant wanted the Tenure in Office Act to be repealed upon his assumption of the office, and his first annual message reiterates this desire.[18] But it was too late; the Rubicon had been crossed. This act had been passed during Andrew Johnson's tenure to prevent Johnson from removing officials from the executive branch without the consent of the Senate, particularly to keep the apostate Johnson from removing Radical Republicans. Early in his term, in March 1869, Grant had closed the channels of patronage to force the Senate's hand in repealing the act.[19] Yet the Senate did not capitulate; instead, it was Grant who gave in and signed a watered-down repeal that preserved the Senate's power in removals (and hence in patronage). "Grant's 'surrender to the politicians' in the first month of his term, when he was regarded with almost superstitious reverence by the population, was held to be an egregious blunder," writes Josephson. As Milkis and Nelson have put it, Grant "never recovered the prestige and power that he lost in his first showdown with the Republican leaders." Had he remained firm, he might have been able to be either a strong and independent statesman or a strong and decisive leader of the Republican Party. But Grant became neither. In fact, as Henry Adams saw it at the time, "The whole executive system has become the avowed plaything of the legislature."[20]

Grant was perhaps even more modest in his requests to the Forty-second Congress. In his third annual message he pushes for the abolition of internal taxes and upholds the Republican standard of "protectionism." He also advocates, though without requesting legislation, a general yet restricted amnesty and, again, a return to specie payment. In his fourth message, Grant does not make any actual requests of Congress that might be considered Republican in character. He does continue to advocate the return to specie payments and supports liberal pensions, but otherwise he does not attempt to outline, even remotely, a Republican program for Congress to consider.[21] He does, though, interestingly enough, engage in some rhetorical flashes in the fourth message in discussing and defending the Ku Klux Klan and "Enforcement" Acts, strong Republican Reconstruction measures to uphold the Fifteenth Amendment, that were passed earlier in his first term. Grant commented on the Ku Klux Klan Act, passed in 1871, in his third message, but more as a technocrat than a partisan. In his fourth message, then, Grant does take the time to defend these acts and seems to rally support for the Radical Republican programs. He says that he "cannot question the necessity and salutary effect of those enactments. Reckless and lawless men, I regret to say, have associated themselves together in some localities to deprive other citizens of those rights guaranteed to them by the Constitution of the United States."[22] Clearly, these sentiments would not have been well-received by Democrats, who bitterly opposed the enforcement acts, or even the Liberal Republicans, who also balked at the "centralism" of the regular Republican Party.[23]

Grant had had an important role in the passage of the Ku Klux Klan Act in the first place. When the Forty-second Congress met for its initial session in March 1871, Grant issued a special message detailing the problems of the South in which he said, "I urgently recommend such legislation as in the judgment of Congress shall effectually secure life, liberty, and property and the enforcement of law in all parts of the United States."[24] Yet although Grant's recommendation and backing of the KKK Act was probably crucial to its passage, he had had to be prodded by Republican leaders to issue a special request and to put his name behind legislation on the issue.[25]

Grant did, therefore, push for or at least advocate Republican programs through his formal messages. He was more a Republican than a Democrat in these messages. But he certainly did not push a consistent Republican program in the way that James Polk had outlined the Democratic program in his messages.[26] Rather, Grant emphasized only some of the platform planks, particularly the return to specie payments, and these only moderately at best. Notably, though, there is no evidence that Grant advanced these ideas because he saw himself as a Republican president elected on a particular platform; it seems more likely that he did so because the people around him advised him to do so (as with the KKK Act recommendation). Grant was largely "managed" as president by Republican leaders in the Senate called the Stalwarts. Thus, the expression of Republican sentiments and policies in his messages was less the work of Grant than of his "directors."[27]

Grant did at times attempt to take the lead in affairs. For instance, he was very much an advocate of a humane Indian policy: his formal messages strongly recommend courses of action regarding Indians, and throughout his eight years in office he pursued, legislatively and administratively, a "peace policy" in their regard.[28] He also inveighed against civil service abuses and actually made some notable strides in his first term toward instituting real reform in the civil service.[29]

Further, there is Grant's conduct in foreign affairs. His foreign policy is generally considered the shining stone of his administration, and with the yeoman help of Secretary of State Hamilton Fish, Grant did distinguish himself in this area as a firm and decisive leader. But although it was in the realm of foreign policy that he made a claim for strong leadership, it was also in this realm that he witnessed the greatest defeat of his presidency. Grant brought the full muscle of his office, through special messages and personal and proxy (cabinet) lobbying, to move the Senate to approve the annexation of the island of San Domingo. Despite his failure, it is important to note the vigor with which Grant lobbied the Senate, sending no less than four special messages urging Senate ratification of the treaty and, as John Carpenter has put it, "shamelessly work[ing] on individual senators to try to win over the wavering and to convince those opposed."[30]

Grant was capable at times, then, of exercising resolute and determined leadership (even if to no avail), but these instances generally were not in the service of party goals and policies. He did naturally reach out to those of his party when advocating those issues that he cared about;

he had come to realize that his position of nonpartisanship would not work in a tremendously partisan era.[31] Cases such as the San Domingo incident may seem like instances of Grant taking strides toward "party government," and in some sense they were. But this party government was not really connected with the popular will as prominently embodied in the platform of 1868; this was a pragmatic presidential party leadership utilized to achieve personally selected ends rather than the publicly mandated goals that I am most concerned with here.

Grant himself explains the likely reason for his minimal role in leading (in any form) as president at the end of his first annual message (a sentiment that is reiterated throughout his first four annual messages): "There are many subjects not alluded to in this message which might with propriety be introduced, but I abstain, believing your patriotism and statesmanship will suggest the topics and the legislation most conducive to the interests of the whole people. On my part, I promise a rigid adherence to the laws and their strict enforcement."[32] Grant clearly believed that it was the responsibility of Congress to make legislation and that his input should, as a rule, be quite limited and certainly not intrusive. This belief was openly embraced by the Republican leadership, too, especially those in the Senate. Henry Adams was exaggerating, but not by much, when he said that Grant was the "plaything of the legislature." It might be more accurate to say, though, that Grant was the "plaything" of Republican leaders in the legislature, particularly the Stalwart Republicans. That he did not exercise strong leadership of any sort, even strong party leadership, was quite agreeable to them as long as he agreed to go along with their programs and policies.

As Grant sometimes expressed one view in public and another in private, it is important to look more closely at his leadership through the informal channels of personal and newspaper lobbying to see whether he routinely veered from his espoused deference to Congress. The record of his first term shows very few instances of his trying to persuade members of Congress through patronage decisions, personal meetings, or newspaper stories—most likely because of Grant's minimal conception of the office of the presidency and consequent lack of a presidential program. But it is also the outcome of a political system that had at this time centered power in the party leadership of Congress, particularly the Senate.[33]

Grant had endeavored to be an "independent" statesman before his election and even for a brief time while president, but he quickly capitulated to Republican congressional power. The story of that capitulation helps to illuminate both Grant's presidency and the function that the presidency played at this time of high partisanship after the Civil War. Many had high hopes that Grant *would* be an independent president, or at least that he would exert strong leadership and "tame his party."[34] Considering his distance from partisan politics and civil administration in general, it was quite reasonable to think that he would be different from the common run of politicians. As Louis Coolidge has phrased it, Grant "was ingenuous as a child in politics" and had never "shown even the ordinary interest in public questions which is supposed to be the birthright of every true American."[35]

That Grant was of a different cut from the normal Washington politician turned out, however, to be a disadvantage rather than an asset, giving the lie to the widespread belief that a nonpolitical leader would bring order and harmony to the political system. Within weeks of his accession to the presidency, his selection of a cabinet took the wind out of his champions' sails: the selections, says Nevins, "betrayed Grant as confused, uninformed, and groping." He had not consulted with party leaders on "his inaugural address, his cabinet selections, or the basic presidential policies," adds Carpenter.[36] His not having done so might have been no problem had he made good cabinet selections. But Grant picked neither a cabinet of distinguished and independent statesmen to help inaugurate a new "era of good feelings" nor a cabinet of party leaders to help facilitate the Republican goals.

In fact, only two of the nominees Grant submitted to the Senate "had ever been guessed" by political observers; only one was a Radical Republican, the dominant faction in the Republican party at the time; and none was a party leader. It seemed, Mayer has said, that "Grant did not propose to destroy the party system but to ignore it." Republican leaders were discouraged and incredulous at this turn of events, but it was not long before they brought Grant under their control. As noted, the Senate demurred about repealing the Tenure in Office Act in March 1869 and indicated early on that Grant's position in the government was to be one of subordination. Republican leaders also effected a reshuffling of the cabinet in the early stages, helping to appoint several strong Republican leaders and associates to the administration, such as Hamilton Fish and George Boutwell.[37]

After handing over patronage control to the Senate with his capitulation on the Tenure Act repeal and then caving in to pressure for Republican leaders in the cabinet, Grant essentially lost firm control of his administration to Republican Party forces centered in Congress.[38] Bowing to Republican leaders, he exerted very little forceful presidential leadership of either major nineteenth-century variety, partisan or independent. In fact, Grant had fallen under the control of Republican leaders by March 1870, and thereafter, Mayer points out, "[Oliver] Morton, [Roscoe] Conkling, and [Benjamin] Butler were regular callers at the White House and had become Grant's main advisers on party policy."[39] Their influence helps to explain the partisan tone of his messages, even though he was not a warm partisan before his elevation to the presidency.

Even had Grant not lacked an understanding of political maneuvering and an interest in exerting even moderate presidential leadership, the state of party organization and its strength in Congress might have made strong presidential leadership difficult, if not impossible. Henry Adams has aptly described the situation that faced the political neophyte: "No distant observer can judge fairly of the difficulties to which a President is subjected when he attempts to maintain such [an independent] position in the face of the party organization which supports him. . . . There are many things that a President cannot evade, and among the first of these is the duty of listening with patience and replying with courtesy to the leading men of his party. A senator may be tedious, ill-mannered, and a notorious rogue, but the double majesty of State and Senate speaks from his lips and commands a hearing."[40] Still, had Grant been a stronger Republican with a better sense of politics, Republican members of Congress probably would have deferred to him at least somewhat. According to Coolidge, one of the most powerful senators of the time, Charles Sumner, believed that "a recognized Republican of ripe political experience would have been better qualified than Grant to meet the problems of the day."[41]

Grant's weakness only reinforced the status of Congress as prime governing authority, and Republican leaders became even more bold and assertive. A Republican member of the House during Grant's tenure described the relationship between the Senate and the president:

> The most eminent Senators—Sumner, Conkling, Sherman, Edmunds, Carpenter, Frelinghuysen, Simon Cameron, Anthony, Logan—would have received as a personal affront a private message from the White

House expressing a desire that they should adopt any course in the discharge of their legislative duties that they did not approve. If they visited
the White House, it was to give, not receive advice. Any little company or
coterie who had undertaken to arrange public policies with the President
and to report to their associates what the President thought would have
rapidly come to grief. . . . Each of these stars kept his own orbit and shone
in his sphere within which he tolerated no intrusion from the President or
from anybody else.[42]

It is difficult, then, to talk about Grant's personal lobbying of
Congress to support party measures or his use of patronage or cabinet
members to push party policies, because he almost never engaged in
such actions. He did attempt, without success, to utilize cabinet pressure
and personal pleading to effect the ratification of the San Domingo
treaty, but that was not a party policy; it was a personal one. What is
more, Grant's efforts greatly provoked the ire of Republican senators,
particularly Charles Sumner, the head of the Senate Foreign Relations
Committee.[43]

Grant's relationship with the press was perhaps even more insignificant than his lobbying of partisans in Congress. The presidential
organ had been discontinued in 1861 by Lincoln, and therefore, Grant
was not in possession of such an administration newspaper as Polk's
Union or Taylor's *Republic*. As Pollard tells it, the *National Republican*
was often regarded as an administration organ, but this was due more
"to the fact that William J. Murtagh, its editor, was intimate with several
who were in the Grant family circle," rather than because it promoted the
policies of the Grant administration. In fact, write John Tebbel and Sarah
Watts, "it was clear from the beginning what Grant's policy (if it could
be called one) toward the press was going to be. He intended to tell it as
little as possible about what he was going to do, an aim made easier by
his naturally secretive nature."[44]

Grant appeared utterly unaware of the potential of the newspapers,
particularly sympathetic administration newspapers, in cultivating support among partisans in the electorate or in Congress. Given his enor-
mous popularity as war hero, he probably could have generated the
support of Democrats as well as Republicans for his policies, and an appeal to the country would perhaps have built support for the ratification
of the San Domingo treaty. But Grant left this avenue of leadership virtually unexplored and unexploited. Pollard's judgment, though a bit

abrasive, is fair: Grant's two terms in office "contributed nothing to the development of [presidency-press] relations except to emphasize the need of putting them on a sound basis."[45]

It is clear that although Grant in his first term tried to be an independent leader in the White House, he ended up far from this ideal. By 1872, writes David Jordan, it "was apparent that he was not any longer the pure-white above-politics leader that he had been in 1868. . . . He would have to be re-elected on a partisan Republican platform, because he was now a partisan Republican."[46] Perhaps someone with Grant's popularity and nonpartisan background could have returned the presidency to an independent status, but more likely the presidency was by this time already too deeply penetrated by the forces of party. In any case, Grant was no George Washington, and his political inexperience and naiveté resulted in his being managed to an alarming extent by Republican leaders in Congress. In fact, he probably brought even less innate political sense to the presidency than Zachary Taylor, who early on showed sense enough to reach out to party leaders in crafting his inaugural message, appointing party men to his cabinet, and establishing a newspaper to support his administration. Even so, Taylor was also to an important extent managed by party leaders and was not himself a preeminent leader of his party.

Both of these former generals aspired to be independent statesmen in politics but were quickly surrounded by partisans and soon found themselves voicing party ideas and positions. Unlike Polk, who should be seen as a willing party president, Grant and Taylor were more reluctant party instruments or agents. The important point is that they did, in fact, capitulate to their parties and, even if modestly, took actions that were in the service of their parties. To reprise Henry Adams, "There are many things that a President cannot evade, and among the first of these is the duty of listening with patience and replying with courtesy to the leading men of his party." The pull of the party system on the presidency was too much for these men to rise above the parties that had elected them.

Grant and Taylor did more than simply aid their parties in Congress, however; they helped to channel the ostensible will of the people as expressed in their party's election. Although there is no evidence that either understood the major tenets of the so-called party constitution and the role of the presidency therein (as James Polk clearly did), they adapted to the party system and became implicated in the collective leadership of their party, the party that had most recently received public validation. When he stated in his first inaugural address that he would not have any policies to "enforce against the will of the people," Grant was unwittingly anticipating his own participation in this collective party leadership.[47]

Surely, Grant, Taylor, and Polk can be distinguished by the degree to which each exerted control over the party that elected him. But all three were caught up in a partisan universe that expected the presidency to be responsive to party demands and leaders. Ideally, this responsiveness to party forces would also imply responsiveness to majority forces in the public represented by these leaders and party forces; thus, both a party *leader* and a party *agent* would be caught up with and responsive to the winds of public opinion, as expressed through parties and elections. Case studies of Benjamin Harrison and Grover Cleveland provide further texture and nuance to my examination of party presidential leadership.

Benjamin Harrison: "Touching Elbows with Congress"

History has not treated well the twenty-third president. When Benjamin Harrison is remembered at all, he is remembered as having an uneventful and unremarkable presidency. One writer, for instance, has called him the quintessential "postage stamp" president, "whose single term (1889–1893) has all but been forgotten, even by most historians."[48] The implication is that Harrison was simply a figurehead who as president made no important contributions to politics, that he was primarily a constitutional officer. Properly told, however, the story of Harrison's presidency is far more interesting than the standard account. In fact, as Arthur Wallace Dunn (a longtime friend of Harrison) put it in 1922, "Harrison was a much abler man than his grandfather [President William Henry Harrison], and ranks to-day as one of the creditable Presidents of the country."[49] Most notable for this book, Harrison's relationship with his party and his role as a redeemer of the party's pledges mark his presidency as a significant one.

Grover Cleveland had set the tone for the 1888 canvass with his precedent-shattering annual message of 1887. He used the message as an opportunity to establish the upcoming contest as one revolving around the issue of the tariff. The Democrats forthwith adopted a low-tariff platform at their convention in June 1888 when they renominated

Cleveland, and the Republicans, accepting the challenge, adopted a high-tariff platform and nominated Benjamin Harrison. Both candidates further fueled the fires by treating the tariff, and other issues, at length in their letters of acceptance; moreover, Harrison further dealt with the issues of the campaign in the forty-nine speeches of his "front-porch" campaign. Harrison won election to the presidency by securing a majority of electoral votes, although Cleveland, building up huge majorities in the South, tallied more popular votes. Even though Harrison did not win the popular vote and Republicans did not have commanding majorities in either house of Congress, Republican leaders believed that the election had conferred upon them a mandate, that the people had approved the Republican platform. They accordingly moved to enact into law the major tenets of their platform of 1888.[50]

The Republican platform of 1888, by nineteenth-century major-party standards, is a long and rambling document that does not neatly list its major tenets. Still, although the tariff is unquestionably the most important, there are no less than fifteen discernible planks: (1) support of a free ballot for all Americans, including blacks; (2) uncompromising support of the tariff for protection; (3) opposition to foreign contract and Chinese labor; (4) opposition to "trusts'; (5) public lands distribution to "citizens," not "aliens"; (6) support for the admission of new western states; (7) opposition to the Mormon Church practice of polygamy; (8) advocacy of bimetallism in currency (i.e., silver and gold); (9) reduction of letter postage; (10) "free schools" for promoting intelligence; (11) rehabilitation of the merchant marine; (12) federal improvements and government appropriations to increase national commerce and security: rebuilding the navy, improving rivers and harbors, fortifying coastal defenses, providing pensions, encouraging shipping, and paying public debt; (13) criticism of Democratic foreign policy, particularly its lack of support of the Nicaraguan canal and American fisheries industry; (14) reform of the civil service; and (15) liberal provision of pensions.[51] Although perhaps half of these were noncontroversial insofar as they echoed Democratic platform planks, there were some very important differences between the parties in this election. The tariff, the admission of new states, the monetization of silver, the support of the merchant marine, the use of government appropriations to foster commerce and provide security, the liberal provision of military pensions, and foreign policy issues all divided the parties.

How actively did Harrison push for legislation on these issues through formal requests in his annual and special messages? His requests to the Fifty-first Congress show a significant degree of activity based on the planks of the 1888 platform.[52] Quite notably, Harrison's initial requests for legislation come in his inaugural address, something not true of the other presidents examined here. What is more, four of the five legislative requests from his inaugural message correspond to the platform: support for a protective tariff, rebuilding of the navy, revitalizing the merchant marine, and liberal provision for soldiers' pensions.

Harrison's first annual message too shows him as a quite partisan president; it reads almost like a reiteration of the platform of 1888 and his letter accepting the Republican nomination. Harrison makes two strong requests for tariff legislation, the most important issue of the campaign; two requests each for rebuilding the navy, revitalizing the merchant marine, and providing liberal pensions; one request each for establishing/ supporting bimetalism, building up coastal defenses through federal appropriations (improvements), limiting "trusts," using the federal government to promote education of blacks, and providing for stronger federal supervision of elections. Additionally, though not "requests" per se, Harrison pledges his support to the construction of a Nicaraguan canal, champions civil service reform, supports homesteaders, and further advocates internal improvements.[53] The plank regarding admission of new states had been discharged before Harrison's first annual message (North and South Dakota, Montana, and Washington were admitted to the Union in November 1889), and the plank calling for restriction of Chinese immigration had been taken care of with the Scott Act of 1888.[54] Harrison's first annual message thus requests legislation on (or champions) eleven of the thirteen "active" planks from the 1888 platform. The only planks that he did not address in that message were fairly insignificant: the reduction of letter postage and the prohibition of polygamy.[55]

Harrison did not, like Grant, blandly list requests for legislation; in fact, in some cases Harrison rivaled James Polk with his rhetorical flourishes. For instance, he said that tariffs "have a direct relation to home production, to work, to wages, and to the commercial independence of our country, and the wise and patriotic legislator should enlarge the field of his vision to include all of these." On the supervision of elections and a free ballot for blacks, Harrison was even more demonstrative: "When and under what conditions is the black man to have a free ballot? When is he in fact to have those full civil rights which have so long been his in law? When is that equality of influence which our form of government was intended to secure to the electors to be restored?"[56] The annual message for Harrison was not simply a constitutionally mandated communication between branches of government but a device for taking, in some cases, a quite strong position of leadership in the attempt to move Congress to support certain courses of legislation.

The requests in Harrison's second annual message do not parrot the platform of 1888 to the same degree. He again asks for legislation to bolster the merchant marine and to assure the freedom of elections, but these exhaust his "partisan" requests. Yet formal requests for legislation cannot be the only standard for evaluating a president's leadership of his party, especially those in annual messages that follow the first. By the time of Harrison's second annual message, Congress had passed legislation dealing with the tariff, bimetallism, trusts, pensions, naval buildup, and Chinese immigration. Bills regarding the merchant marine, supervision of federal elections, and federal promotion of education were stalled in Congress.[57] Harrison's second message discusses most of these passed and pending measures.

Further, Harrison champions certain planks of the platform without making strict recommendations. For instance, he expresses his continued support of Chinese immigration restriction, development of a Nicaraguan canal, and the buildup of coastal defenses; he also inveighs against the Mormon practice of polygamy.[58] What is more, since he was able to address and take care of his pledges to civil service reform and land (homestead) policy largely through administrative means,[59] absence of specific requests in a formal message does not necessarily indicate a lack of party leadership. In fact, the second message touches again on nearly all the Republican planks of 1888, either by championing bills passed or pending in Congress, by making requests for new legislation, or by announcing his support of a particular position.[60]

Indeed, one can see Harrison as using his second annual message to occupy a position of party leadership. With the knowledge that his Republican Party had received a crushing blow in the 1890 elections, losing control of the House and being left with a razor-thin majority in the Senate, he used the message to "keep the faith" among partisans regarding the bills they had passed and to urge them to pass pending pieces of legislation before the end of the Fifty-first Congress (and subsequent end of Republican control of both houses). He defends the antitrust, silver, pension, and navy legislation passed by Congress but reserves his strongest comments for the tariff legislation. After congratulating "the Congress and the country upon the passage at the first session of the Fifty-first Congress of an unusual number of laws of very high importance," he launches into a strident defense of the McKinley Tariff of 1890:

> No bill was ever framed, I suppose, that in all of its rates and classifications had the full approval even of a party caucus. Such legislation is always and necessarily the product of compromise as to details, and the present law is no exception. But in its general scope and effect I think it will justify the support of those who believe that American legislation should conserve and defend American trade and the wages of American workmen. . . . The criticisms of the bill that have come to us from foreign sources may well be rejected for repugnancy. . . . [I]t will be found that our markets are open to friendly commercial exchanges of enormous value to the other great powers.[61]

This defense of the tariff bill is not unlike Polk's defense, in his second and later messages, of the constitutional treasury, tariff, and other bills passed by his Democratic Congress in response to the ostensible mandate of the people in the 1844 election.

Harrison clearly identified himself with the major legislation passed during the first session of the Fifty-first Congress. He was not simply a constitutional executive elected to administer the laws impartially and sign all bills coming from Congress unless unwise, hasty, or unconstitutional. He evinced a fidelity to the Republican Party, its principles and constituencies, and he ardently defended the major pieces of legislation that he had had an important role in crafting. Additionally, Harrison urged passage of remaining pieces of party legislation by the Fifty-first Congress; not surprisingly, he was afraid that Democratic control of the House would impede indefinitely the major Republican programs that had not yet made their way through Congress: merchant marine, education, and election bills.[62]

The bill to secure black voting rights in the South, also known as the Lodge Bill, receives particularly strong support in Harrison's address: "It is not . . . a question whether we shall have a Federal election law, for we now have one and have had for nearly twenty years, but whether we shall have an effective law." Further, he says that if sections of the country (read: the South) do not see him as friendly to their interests, "I can not add connivance at election practices that not only disturb local results, but rob the electors of other States and sections of their most priceless political rights." After this strong support of the Lodge Bill, Harrison again reminds Congress that "the brief time remaining for the consideration of the important legislation now awaiting your attention offers no margin for waste. If the present duty is discharged with diligence, fidelity, and courage, the work of the Fifty-first Congress may be confidently submitted to the considerate judgment of the people."[63]

It is striking that Harrison speaks of submitting the work of the Fifty-first Congress to the judgment of the people. There has just been a congressional election, so Harrison cannot be speaking of the elections of 1890; he obviously is thinking ahead to the election of 1892, a presidential year; he is concerned that he and the Republican Congress of 1889–1891 make good on their 1888 promises to the people. Given Democratic control of the House in the Fifty-second Congress, they would likely not have another opportunity to do so before the 1892 election. Only if they can pass their program before the end of the Fifty-first Congress would the voters be able to evaluate their work and their responsibility to their pledges of 1888. Chauncey Depew, the Republican industrialist and politician, laid out this sentiment quite well in the 1892 campaign: the choice of the people would turn on "whether the country has been in a better condition at home and stood more honorably abroad—under these last four years of Harrison and Republican administration than during the preceding four years of Cleveland and Democratic government."[64] Harrison himself offered this assessment in his letter accepting renomination by the Republicans in 1892: he had worked strenuously "to carry out the pledges made to the people in 1888. If the policies of the Administration have not been distinctively and progressively American and Republican policies, the fault has not been in the purpose but in the execution."[65]

Harrison's formal requests of the Fifty-second Congress are those that one might expect from a president faced with a nonreceptive and even hostile legislature—and, in fact, the divided Fifty-second Congress produced no important or substantive legislation.[66] In both his third and fourth annual messages, Harrison continues to request legislation consistent with the Republican platform on internal improvements (coastal defenses), immigration (particularly Chinese) restriction, buildup of the navy, federal supervision of elections, and the development of a Nicaraguan canal. His final message also requests legislation aimed at civil service reform, federal prevention of lynching, and further development of the merchant marine.[67]

Harrison's formal requests, though, did not exhaust his party leadership in his final two messages. His third annual message defends the tariff, silver-coinage, pension, navy, and ocean mail laws passed by his Republican Party and urges their continuation.[68] Moreover, Harrison takes positions supporting the Republican stand on civil service reform, homestead policy, polygamy, and regulation for railroad safety. In the fourth message, similarly, he defends the tariff, silver, pension, and ocean mail/steamer laws and espouses continued support of safety regulation for railway employees.[69] Harrison's messages to the Fifty-second Congress, then, exhibit notable fidelity to the Republican platform of 1888 and Republican principles in general. Although he does not treat every single plank of the platform, a sizable majority of them again receive his attention. Furthermore, the tone that Harrison takes in regard to the tariff, silver, and election issues deserves comment. He vigilantly defends the protective principle and bimetallism as embodied in the McKinley Tariff and Sherman Silver Purchase Acts and in both messages continues to urge the necessity of a federal elections act. In his third, for instance, he says of the tariff law that a look at U.S. prosperity should "satisfy any impartial inquirer that its results have disappointed the evil prophecies of its opponents and in a large measure realized the hopeful predictions of its friends."[70]

Perhaps even more interesting than Harrison's strong position of leadership on these Republican issues is his interpretation of the 1892 election in his fourth and final message. Although continuing to support the Republican program, he is resigned to the meaning of the victory of Cleveland and the Democrats: that is, likely revision of Republican policies. Regarding the tariff, he concedes that the "result of the recent election must be accepted as having introduced a new policy," because "it would be quite offensive to suggest that the prevailing party will not carry into legislation the principles advocated by it and the pledges given to the people."[71] He does not specifically mention Cleveland but is undoubtedly speaking of Cleveland as an important part of this "prevailing party." The presidency, on Harrison's own view, was bound up inextricably with the parties, which, in turn, had a definitive linkage with public opinion.

Harrison's final message is quite similar to James Polk's final message. Just as Polk knew that the Whigs had captured the presidency, so Harrison knew that the Democrats had secured the presidential prize, and both of their messages reflect this context. Each continues to defend his party's policies and rally partisans to its standards but also resigns himself to the change of governmental affairs. Harrison is perhaps more magnanimous than Polk, whose final message was vitriolic and bitter at times, whereas even in defeat, Harrison shows a poignant respect for the party system. Seeing the victory of Democrats as an opportunity for experimenting with new policies, he concludes, albeit with a hint of ill will, that "this brief exhibit of the growth and prosperity of the country [his own administration] will give us a level from which to note the increase or decadence that new legislative policies may bring us."[72]

Overall, it seems that Harrison was very much the party president in his formal messages to Congress, advocating and championing Republican programs, at times strongly. He assumed a position of leadership of the Republican Party through his messages and thereby worked to help ensure the passage of major Republican policies. In fact, Harrison's first two years were among the most productive legislatively of any presidency.[73] But from the formal messages one can only partially gauge Harrison's role within the leadership of his party. The formal messages indicate that he occupied an important party leadership role and was not—like Taylor or, particularly, Grant—blandly recommending policies simply at the prompting of his managers. But for a fuller answer, one needs to look at his informal activities to cultivate party support.

Harrison has often been cast as a nonentity president of the Gilded Age, when Congress reigned supreme and presidents were weak and inconsequential. This standard conception, however, does not jibe with either his formal actions or his informal relationships vis-à-vis Congress. An oft-told story gets at only a piece of Harrison's role and conduct as president: John Sherman, a Republican senator, is supposed to have said to Harrison after the 1888 election, "The President should touch elbows with Congress. He should have no policy distinct from that of his party; and this is better represented in Congress rather than in the Executive."[74] Harrison, according to most accounts, willingly agreed with Sherman—but supporting the notion of a president having no policy distinct from his party was not the same thing as being a congressional sycophant. To be sure, Harrison championed very few policies that were not in the Republican platform of 1888, but he had specific ideas about how those policies should look, and he did not hesitate to use informal means to pressure his partisans in Congress for legislation that he could willingly support. He was also protective of his powers as executive and did not, like Grant, allow his presidency to be directed or managed by a congressional cabal of party leaders.

Harrison showed quickly the role he aimed to play within the Republican Party when he announced his cabinet selections. Although there was no way of getting around nominating the "Plumed Knight," James Blaine, as secretary of state (Blaine had earned it, having been the preeminent Republican leader for more than a decade), Harrison did not capitulate to the wishes of party bosses on many other appointments, cabinet and otherwise. In addition to Blaine, Harrison picked solid Republicans for his cabinet, but none was a major party leader. He had ignored the bosses in his major cabinet selections.[75]

The same goes for Harrison's patronage decisions. He was careful to distribute the patronage geographically and to all factions of the Republican Party, but unlike Grant, he did not turn over the patronage decisions to prominent party bosses and senators. What is more, he strategically doled out the patronage so as to prevent any one Republican leader from gaining too great a foothold in the administration. Harrison wanted to make sure that he satisfied the party by his appointments, but as Homer Socolofsky and Allen Spetter point out, he did not "want among his list of appointees in public office those who had too much political power, such as state party bosses."[76] He did choose partisans affiliated with or beholden to major powers within the party but often avoided selecting the actual major leaders themselves.

What Harrison was trying to do was conciliate party leaders while at the same time keeping his administration firmly under his own control. If he did not accomplish the former, he certainly did achieve the latter: "It soon became apparent," observed Dunn, "that Harrison would himself attend to every important matter in the government. Cabinet members could look after details, but the big things were always taken to the President." But this strategy definitely did not appease the major forces, particularly the bosses, within the party—which led to problems when he tried to gain support for his favored policies in Congress. Although it is an exaggeration to say, with Mayer, that no president was "less effective as a party leader than Benjamin Harrison," it certainly is true that Harrison's relations with his partisans in Congress could have been more harmonious.[77]

Perhaps the biggest (and most condign) criticism one can make of Harrison's party leadership is that he did not use his control of patronage to smooth over differences with congressmen. As Arthur Wallace Dunn said, "Generally the first break which occurs between a President and his party is over patronage. That was the trouble with Benjamin Harrison and his party leaders." He "was one of the Presidents who did not use patronage as a club to secure legislation." There is no evidence that Harrison, like Polk, called members into his office to suggest that they would or would not get patronage in exchange for support of the administration. Over time, however, his active strategy of undermining the major party leaders and his surly treatment of them made leaders cantankerous and confrontational who would otherwise have been friendly to his favored policies. In fact, by 1890, major Republican leaders such as Thomas Platt, Matthew Quay, and Thomas Reed were routinely hostile to the administration, most prominently because of Harrison's active control of the federal patronage trough.[78]

But Harrison's ineptitude in managing his partisans in Congress through patronage should not obscure the important role he did play in the legislative successes of the Fifty-first Congress. His somewhat Whiggish understanding of his role as president went only so far. Not a domineering executive, he nonetheless took an active hand in legislation that Congress was considering, beyond making strong formal recommendations. Although they overstate a bit, according to his most recent biographers, Harrison "established new precedents for providing presidential input for bills while they were still in Congress. He held informal dinners or receptions for congressional leaders, and he let them know about specific items that he would need in order for him to sign certain bills. He used a threat of veto on some measures, although his actual vetoes were few. Later, Harrison wrote that his primary influence on legislation had come from his veto power. Sometimes, members of his cabinet carried instructions to Capitol Hill. William McKinley, a frequent visitor at the White House, would use these Harrison techniques when he became president."[79]

One excellent example of the behind-the-scenes lobbying in which

Harrison engaged was his participation in the passage of the Sherman Silver Purchase Act. In his first message he had asked Congress to pass a bill that would be supportive of the monetization of silver. But beyond making this recommendation, he personally met with and appealed to "free-silver" senators to support the legislation, even though it fell short of their hopes. Also, it appears that Harrison's secretary of the treasury had a hand in lobbying silverites to accept the Sherman Silver Purchase Act. Similarly, Harrison's strong support of the Lodge (election) Bill extended beyond his formal messages; he went so far as to bring obstinate members of Congress to the White House to urge them to do what they could to pass the bill. Finally, he reportedly worked quite closely with Congressman William McKinley when the latter was crafting the tariff bill that would pass in 1890.[80]

Whether Harrison was successful in cajoling his partisans in Congress to support his policies (he did fare reasonably well with the Fifty-first Congress) is of less importance than that he saw himself as much more than a constitutional executive. To a significant extent he saw himself as a major Republican leader in Washington who would not only use his formal messages to help lead the party but also personally lobby his partisans in Congress and use his cabinet to do the same—all largely in the service of party, not personal, goals.

Nor was personal and cabinet lobbying of members of Congress Harrison's only informal means of leading and rallying the Republican Party and helping to institute its program. True, he only indirectly used the newspapers to generate public support for party policies, for like Grant, Harrison came to the presidency in an age when the administration organ was no more; no newspaper in Washington had as its primary task defending his administration's policies. This is not to say that the presses were not still fiercely partisan at this time. Despite a growing number of independent papers, most were still controlled by either Democratic or Republican editors.[81] And notably, writes Pollard: "Like other Presidents, Harrison found newspaper editors and publishers among the most numerous and insistent applicants for patronage. This was entirely in character since many of them were active in politics and looked upon office and perquisites as their just due in return for editorial support and party regularity." Of course, there was never enough patronage to go around, but Harrison did manage to find enough positions to prompt the *Nation* to list twelve Republican editors, including Whitelaw Reid of the formidable *New York Tribune,* who were "subsidized" by the Harrison administration and the Republican Party.[82]

Although Harrison undertook the ostensibly common practice of rewarding sympathetic editors with federal patronage, there is no evidence to indicate that he ever cultivated editors in order to build support for his policies through the press. The subsidized Republican editors most likely showed a strong degree of support for his administration, but Harrison probably did not proceed beyond this indirect influence: "Harrison seldom dealt with the press in a direct way, preferring to remain withdrawn and aloof as much as possible," write Tebbel and Watts.[83] Yet it appears clear that the option was open to him, had he preferred to work with and cultivate the press.

It is important to note the keen attention paid to the executive office by the press and the public at this time. When Polk's annual messages were ready for delivery to Congress, the papers eagerly snagged copies for publication. Annual messages, by the 1840s, were not simply communications between institutions; they were communications to Congress, partisans, and the public in general. Harrison's care in delivering his first message to Congress suggests that the public was still eager for presidential communications over forty years later. As related by Tebbel and Watts, to prevent his first message from leaking to the press, for example, he "sent a confidential White House clerk, Col. William H. Crook, to carry sealed copies by train to Baltimore, Philadelphia, and New York," which were not to be released "to newspapers and press associations until the message was safely in the hands of Congress."[84] It would seem a safe guess that when he was preparing his messages, replete as they were with support for Republican policies and programs, he had in mind the cultivation of partisans not only in Congress but in the general public.

Although Harrison's use of the press falls short of that of James Polk, he did something perhaps even bolder than Polk for the promotion of his party: he undertook many travels while occupying the presidential office. Of nineteenth-century presidents, Harrison was second in the number of tours taken and first in number of speeches delivered on those tours. He actually engaged in midterm campaigning (though it was very primitive in form) throughout the Midwest in October 1890 to help drum up support for members of his party running for Congress.[85]

In a certain sense, Harrison was engaging in a species of the modern-day tactic of "going public": he was appealing to the people to influence Congress, although he was trying to influence congressional *elections* rather than *legislation*. As Socolofsky and Spetter have explained: "Polls that were taken in the fall of 1890 indicated that the Republicans were slipping badly and that they would lose many races in the November elections. . . . So Harrison took a week-long circuit around the states of Ohio, Indiana, Illinois, Iowa, Kansas, and Missouri then back to Washington, in an effort to prop up midwestern candidates." The trip was made "officially" to attend a reunion of Harrison's Civil War brigade, and he did not make overt appeals to the public to vote for Republicans for Congress; the presidency had not yet evolved that far. He did, however, capitalize on the massive crowds that turned out to greet him along the way, and most of his speeches emphasized "the flag, loyalty to the nation, the value of education, and the prosperity enjoyed by all American citizens."[86] The emphasis on prosperity was most likely a not-so-subtle reference to Republican tariff policies and the professed prosperity that they would foster.

Even without overt appeals to the people to vote Republican, it was a significant development that Harrison used his position as president to help rally support for his fellow Republicans in their quest for office. He putatively hoped that by putting himself in front of the voters and generating feelings of goodwill for his administration, he could also generate goodwill and support for Republican candidates, who would be assumed to be affiliated with the Harrison administration.

Such actions on the part of a president undoubtedly would have troubled the founders. Not only did it undermine the separation of powers in that a president was taking steps to influence the composition of the legislature; more important, Harrison was campaigning to help the Republican Party maintain majority control of the executive and legislative branches and enact its full program of policies. Further, his tour demonstrates the degree of loyalty and fidelity he felt to the Republican Party and its principles. He saw himself as a Republican leader, and he took a nearly unprecedented step as president to try to assure the continued success of the party and its principles in government. That his endeavor was unsuccessful—the Republicans fared miserably in the 1890 elections—is beside the point. Even though he failed to generate enough support for the Republican ticket, he took on an important role as party leader in his tour of the Midwest. What is more, his effort to establish a direct connection with the public was a major facet of this party leadership.

On closer inspection, then, the Harrison presidency appears much more textured and interesting than the clichéd accounts allow. Harrison strongly affiliated with the Republican Party at the time of his nomination, actually gave partisan speeches during the campaign of 1888, and clearly staked out his relationship to his party in his inaugural message. Once in office, he was quite serious about his role as a party leader. Interpreting the 1888 election as a mandate from the people for the passage of Republican programs, he worked actively to promote the major programs of the party and, in doing so, showed the presidency to be an important seat of popular leadership.

Although Harrison's force in promoting the party agenda did not approach that of James Polk, he can certainly be considered more of a party leader than Taylor and Grant; they were carried along by the partisan centers of power in Washington to their positions as partisan presidents. But Harrison actively embraced a partisan role and utilized various means, formal and informal, to influence the direction of party policies. The conventional view that he was simply a figurehead who rubber-stamped congressional policies and took no position of leadership on his own is too pat. Yet "leader" is not quite the proper term. Harrison probably should be termed a party "facilitator," denoting someone who is not simply bowled over by his partisans but who also makes important contributions to the direction that the party is taking.[87]

Although Harrison may for the most part have "touched elbows with Congress," as Senator Sherman put it, he did not hesitate, at times, to set his elbow to the ribs of his congressional partisans. Certainly, he did not dominate the political landscape as did Polk, Jackson, or many modern presidents. Yet one should not fixate on the strength or power of presidents when examining their activity as partisans and popular leaders. As Harrison's tenure clearly demonstrates, presidents could be warm and active partisans without dominating their parties. They could be an active part of the "collective leadership" of the party—could be party presidents—without being the dominant figure in Washington. As the inaugural addresses demonstrate, party-era presidents generally saw themselves as bound up with their partisans and the "popular will" that had elected them, but they did not see this validation as altering their constitutional role so much as bolstering it. Polk, in fact, in his domination of his party was pressing up against the limits of a system in which presidents were considered only one of several major party leaders in government. Even Benjamin Harrison's moderate facilitation of party goals was regarded as excessive in some circles, as evidenced a cartoon of the period showing him astride a GOP elephant and party leaders scurrying after him.[88]

My concern is to what extent presidents considered themselves bound (as either leaders, agents, or facilitators) to their parties and to the ostensible will of the public as embodied in their party's electoral success. In other words, was the presidency, through the workings of the party system, considered a seat of popular leadership? It is important to stress the article *a* preceding the term *seat;* the office was not the exclusive seat of popular leadership that the modern presidency clearly appears to be today. But the presidency under Harrison's direction does seem to have been bound to the Republican Party and the people who offered it the reins of government in the 1888 election; it was *a* seat of popular leadership.

Grover Cleveland: Refashioning the Party in His Own Image

Grover Cleveland's rise to the presidency was nothing short of meteoric: he went from newly elected mayor of Buffalo to president of the United States in three short years. His entrance into national politics and his first term as president (preceding Harrison) warrant brief consideration as prelude to a discussion of his second term in office. Cleveland was the man for the Democrats in 1884, for as governor of New York he had developed a strong reputation as a "reformer." His reformist tendencies and his professed "independence" in politics were seen as crucial assets to the Democracy in the election of 1884. Not only were the Democrats a diverse and divided party in need of a factionally untainted leader at the time, but James G. Blaine, a regular Republican organization man, had been nominated by the Republicans. In this era of growing distrust of the parties, writes Josephson, "the naming of Blaine as the Republican candidate, and the news of Mugwump [reformist Republicans] disaffection, made Governor Cleveland the most 'available' standard-bearer for the opposition party."[89]

Cleveland carried the election of 1884—a contest largely about the candidates' probity—thanks in part to defections from the Republican ranks to the so-called independent Cleveland. These defectors, however, would soon be disappointed, particularly with the patronage policies of Cleveland the president. As his first term progressed, he gave in more and more to the Democratic Party when it came to patronage. In fact, he began to feel justified in this course: he increasingly thought, according to Richard Welch, that "Republican officeholders were, for the most part, ill-wishers for the success of a Democratic administration."[90] Moreover, although Cleveland often expressed the Whiggish idea that a president was simply an executive, an impartial administrator of laws, over the course of his first term he became more involved in legislation and in setting the direction of Democratic Party policy. This gravitation toward a larger party role culminated in his famous third annual message, in which he laid out the Democratic cause of tariff reform for the election of 1888. Cleveland also saw himself as bound to public opinion through his party. He very much believed that Democrats (himself included) should redeem their electoral pledges to the people, that the popular voice spoke through elections, and that it was the Democracy's job to follow its dictates.

But Cleveland did have an independent streak that would pervade both his terms in office. At times, he seemed to embrace an understanding of the presidency consistent with that of the founders, often taking a hands-off approach to Congress; even when he did get involved, it was never to the extent of modern presidents. His face-off with the Senate over the Tenure of Office Act in 1887, which resulted in its repeal, was a shining example of executive independence from Congress and a reclamation of presidential prerogative. Additionally, he would never let himself be bullied by a popular opinion, believing it more important for the executive to do what was right than what was popular. His veto of a popular bill for the relief of Texas drought victims in 1887 was only the most notable instance of this independence from popular opinion.[91]

Furthermore, despite Cleveland's strong relationship with his party, it too was characterized by an independence seldom seen in previous administrations. He did not believe that the executive should be bullied by Democratic members of Congress or factions within the party. In fact, it appears that over the course of his first term, Cleveland came to believe nearly the opposite: the executive should strongly lead members of Congress and factions within the party. He certainly believed in and embraced the principles of the Democratic Party, and he continued to feel an electoral connection with the people, but his Democratic principles were those interpreted and outlined by himself. In his third annual message (1887) on tariff reform, for instance, Cleveland saw himself as making the Democratic Party "stand for something."[92] Through his forceful personality and exertion of presidential will, he did make the party stand for something, and by the late 1880s it had the national purpose, most notably, of tariff reform. Moreover, the Democratic Party would be for nearly the next decade intimately bound up with the person of Grover Cleveland.

In 1892, Grover Cleveland and Benjamin Harrison reprised their battle of 1888. Again, the campaign was largely devoted to the issue of the tariff, with the candidates taking quite opposed positions. The "currency" question (gold versus silver) was also of moment in the campaign. Cleveland had issued the call for Democrats to oppose the Republican Silver Purchase Act of the Fifty-first Congress and embrace the gold standard in a famous letter he publicly released in 1891, inveighing against "the dangerous and reckless experiment of free, unlimited and independent silver coinage."[93] Republicans had taken quite a beating in the midterm elections of 1890, and the 1892 election was a consummation of this trend away from the Republicans. Cleveland and the Democrats won handily, assuming control of both the executive and legislative branches of government for the first time since before the Civil War.[94]

Not surprisingly, then, Democrats felt the need to follow through on their pledges to the people, particularly the tariff reform pledge. As Cleveland put it in his inaugural message: "The people of the United States have decreed that on this day the control of their Government in its legislative and executive branches shall be given to a political party pledged in the most positive terms to the accomplishment of tariff reform. They have thus determined in favor of a more just and equitable system of Federal taxation. The agents they have chosen to carry out their purposes are bound by their promises not less than by the command of their masters to devote themselves unremittingly to this service."[95] Further, when asked in January 1893 (as president-elect) by a reporter whether tariff reform would be forthcoming, Cleveland curtly responded, "What were we elected for? What were we elected for?"[96]

But tariff reform was only one of many planks in the 1892 platform. Like the Republican platform of 1888, the Democratic platform of 1892 is a sprawling document, with no less than eighteen planks: (1) opposition to the Republican "Force Bill" (the federal elections bill that stalled in Congress during the Harrison administration); (2) tariff reform—"tariff for revenue only"; (3) strict enforcement of antitrust legislation; (4) fair public lands policy; (5) opposition to the Sherman Silver Act (support for "sound money"); (6) civil service reform; (7) strengthening of the navy; (8) support for Russian Jews and Irish; (9) immigration restriction; (10) honest military pension distribution; (11) improvement of major waterways; (12) support of the Nicaraguan canal; (13) support for the World Colombian Exposition; (14) support for "free schools"; (15) admission of new territories and institution of "home rule"; (16) passage of legislation protecting railway employees; (17) support for state laws against labor exploitation; and (18) opposition to sumptuary (regulation of personal behavior) laws.[97]

In examining presidential requests, one is immediately struck by the large difference between Cleveland's requests to the Fifty-third Congress and Harrison's to the Fifty-first.[98] Whereas Harrison promoted well over half the planks of his party's platform of 1888, Cleveland's requests touch on only a few platform planks. In two annual messages and two special messages, though, he makes a whopping total of twenty-one legislative requests regarding the currency question. (One special message, moreover, calls for a special session of Congress for the sole purpose of repealing the Silver Purchase Act.) His first and second messages also ask Congress for tariff revision (four requests), navy buildup (two), and fair land policy, including forest preservation (four). It would seem that Cleveland's legislative requests neglected well over half the planks of the 1892 platform.

Beyond the confines of actual requests to Congress and including his championing of Democratic planks in the annual messages, Cleveland fares a bit better as redeemer of his party's pledges, but much is still missing. His first annual message supports the construction of a Nicaraguan canal, honesty in pension distribution, and civil service reform, topics also broached in the second annual message. In his communications to the Fifty-third Congress, then, Cleveland addresses only seven of the eighteen planks of the Democratic platform of 1892, and some of these only weakly.[99] Although it was perhaps unnecessary for him to speak on the need *not* to adopt a Republican-style "Force Bill" or *not* to pass sumptuary laws, he might at least have referred to the problem of trusts, immigration policy, the idea of "free schools," protection of railway employees, and other planks that would have called for government action. The Fifty-third Congress would pass two quite important Democratic bills, one repealing the Sherman Silver Purchase Act and the other reforming the McKinley Tariff; nevertheless, Cleveland's support of the vast range of Democratic Party policies seems rather tepid.

Cleveland's partisan requests of the Fifty-fourth Congress are even more meager, when measured against the Democratic platform of 1892. He makes ten requests (five in each annual message) for legislation establishing a sound currency, three requests (via a special message) for fair public lands policies, and one request (in his fourth and final message) for tighter restrictions on "trusts." Beyond requests, his third annual message champions the 1894 Democratic tariff reform law and the need to do something about immigration and foreign labor. And his fourth annual message asserts his support for naval buildup, fair public lands policies, honesty in pensions, civil service reform, and the 1894 tariff reform.[100] To be sure, Cleveland's third annual message is somewhat unusual in that it is purposively restricted to foreign policy and the finances of the country, but his fidelity to the Democratic platform of 1892 is limited in the fourth message as well.

Still, this ostensible infidelity to the platform of 1892 need not prejudice an understanding of Cleveland as a partisan. Though he did not, like Harrison, pay heed to most of the planks of his party's platform, he did undoubtedly play the role of party leader through his annual messages and requests; yet again, then, excessive attention to his lack of fidelity to the *whole* platform can be misleading. Given that the United States experienced a severe depression two months after Cleveland assumed office, he naturally chose to focus on sound money and the tariff above other matters, for he saw those two planks as intimately connected to the financial situation of the country (a sentiment expressed at length in his third annual message).[101] In any case, those had really been the most important two issues in the 1892 campaign. In his first annual message, Cleveland said as much in regard to the tariff: "After a hard struggle [the election of 1892] tariff reform is directly before us."[102] His lack of exertion for the entire Democratic agenda was probably also a result of his regarding the Democratic Party as an extension of his person more than himself as an extension of the Democratic Party. Cleveland, after all, virtually dominated the national politics of the Democracy from 1884 to 1896; to him, it would most likely have been better termed the Cleveland Democracy, since the policies it would pursue would be chosen by Grover Cleveland.

His annual messages often put the full force of his rhetoric behind his favored party policies, as in his arguments for a change in tariff laws. According to Cleveland in his first annual message, "Nothing so important claims our attention and nothing so clearly presents itself as both an opportunity and a duty—an opportunity to deserve the gratitude of our fellow-citizens and a duty imposed upon us by our oft-repeated professions and by the emphatic mandate of the people." He is undoubtedly speaking to his fellow Democrats about the mandate of the 1892 election. He continues: "The world should be open to our national ingenuity and enterprise. This can not be while Federal legislation through the imposition of high tariff forbids to American manufacturers as cheap materials as those used by their competitors. . . . [T]he intelligence of our workmen leads them to quickly discover that their steady employment, permitted by free raw materials, is the most important factor in their relation to tariff legislation."[103] Cleveland is not simply recommending a path of legislation; he is urging Congress to take action.

Another example is Cleveland's strong criticism of the free coinage of silver in his third annual message: "Those who believe that our independent free coinage of silver at an artificial ratio with gold of 16 to 1 would restore the parity between the metals, and consequently the coins, oppose an unsupported and improbable theory to the general belief and practice of other nations and to the teaching of the wisest statesmen and economists of the world, both in the past and present, and, what is far more conclusive, they run counter to our own actual experiences." He presses his criticism of the free silver movement later in the same message, hoping ultimately to return wayward silverite Democrats to the flock: "I will not believe that the American people can be persuaded after sober deliberation to jeopardize their nation's prestige and proud standing by encouraging financial nostrums, nor that they will yield to the false allurements of cheap money."[104]

It seems eminently reasonable, therefore, to ascribe the term "party leader" to Grover Cleveland on the basis of his annual messages to Congress and especially of the strong rhetorical support he gave to his prioritized party policies. In his second term, Cleveland also showed himself the party standard-bearer in his use of the veto, which he was much more likely to wield than Taylor, Grant, and Harrison. In fact, early on in his political career, he had earned the appellation, "Veto Mayor" of Buffalo.[105] He brought this disposition to the White House, vetoing 413 bills in his first administration and 170 in his second.[106] Of the 170, many were vetoes of pension claims that Cleveland believed did not bear scrutiny; these can be seen as upholding the pledge in the Democratic platform and Cleveland's letter of acceptance (one that he frequently repeated in annual messages) that "our pension roll should be a roll of honor, uncontaminated by ill desert and unvitiated by demagogic use."[107]

The remainder of Cleveland's vetoes, with a few signal exceptions, were not primarily partisan.[108] Perhaps the most important veto of his second term came with his disapproval of the "Seigniorage Bill" of 1894. This bill was passed to conciliate pro-silver forces in Congress, particularly silverite Democrats, who were displeased by the Cleveland administration's 1893 repeal of the Sherman Silver Purchase Act. Cleveland continued to hold his "sound currency" (pro-gold standard) ground in the Seigniorage veto message and exhorted his party to follow along, attributing his stance to "my conception of the obligations and responsibilities attached to the great office I hold [which] forbids the indulgence of my personal desire and inexorably confines me to that course which is dictated by my reason and judgment and pointed out by a sincere purpose to protect and promote the general interests of our people."[109] This explanation implies that he was exercising his "independent" judgment as constitutional officer—and, indeed, he was.

Yet there is more to Cleveland's veto than his obligations as constitutional officer. As he further notes, "The necessity of preserving this parity [between gold and silver] is obvious. Such necessity has been repeatedly conceded in the platforms of both political parties and in our Federal statutes. It is nowhere more emphatically recognized than in the recent law which repealed the provision under which the bullion now on hand was purchased."[110] Not only have both political parties supported Cleveland's current view, but this view has also been embodied in the Democracy's repeal of the Silver Purchase Act in 1893. Cleveland, while surely doing his "constitutional" duty, is also making good on the pledges he and his party made to assure that the United States maintained a sound currency. And what is more, his message is hortatory and rhetorical, not simply giving reasons for the veto but making strong arguments and appeals for support of his action.[111]

Of final note is Cleveland's veto of the Lodge Immigration Bill of 1896. Two days before leaving office he vetoed that Republican measure (Republicans had gained majority control of Congress in the 1894 elections), which sought to restrict the immigration of illiterate foreigners. It had passed the House and Senate by large numbers and likely had solid public support.[112] Yet Cleveland vetoed the measure. As with the Seigniorage bill, he most likely acted partly out of his felt duty as a constitutional officer. But he also was paying fidelity to the Democratic platform of 1892, which was quite explicit in "condemn[ing] and denounc[ing] any and all attempts to restrict the immigration of the industrious and worthy of foreign lands." This was precisely Cleveland's main justification for the veto: "The ability to read and write, as required in this bill, in and of itself affords, in my opinion, a misleading test of contented industry and supplies unsatisfactory evidence of desirable citizenship or a proper apprehension of the benefits of our institutions."[113]

In sum, when looking at Cleveland's formal relations with Congress as reflected in requests, messages, and vetoes during his second term, one must conclude that for him the presidency was to a significant extent a party office, even if he conceived that differently from his predecessors. To be sure, his support of the party agenda, as embodied in the platform of 1892, was limited. He did not seem to feel bound to all the planks of the platform and did not, like Harrison, willingly make it his business to speak to most of them in his annual messages. But Cleveland did feel bound to the major tenets of his party and its philosophy. He strongly supported what were arguably the most important planks of the Democratic platform and campaign of 1892, currency and tariff reform, and several other planks as well. Also unlike Taylor and Grant, who espoused party policies seemingly at the behest of their advisers, he was his own person, with his own agenda and priorities.

Cleveland used the full force of his messages on behalf of his favored policies, rivaling Polk in the strong rhetoric with which he lobbied for them. He seemed to indicate that he was championing these policies, particularly tariff reform, in response to the popular will, yet his obeisance to the popular will and his party went only so far. This is the vexatious quality of his party leadership, distinguishing him from Polk. His party leadership was, to an almost unprecedented degree, on his own terms. He chose what he considered the most important Democratic issues to pursue, defined them in his own way, and expected his party to follow along (he had, after all, had a big part in defining the Democratic Party's official stance on the free-silver question). His party was the "Cleveland Democracy," with emphasis on the former as well as the latter term. Certainly, the Democratic Party was still strong enough to give shape to and structure Cleveland's actions, but it also bore the stamp of Cleveland's personality in a way that Polk's Democracy had not. In fact, Cleveland's notion of parties and presidential party leadership presages the conception of them that Woodrow Wilson would later espouse: namely, parties as temporary organizations supporting and following a particular presidential candidate or president.[114]

Cleveland's cabinet selections in his second term further evidence his conception of his role in the Democratic Party. The cabinet was composed of capable men, and almost all were Democrats, but few of them, writes Welch, "had played an important role in party politics, and they would have little influence with party members in Congress." One, in fact, Secretary of State Walter Q. Gresham, was a Republican, which, of course, did not endear Cleveland to his party, although it did please the country's reform-minded men. To be sure, Cleveland's selections were partly influenced by the difficulty he had in getting the men that he wanted (a number of his original designees declined), but they also reflected his concern to surround himself with men who were not rivals within the party, so as to assure loyalty to himself.[115]

Nevins points out that two of Cleveland's appointments, Postmaster General Wilson S. Bissell and Secretary of War Daniel S. Lamont, were "old friends who had never held important public office and who possessed no political following whatever." Cleveland could have put himself in better stead with his party by appointing men who had substantial party followings that they could bring behind his administration; such individuals likely would have had better contacts and influence with Democratic members of Congress, as Polk's cabinet did. But Cleveland was much less concerned with pandering to forces in his party than he was with securing a cabinet loyal to him. As Welch has aptly cast it, he viewed his cabinet as a "privy council, not a party council representative of the diversity and leadership of the Democratic party"; its members, although they did cultivate relationships with members of Congress and push Cleveland's policies, did not have great influence with Congress.[116]

Cleveland himself, however, was not above directly meeting with and appealing to members of his party to support his policies, applying reasoned appeals and his power of patronage to gain congressional support. He was also willing to use public opinion to pressure members of his party. Almost immediately after assuming office in 1893, exercising his constitutional prerogative, Cleveland called a special session of Congress for August to repeal the Sherman Silver Purchase Act of 1890. Although the financial crisis prompted the calling of the special session, repeal of the act was likely, given Cleveland's sound-money stance and the Democratic platform's criticism of the act. Not only had Cleveland written a strong message urging repeal, but he let it be known that patronage assignments for Democratic congressmen would be contingent on their support. With this general patronage threat and his cultivation of several "administration" congressmen—key among them William L. Wilson—the repeal bill passed the House smoothly.[117]

It faced stiffer opposition in the Senate, however. Cleveland had his champions there—for instance, Senator Daniel Vorhees—as he had in the House, but senators were less easily coerced.[118] Many Democratic senators feared party division, given the growing contingent of silverites from the West in the Democratic Party, and looked toward a compromise with the silver forces. Cleveland would have none of it and demanded unconditional repeal, again threatening to deny patronage to resistant Democratic senators, especially silverite Democrats. As a member of his administration put it, Cleveland "said that if they wanted a fight, he would give them one. Senator [William F.] Vilas had written him suggesting that he should hold back appointments. He said that he should telegraph Vilas that his idea was a good one and that he had better suggest it to the Cabinet officers."[119]

Even more interesting, to help force the hand of the Senate, Cleveland resorted to publishing a letter he had written to Georgia governor W. J. Northen, a silverite Democrat. In it, Cleveland reiterated his mantra that he was "opposed to free and unlimited coinage of silver" and that he was "in favor of the immediate and unconditional repeal of the purchasing clause of the so-called Sherman Law." He concluded with the hope that the Senate would pass the unconditional repeal bill because he did not want the Democratic Party held responsible for the catastrophe that would result from Senate failure to do so.[120] There is no way to know just how much influence this letter had (not surprisingly, it irritated some silverite Democrats), but it is quite important to note that Cleveland did not refrain from utilizing newspapers and public opinion to strong-arm his partisans in Congress. The Senate passed the unconditional repeal bill.

Its passage was clearly a triumph for Cleveland but less so for the Democratic Party, given the dissension created in its ranks by the agitation on silver. What is more, the victory was somewhat hollow for the president, because his extensive use of patronage threats for this bill weakened his hand for the next round of negotiations with Congress— this time over tariff reform, which was, as Cleveland saw it, what the Democrats had been elected for. The Congress got around to considering tariff reform in the first regular session of the Fifty-third Congress in December 1893.

As was clear in his first annual message, Cleveland wanted to reform the rates established by the McKinley Tariff of 1890, and he had very distinct ideas about how to do so. In fact, he played an important part in crafting the tariff reform legislation in the House, from the committee stage to the conference committee. Cleveland and his first lieutenant in party matters in the House, William Wilson, were in close communication and consultation as Wilson's committee, Ways and Means, put together a tariff bill. "When the Wilson bill was reported by the committee to the House, it was in nearly all respects a bill that matched Cleveland's demand for cautious and safe revision," writes Welch. That bill, with minor modifications, passed the House under strong Democratic leadership. As in the Silver Purchase repeal, the president all the while used the potential denial of patronage as the stick with which to gain Democratic support.[121]

But Cleveland again ran into problems in the Senate, where the Democratic majority was slimmer. Moreover, he had used up much of his patronage reserve in gaining support for the silver bill repeal and for House passage of the Wilson tariff. Consequently, the Wilson bill became subject to many amendments, even though Cleveland personally met with and lobbied senators to retain its original intentions. When it did pass the Senate, it hardly resembled the House bill: the Senate had attached more than six hundred amendments, and it was now called the Wilson-Gorman bill, adding the name of its Senate manager. Cleveland nevertheless urged passage because he was optimistic that many of the amendments could be dropped in the conference committee between the two houses. Yet although he tried mightily to persuade members of the conference committee to hold the ground of the Wilson bill, he met with little success.[122]

With the conference committee deadlocked because of Senate recalcitrance, Cleveland took one of the more dramatic actions of his second term. Goaded by Congressman Wilson, Cleveland allowed him to release a letter the president had written to him regarding the course of the tariff bill. In the letter, very much a rallying call for the Democratic Party, Cleveland had argued that the tariff reform embodied in the Wilson bill would mean "the fulfillment of Democratic pledges, and the redemption of Democratic promises to the people." A rather inflammatory statement later in the letter admonished Democrats that "abandonment of the cause [tariff reform] or the principle upon which it rests means party perfidy and party dishonor."[123]

The letter was not a hit with several prominent Democratic senators, who deeply resented being accused of "party perfidy and party dishonor." But it was a hit with the public, having "all the desired effect in calling forth a burst of remonstrance against the Senate obstructionists," according to Allan Nevins. "Democratic State conventions in Iowa, Indiana, Florida, and Massachusetts passed resolutions endorsing the letter; public meetings for that purpose were held in Maryland"; and many newspapers as well greeted the letter with praise and support.[124] But the appeal to public opinion was essentially too late; the "obstructionist" senators' position had hardened, and they could not be budged. The House acquiesced to the Senate version, and the Wilson-Gorman tariff bill was passed. Deeply disappointed, Cleveland let it become law without his signature.

Despite not gaining the tariff legislation he wanted, the leadership position Cleveland attempted to assume is remarkable. Not only did he personally lobby members of Congress and threaten to withhold patronage, but he also reached out to public opinion to influence Democratic votes. If Democratic senators were enraged at his questioning of their party loyalty and their institutional positions as senators, rank-and-file Democrats did indeed seem to be on Cleveland's side to an important degree. But, like Polk's, Cleveland's public appeal was not mainly an appeal to the general public to support his policies, as is the modern convention; rather, it was an appeal to Democrats not to abandon their party standard. Cleveland was using public opinion to maintain and cultivate partisan support, hoping that rank-and-file Democrats would pressure their leaders in the Senate. He was, again, attempting to mold *partisan* opinion.

There are two additional major examples of Cleveland's lobbying his partisans in his second term. First, he elicited the support of Democrats in Congress to uphold his veto of the Seigniorage Bill of 1894, using his veto message as justification and also as a means to rally the support of his partisans to sustain it. Cleveland went beyond this formal maneuver, though: by personally lobbying the Democratic Speaker of the House, he succeeded in blocking debate on the veto, which was thereby sustained. Second, and less notably, he rallied Democratic forces in the Senate to defeat an important resolution introduced by Henry Cabot Lodge which would have favored silver currency.[125]

Cleveland, then, was certainly not above personally lobbying members of Congress to support his plans, nor was he averse to using public opinion to help his cause. It is instructive to observe his dealings with the press and public opinion more thoroughly. George Parker was a friend and confidant who served as Cleveland's "self-appointed press secretary" in the presidential campaigns.[126] Just before Cleveland's death in 1909, Parker recorded his revealing thoughts about the presidency and the press:

> If an official, with a duty to the whole public, so far forgets his dignity or that of his great office to court some part of the people by appeals to that vanity which, for reasons I could never understand, wants to shine with a reflected light, retribution is certain to come when power has gone, if not before. No, I should prefer, for reputation's sake, to take my chances, even in the face of the opposition, than to have resorted to methods which now seem to be accepted as a necessary way for moving public opinion. I am really thankful that the efforts to create an unconscious, but effective, censorship of the press never had encouragement from me at any point in my public career.[127]

The passage expresses an important truth about Cleveland's dealings with the press, but it is only part of the truth.

Cleveland clearly did not go out of his way to cultivate reporters or use them to gain support for his positions, in his second term even denying patronage to newspapermen. This undoubtedly vexed Parker (and probably prompted his decision to be Cleveland's self-appointed go-between with the press at election time), who believed that there "was no time when he [Cleveland] could not have had the most enthusiastic support of the newspapers of his own party for anything that he might have wanted, within reason." After all, Parker continued, he "had only to do as others had done before him and have done after him; but it was impossible"; good relations with the party newspapers were "impossible" because of Cleveland's personal decision to keep them at bay. Such a view is an exaggeration, however, because he did release public letters through the press, as cited above, to move partisan public opinion behind his positions. As Pollard puts it, "He held the newspapers mostly at arm's length but Cleveland was wise enough to use them when he thought it was in the public interest."[128]

But I have not yet detailed Cleveland's most aggressive appeals to public opinion in his second term, after the Democrats had been trounced at the polls in the midterm elections of 1894. They were stripped of their majority status in both houses of Congress, and many of those remaining were of the free-silver persuasion. In 1895 and 1896, Cleveland undertook a public campaign to win the Democracy back from the silverite Democrats whom he regarded as apostates.

Cleveland began his campaign in April 1895 by releasing a letter to Chicago businessmen who had asked the president to address a sound-money group. His response, a letter of heavy rhetoric and strong sentiment concluded with the admonition, "Disguise it as we may, the line of battle is drawn between the forces of safe currency and those of silver monometallism." He stepped up the campaign with another public letter read at a gathering of Democratic editors from the state of New York in May 1895. It opened with an unambiguous statement of his case: "Our party is so much a party of principle, and its proper action and usefulness are so dependent upon a constant adherence to its doctrines and traditions, that no tendency in our ranks to follow the misleading light of a temporary public misapprehension should go unchallenged." Cleveland then proceeded again to defend "safe money" and criticize the pro-silver forces in a clear attempt to persuade Democrats back to the party standard. He said as much in the conclusion of the letter, where he also demonstrated a keen understanding of the influence of the press: "I have referred to this subject in the belief that nothing more important can engage the attention of the American people or the national Democracy, and in the conviction that the voice of Democrats of New York, through its press, should constantly be heard in every State."[129]

And Cleveland's public campaign of letter writing was not finished. Before the meeting of the Democratic National Convention in June 1896, he released a letter to Democratic voters through the *New York*

Herald. Worried that there would be "engrafted upon our Democratic creed a demand for the free, unlimited, and independent coinage of silver"—which, of course, he saw as a catastrophe that would signal the party's demise—he appealed to Democrats to ensure that at the convention "those Democrats who believe in the cause of sound money should be heard and should be constantly in evidence."[130] On July 4, 1896, another Cleveland letter was read at a gathering at Tammany, urging the party to abandon its turn toward free silver. And finally, in despair, Cleveland released a letter urging support for the "National Democracy" party-bolters who refused to accept Bryan and the silverites' capture of the party at the convention of 1896.[131]

In 1895, while he was fighting his battle in the press for the soul of the party, Cleveland was also trying to cultivate support in the South for his sound-money brand of Democracy. Apparently he again used public letters and engaged in some other interesting tactics of public opinion mobilization as well.[132] He not only lobbied southern Democratic leaders but also ordered published material (on "sound money") to be distributed in the South, sent Secretary of the Treasury John G. Carlisle on a speaking tour in May, and personally toured the region in the autumn.[133] Even though Cleveland's tour was far more ceremonial than Secretary Carlisle's, his intention was the same: to generate southern support for his brand of Democracy.

Although a significant part of Cleveland's second term was spent aspiring to a position of party leadership, his relationship with his party was unlike that of the other presidents I have considered, with the exception of Polk. Cleveland and Polk were much more clearly *leaders* of their parties than were Taylor, Grant, and even Harrison, each very active in pushing his party's policies through force of presidential will. Each utilized his formal messages, veto power, personal relations with members of Congress, cabinet members, and the press to gain support for and institute important party policies. Both similarly expected to lead and congressional partisans to follow.

Yet there is a crucial difference between Polk's and Cleveland's relationships to their parties. Polk exerted strong leadership but was also quite concerned about deference to the major forces within the party; he understood that they had to be conciliated. This explains, among other actions, his putting James Buchanan, a major Democratic leader, in his cabinet, his detailed concern with press relations, and his decision not to seek a second term. Polk may not have been a keen party manager all the time, but he clearly knew where the power lay in his party and he knew how to compromise.

Cleveland, however, was a president who did not seem to understand or care about the management of partisans and who disliked compromise. As George Parker put it, Cleveland "welcomed that large independence [from party] which was founded upon principle. If he was himself, in some degree, the beneficiary of this quality, he was, to perhaps still larger degree, its victim."[134] Cleveland made his reputation, in part, through his supposed independence from regular party politics and his strong, principled stances. Yet his reputation also suffered the most as a result of this same independence on the issue of the gold standard, and he was repudiated by his party at the 1896 Democratic convention.

Still, this was Cleveland's way, illustrating not so much the resurgence of a founding understanding of the presidency (as an independent office) as a more modern understanding of the party presidency. Cleveland's party leadership in his second term anticipated the political thought (and, to a lesser extent, practice) of Woodrow Wilson. Certainly, he was not as adept as Wilson at party leadership and management or at public relations, but he clearly approximated the Wilsonian notion of party leadership as personal leadership. As James Ceaser has said, Wilson's party seemed "to be a temporary organization—perhaps under a traditional party label—that is 'owned' by a particular leader and that exists to promote that leader's interest."[135]

Richard Welch, in concluding his excellent study of Cleveland's presidencies, perceptively remarks that they serve as an "introduction to the development of the modern presidency and to the identification of executive power in the person of the president."[136] It is with Cleveland that one begins to see the tension between party and "person" resolve in favor of the latter. To be sure, Cleveland cared about the Democratic Party and its traditions, but he was not above recasting the party along his own lines and seeing it embodied in his person, something that previous party presidents were hesitant to do. Cleveland, after all, had made the party "stand for something" with his tariff message of 1887. And indeed, he expected the party to follow his lead on tariff reform and currency issues. When it did not, he was willing to exert considerable energy to make it do so, even to the extent of publicly skewering fellow Democrats. It did not seem to strike him that a large part of his party role should be compromising with and at times deferring to congressional Democrats rather than commanding or strong-arming them.

The Democracy had not been the Polk Democracy in the 1840s, but it was the Cleveland Democracy in the late 1880s and early 1890s—at least in Grover Cleveland's view. Thus, although Polk and Cleveland can both be considered party leaders, as opposed to party agents or facilitators, it is important to differentiate the character of their leadership. For lack of better terminology, Polk's might be designated "traditional" party leadership, whereas Cleveland's, with its emphasis on the personality of the president more than on the party, might be called "modern" party leadership. Both should be seen as taking strong leadership roles vis-à-vis their parties, but the former would be more obedient to other centers of power in the party, while the latter would regard himself and his person as the power center and embodiment of the party.

My five case studies illustrate a range of presidential party behavior along an agent-leader continuum. It is worth noting the rather obvious partisan differences: the Whigs and Republicans were agents or facilitators; the Democrats were leaders. This distinction is consistent with established nineteenth-century partisan interpretations of the role of the presidency within constitutional and party frameworks. Democrats, after Jackson, tended to be more receptive to popular presidential party leadership, while Whigs and then Republicans favored a Congress-centered (although not Congress-dominated) party leadership.[137]

Although Harrison's facilitator role was probably the most consistent with the dictates of the party constitution, across all five cases one finds a presidential concern with party principles and with redeeming party pledges made to the public. The leadership style that most pressed against the conventions of the party constitution, however, was that of Cleveland, in the twilight of the nineteenth century. There would not be a sharp break with the party model, but with Cleveland one sees most clearly the beginnings of modern presidential leadership and the identification of the presidency with the person of the president, rather than with the collectivity of the political party.

On my view, this development may well be a cause for concern. What might be done to temper the modern presidency and reassert the party constitution's emphasis on representation and accountability in presidential leadership?

Conclusion
Presidential Leadership and Political Parties in the Twenty-first Century

As the parties wasted away, the Presidency stood out in solitary majesty as the central focus of political emotion, the ever potent symbol of national community. When parties were strong and media weak, Presidents were objects of respect but not of veneration. There were no great personal cults of Rutherford B. Hayes and Benjamin Harrison.

Arthur Schlesinger Jr., *The Imperial Presidency*

Created to be largely insulated from the influence of mass publics, the presidency came under their sway by the 1830s and 1840s with the development of mass political parties and their control over the nomination and election of candidates. The presidency became, to a significant extent, a seat of popular leadership. In fact, following James Mac-Gregor Burns, I have argued that political parties loomed so large in the nineteenth century that a "party constitution" was "adopted" which altered the original constitutional setup between the branches of government and especially between the presidency and the people.[1]

I have focused specifically on the popular presidency that was forged by mass political parties in the nineteenth century. Beginning in the 1830s, the presidency became subject to the pull of the partisan universe and would no longer be—if, indeed, it ever truly was—the independent, constitutional office advocated by the founders. It would be a partisan and, hence, decidedly popular office. Although the nineteenth-century presidency was clearly not a plebiscitary office, presidents exercised a popular, democratic leadership that had considerable merit.

These claims about nineteenth-century presidential leadership have been borne out in the previous chapters. My examination of the nineteenth-century presidential electoral milieu, through extensive use of campaign biographies and nomination acceptance letters, evidences the tendency of presidential candidates, beginning in the 1830s, to espouse issue positions and political principles affiliated with political parties in their quest for office. Chapter 2 shows that candidates were expected to pledge allegiance to parties and their principles and that the people were to make a decision not only about whom to elevate to office (the founders' desideratum) but which principles should inform government conduct and policy as well. Chapter 3, however, highlights the nuance in this party period, tracing the evolution of the presidency from a party office toward a more plebiscitary one.

The fidelity of presidents and presidential candidates to their parties in this period was not merely an electoral phenomenon, though. The analysis of inaugural addresses in chapter 4 shows that most presidents in the party period of the nineteenth century expressed fidelity to a party and its principles upon assuming the office. A number of presidents outlined a notion of the American political system quite in line with my understanding of the party constitution, each seeing himself as the head of his political party, elected in response to the popular will. But presidents' loyalty to their parties went beyond the rhetoric of their inaugural addresses, as chapters 5 and 6 demonstrate; five case studies illustrate the extent to which presidents in the party period acted with and on behalf of their parties while in office. Although their kind and degree of partisanship differed, it can with confidence be said that all five were to a significant extent partisans and thus were exercising popular leadership.

Responsible Parties or Electoral Machines?

To make these claims about the nineteenth-century presidency and parties is to court controversy. A standard assumption of scholars and political commentators is that the presidents between Jackson and McKinley, with the exceptions of Polk and Lincoln, are hardly worthy of attention. There is a similar assumption in the scholarly literature about nineteenth-century political parties: that is, that they were really not much more than sophisticated electoral machines concerned with the spoils of office. My analysis, however, offers a contrarian perspective. Even though the picture of the nineteenth-century party system that has emerged in this book does not evince an overwhelming fit with the party constitution model, there are substantial similarities. Nineteenth-century political parties were much more than just useful vehicles for electing persons to office, and party presidents offered sophisticated and substantive models of democratic leadership.

But mine is a minority view. For instance, the political scientist Anthony Downs, characterizing the American party system in general, has argued famously that "politicians in our model [of political parties] never seek office as a means of carrying out particular policies; their only goal is to reap the rewards of holding office per se." The historian Richard P. McCormick, talking less generally, says of nineteenth-century parties that they "functioned best in securing agreement on candidates, conducting campaigns, mobilizing their partisans in the electorate, and sustaining and rewarding a large corps of organizers."[2] Primarily by highlighting the similarities between the parties, or the ostensible lack of ideological difference, this view suggests that American parties have fallen well short of being conduits for the will of the people. By not taking strong opposing positions on issues, they have not provided the public, through elections, with a full-bodied control over government policy and thus have been electoral machines first and foremost.

Such characterizations are too heavy-handed, however; parties were much more than electoral machines in the nineteenth century. It is insufficient to argue that they were even primarily concerned with the mere winning of office, that they were organizations designed mostly to help office seekers attain their goals. As my empirical analysis makes clear, nineteenth-century parties are better seen as coalitions of diverse interests, organized around certain principles and ideas that, upon electoral validation, they tried to enact into government policy.[3] Parties in the nineteenth (as well as the twentieth) century lacked the cohesion, unity, and sharpness of principles to meet fully the dictates of the party constitution (or, what is the same thing, the responsible party) model, but in articulating principles or "persuasions" and, having gained office, working to institute them, they approximated the party constitution model.[4] Parties, on this view, were what Paul Beck calls "broad-based organizations that transcend[ed] the office seekers and officeholders. . . . [P]olitical parties reside[d] in both citizen and elite circles."[5]

Nineteenth-century parties insinuated themselves into the lives of regular citizens through party conventions, newspapers, parades, and elections; and they developed long-standing sets of principles and commitments to voters. Their leaders, writes Joel Silbey, "articulated political appeals and shaped the grounds of battle effectively and repeatedly. But they did their work in conjunction with other forces: their fellow party members, the mass of party voters."[6] They were not simply crafty and unprincipled leaders who engaged in empty rhetoric to woo the public at election time and gain the spoils of office; they actually aggregated and articulated the interests of their supporters (elite *and* mass) into relatively coherent platforms.

There were notable ideological differences between the nineteenth-century parties, and their platforms treated salient and controversial issues, as a number of writers have pointed out.[7] Among other things, the parties were quite concerned about—and disagreed over—financial systems, tariff rates, the constitutionality of internal improvements, the involvement of the federal government in citizens' lives, and the proper way of rebuilding the South after the Civil War. For instance, John Gerring explains, "On economic matters, Whig-Republican policy could be summarized as mercantilist, Democratic policy as laissez-faire. . . . Whereas Whig-Republican economic policies favored industry, Democratic policies were slanted toward agriculture." And the parties can be said to have been at least moderately principled; even the much-maligned and supposedly "issueless" Whig Party was somewhat issue-oriented in its campaigns and actions. As Michael Holt has recently argued, the traditional interpretation of the 1840 election—that it was all hullabaloo and no substance—"belittles the importance of issues in the election, both what was said during the campaign and, more important, the concrete records and programmatic alternatives the parties had created in state legislatures and Congress since 1837."[8]

To be sure, when the parties squared off at election time, they would often champion a number of the same issues, disagreeing only on a few. Yet this fact should be taken to indicate not a lack of choice for the public but, rather, the large degree of agreement among a majority of Americans on many salient public issues.[9] But although there is much that Americans agree on, there are also substantial disagreements, and it was the rare presidential election in the party period in which there were almost no differences between the parties on important issues.

Further, my analysis indicates that presidents, once elected, worked with their partisans—with varying degrees of success—to help implement the platforms and programs of their parties. The nineteenth-century presidency, in its electoral and governing manifestations, was a partisan office. Parties were the intermediaries between officials and the public, and the relationship was two-way: the public helped the parties define their principles and win elections, and the party then was expected to reward the public by redeeming its pledges (of offices *and* policy direction). The presidency was an office to which the public, through partisan opinion, laid an important claim; the presidency was a seat of popular leadership.

Several presidents even saw their relationship with partisans as breaking free of the conventional electoral nexus. That is, they used the powers at their disposal—formal messages, public appeals, personal lobbying—to cultivate the support of and to rally partisans (both leaders and masses) between elections. James Polk and Grover Cleveland were particularly noteworthy on this front. Polk used his messages and his administration organ—the *Union*—to cultivate Democratic support for his policies (which he believed had been publicly mandated in 1844) throughout the course of his administration. Grover Cleveland used the force of his personality, his formal messages, and public letters to move the Democratic Party toward a "sound money" financial standard during his second term.

To be sure, the nineteenth-century party system in certain respects, and at different times, fell well short of the party constitution. Antiparty movements, culminating in Progressivism, certainly had some solid reasons to be skeptical and critical of the parties. Even though from the perspective of the founding generation the mass party system was quite progressive and "democratic," it hardly needs mentioning that black Americans and women were almost completely excluded from participation in the party universe of the nineteenth century. Indeed, democracy is rather a misnomer, for how can one talk of "representation" and "accountability" and the "public will" in any full sense when only a minority of the population is able to participate in politics? A truly democratic party system would have to include all citizens, regardless of race and sex.

In addition to this obvious limitation, there were widespread accusations of corruption against nineteenth-century parties. Partisans often saw their offices not as public trusts but rather as opportunities for private gain. President Grant surely did not surround himself with the most reputable of gentlemen. The popularity of the Mugwumps and Liberal Republicans, and the comeback of the Democratic Party through

Grover Cleveland, were made possible by the very real and objectionable corruption of party leaders and officials in the postwar period. Patronage was often at the heart of the problem. The power to dispense jobs was critical to the power and strength of the parties, but it also opened the door to corruption. That party leaders would often confer jobs and appointments only after receiving something in exchange—political support or money or lucrative business deals—was clearly a cause for concern. As the famous machine politician George Washington Plunkitt would have put it, many party leaders "seen their opportunities and took 'em."[10]

Further, although it was rare for a presidential campaign in the party era to be completely issueless, several elections in the Gilded Age were remarkably vacuous. The Republican Party during Grant's tenure became an "organization" first and foremost and a principled party a distant second. As Josephson tells it: "The General Grant Era witnessed the full flowering of the spoils system in our Government in stronger and purer form than ever before. For seven years, until they faced detection and punishment, the spoilsmen who invaded every branch of the National Government moved in the pursuit of 'beauty and booty' solely. Gathered in overwhelming majority, with the great silent soldier present to keep order in the country, they needed to concern themselves with no threat from a beaten opposition party, no serious problems of national policy—such as troubled the prewar era—nothing, in short, but the uninterrupted use and enjoyment of the offices."[11] Although that passage is somewhat hyperbolic, there is no doubt that many Republican leaders were more concerned with securing patronage for themselves and their constituents than they were with promoting a decisive set of principles and policies. The party system at that time was not doing its job of organizing and conducting public opinion. In the parlance of responsible-party theory, the responsibility of the Republican Party to the public will was moderate, if not negligible. The partisan opinion to which President Grant was clearly bound was significantly severed from the public and popular opinion at large.

This period was not characteristic of the era as a whole, however; in general, parties in the nineteenth century were not issueless, not concerned only with winning elections. Clearly important issues divided them and their presidential candidates in the antebellum period. Voters were undoubtedly opting for different products in voting for James Polk or Henry Clay, Lewis Cass or Zachary Taylor, James Buchanan or

Charles Fremont. And by 1876, the postwar corruption of the parties having been exposed, they would begin again, if tentatively, to promote and embrace issues and principles rather than just seek the spoils of office.

The five presidents studied in chapters 5 and 6—whether party leaders, agents, or facilitators—were all popular, democratic leaders (as were all the presidents in the party period). Because they were all bound up in the collectivity of their political parties, the presidency was, to greater or lesser degree, a seat of popular leadership. To be sure, Polk and Cleveland were more popular leaders than Grant, Taylor, and even Benjamin Harrison, because they more actively and aggressively pushed for the support and passage of their party's programs; what is more, they reached out between elections to cultivate the support of partisans for the party's programs. They were, I have argued, party leaders. Harrison too had an important role in the passage of his party's policies—namely, the tariff, pension, silver, and antitrust acts—even though he tended to be one of many party leaders rather than the preeminent party leader in Washington; he was a party facilitator. And even Taylor and Grant, who served as agents or instruments of their parties rather than leaders or facilitators, were to an important extent caught up in the winds of public opinion as expressed through their parties.

It should not be controversial to say that this state of affairs ran counter to the founders' ideas about the place of the presidency within the American constitutional system. Whatever the extent of his active party leadership, a president who submitted to the dictates of the party system would be, through these actions, contravening the proper position of the presidency within the U.S. constitutional system. The presidency, under the nineteenth-century party system, was not the independent office that the founders envisioned but a notably partisan and popular office, one tied to the public will.

Although nineteenth-century presidents and political parties did not embody fully the party constitution model, they did approximate it; they did make pledges to the people which they tried to "redeem" when they won election. Given the differences between the parties at most times during the century, it did matter, in terms of policy direction, that one party was elected instead of another. And although spoils were important, they were not the summum bonum of nineteenth-century politics. Despite distinct drawbacks, the essence of the party system, though often not fully realized, offers a powerful model for the reorganization of the contemporary political system. Most particularly, it offers a template for presidential leadership that could help to bring balance back to the constitutional system and serve the values of representation, accountability, and deliberation, instead of those preeminent values of the modern presidency: power and efficiency.

The Modern Presidency and the Pitfalls of "Democratic" Leadership

The party model of presidential leadership has distinct relevance to present-day debates over the appropriate structure and scope of presidential leadership. Seen through the lens of the nineteenth-century party presidency, the modern presidency and modern presidential leadership are found wanting. What is more, however Panglossian and misguided it may be to argue for a full return to the party era and its assumptions about presidential leadership, it is far from foolish to suggest that presidents, presidential scholars, and interested citizens would do well to become (re)acquainted with a reserved yet popular style of presidential leadership culled from the pages of presidential history. Indeed, modern presidential leadership needs to embody far more fully the key values of representation, accountability, and deliberation, which were the essence of the party model.

To argue for a revitalization or "modernizing" of the party model of presidential leadership logically demands a critique of the modern presidency highlighting particularly those drawbacks that would likely be remedied by a return to the party model. Why, after all, is a different model needed, if modern presidential leadership is exemplary, satisfactory, or at least acceptable? There is no shortage of studies critiquing the modern presidency, and many of the arguments against it are well known and often mentioned. Although a sustained attack has been made by scholars who favor a more "constitutional" understanding of the office, such as James Ceaser and Jeffrey Tulis, criticism has come from sundry sources.[12] Among the most important indictments of the modern presidency are these three: (1) it undermines deliberation in Congress; (2) it promotes demagoguery (and personalism) on the part of presidential candidates and presidents; and (3) it results in a "pseudodemocratization" of the presidential office while feigning a thoroughgoing and substantial democratization.[13]

Although there are significant disagreements about exactly when the "modern" presidency began, many writers look to the presidencies of Theodore Roosevelt and Woodrow Wilson. Perhaps T. R.'s campaign in 1912 offers the clearest picture of what the twentieth-century presidency would bring. Gearing up for his 1912 presidential bid, Roosevelt canvassed the country in the summer of 1910, making a controversial and notable speech at Osawatomie, Kansas. Among other things, he laid out very clearly his notion of the executive authority when discussing the Progressive movement and its "New Nationalism" creed:

> The American people are right in demanding that New Nationalism, without which we cannot hope to deal with new problems. The New Nationalism puts the national need before sectional or personal advantage. It is impatient of the utter confusion that results from local legislatures attempting to treat national issues as local issues. It is still more *impatient of the impotence which springs from overdivision of governmental powers,* the impotence which makes it possible for local selfishness or for legal cunning, hired by wealthy special interests, to bring national activities to a deadlock. *This New Nationalism regards the executive power as the steward of the public welfare.* It demands of the judiciary that it shall be interested primarily in human welfare rather than in property, just as it demands that the representative body shall represent all the people rather than any one class or section of the people.[14]

After failing to win the Republican nomination in 1912, Roosevelt bolted the party for the independent Bull Moose Party. In his nomination acceptance speech, he further articulated his decidedly "modern" understanding of the presidency:

> I believe in a larger opportunity for the people themselves directly to participate in government and to control their governmental agents, because long experience has taught me that without such control many of their agents will represent them badly. By actual experience in office I have found that, as a rule, I could secure the triumph of the causes in which I most believed, not from the politicians and the men who claim an exceptional right to speak in business and government, but by *going over their heads and appealing directly to the people themselves.* I am not under the slightest delusion as to any power that during my political career I have at any time possessed. Whatever of power I at any time had, I obtained from the people. I could exercise it only so long as, and to the extent that, the people not merely believed in me, but heartily backed me up. *Whatever I did as president I was able to do only because I had the backing of the people.*

When on any point I did not have that backing, when on any point I differed from the people, it mattered not whether I was right or whether I was wrong, my power vanished. I tried my best to lead the people, to advise them, to tell them what I thought was right; if necessary, I never hesitated to tell them what I thought they ought to hear, even though I thought it would be unpleasant for them to hear it; but I recognized that my task was to try to lead them and not to drive them, to take them into my confidence, to try to show them that I was right, and then loyally and in good faith to accept their decision. I will do anything for the people except what my conscience tells me is wrong, and that I can do for no man and no set of men; I hold that a man cannot serve the people well unless he serves his conscience; but I hold also that *where his conscience bids him refuse to do what the people desire, he should not try to continue in office against their will.*[15]

Within these two passages is contained the essence of the contemporary presidency, not only the glorification of the "executive power" and the denigration of "overdivision of governmental powers" but also the grounding of this far-reaching executive authority in public opinion or the "backing of the people." Anchored in public opinion, the modern presidency gains power and authority vis-à-vis coordinate branches of government and other sites of political power and becomes, on the Rooseveltian view, the "steward of the public welfare." It is hard not to see today's presidency in these passages crafted by Roosevelt. Although he was considered radical by many at the time, including both of his 1912 presidential opponents, William Howard Taft and Woodrow Wilson, these ideas have since become accepted tenets of U.S. political culture. Presidents are expected to dominate Congress and the political landscape, rally the public behind an ambitious legislative agenda, fend off the "special interests," and lead America to the political promised land.

Admittedly, the political dominance of the presidency has been an uneven development in the twentieth century, but a development largely in one direction: increasing power for the presidency. Constitutional imbalance, as such, need not bode ill for the American body politic; in some circumstances, many would argue, constitutional imbalance has served America well. For instance, presidential dominance was essential, on this view, to the passage of the New Deal programs, or to leadership in times of foreign crisis. But it is one thing to have dominant presidential leadership during brief (and rare) times of crisis; it is another thing entirely to have dominant presidential leadership at all times.[16] Modern presidents, it would appear, to feed their insatiable appetite for the spotlight (and the public's demands for them to step into the spotlight), see crisis lurking around every corner. There are no quiet times for the modern presidency; modern political values and expectations will not allow for presidential restraint or humility.

Thus, although there are undeniable benefits to strong, modern presidential leadership, because this leadership apparently cannot be contained to simply "crisis" situations, it poses at least three significant drawbacks to the body politic. The first is that strong presidential leadership often usurps the deliberative function of Congress in the legislative process, a point made effectively by numerous commentators.[17] As the *Federalist* indicates, the founders created the House and Senate in such manner as to promote, and certainly not obstruct, deliberation in the course of legislating. To be sure, they did not believe that logrolling and compromise would be absent from the process of representation, but they did expect dialogue and deliberation to be central features of the process.[18] What is more, they clearly did not envision a legislative process directed and dominated by the president. Presidents were to be one of numerous participants in the deliberative process.

When presidents usurp the legislative function in the political system—amid calls that Congress is dominated by "special interests" and "parochialism"—the body politic is not usually well served. Although some very important and needed legislation may pass Congress as the result of presidential strong-arming, more frequently the result is poorly crafted legislation. President Bill Clinton's health care initiative, developed during the 103d Congress, is just one in a long string of major presidential policies crafted largely in the executive branch, by political appointees and policy advisers, rather than by the people's representatives. That it did not pass should not be a cause for complacency. Although its failure was indeed a triumph of deliberative legislative democracy over insulated, presidency-centered dictation of legislation, lack of merit may not have been the primary cause; rather, Clinton's unpopularity—and thus representatives' willingness to challenge him—was probably at the heart of the failure. Had he presented his health plan in the early days of his presidency (before numerous missteps eroded his popularity), and capitalized on the goodwill that the electorate provides a new president, he might, regardless of the plan's merits, have notched a major legislative victory. After all, many members expressed suspicion of President Ronald Reagan's 1981 budget yet felt compelled to support it because of the president's popularity.[19]

Let me stress, however, that public and elite expectations are such that a president can hardly avoid promoting an ambitious agenda and trying to force it through Congress. Eisenhower's failure to submit a legislative program to Congress in 1953, for example, was not well received, particularly among opinion leaders, and Ike would not make this "mistake" again.[20] According to our contemporary political morality play, presidents are champions of the "whole people," and Congress is the home of "special interests" and narrow views.[21] Thus, public and media pressure is certainly on presidents to bend Congress to their will. Former Senator Bill Bradley made these expectations a centerpiece of his 2000 presidential campaign. In discussing the likelihood of health care reform, Bradley spoke of "leadership at the very top, leadership that is willing to take a big issue and push it—not a small issue, not something step by step—but something that is comprehensive and that will deal with the problem. . . . I'm running for president, because I want to offer that kind of leadership on big things just like health care for all Americans."[22] Impatience with incrementalism, with the give-and-take of deliberative, Congress-centered legislating, has led to a preference for presidential dominance and direction in legislative affairs. It would be unthinkable, in our era, for a president to defer to Congress on major legislative initiatives, let alone extol the virtues of a cumbersome, deliberative system. Few would today agree with President William Howard Taft, writing not long after leaving office, that the principal "danger to the best interests of the country, is in the overwhelming mass of ill-digested legislation."[23]

But "ill-digested legislation" is not the only problem that a presidency-centered political system engenders. The second major drawback, related to the first, is that modern presidents in their attempts to rally Congress and the American people often engage in demagogic rhetoric and appeals. James Ceaser has identified two main types of demagoguery, "soft" and "hard."[24] The former refers to rhetoric that appeals to the public on the basis of flattery and intimacy. The latter is rhetoric that seeks to pit citizens against one another and rouse their resentment or even hatred of certain groups or classes. Neither type is conducive to reasoned public debate, as each appeals to emotional, irrational, or base instincts of the population. "Hard" demagoguery, at least on the part of presidents, is fortunately rare, although it does sometimes appear at the margins of presidential rhetoric.[25] But soft demagoguery is far more prominent and, because of its ubiquity, should elicit concern. Given their tendency to flatter the people and maintain an intimate relationship with them, presidents are often compelled to support legislative proposals and ideas that have little chance of success or, worse, that are misguided and quixotic. Presidents, because they must flatter the people, tell them what they want to hear: that our problems can be solved quickly, efficiently, and in a fashion that produces few losers. But quick and painless legislative solutions with no "zero-sum" implications are very rare, of course, if not chimerical. As James MacGregor Burns admonishes, the modern president "embraces his role as chief of state, 'adjourning politics,' evading the mean problems created by the separation of powers and checks and balances, and creating a relationship with the mass public based on symbol, myth, and ritual."[26]

Even mild demagoguery is detrimental to public discourse and debate and also to political trust. Not only does it contribute fundamentally distorted views of the political world to public debates, but it promotes an impatience with government and public officials. In the process of trying to meet the expectations of modern presidential leadership, presidents and presidential candidates, through their ambitious promises and "visions," often undermine reasoned public argument. But, as Marc Landy and Sidney Milkis have pointed out, "What special qualities of mind, heart, and soul endow a working politician with the mystical gifts necessary to foresee the future and the license to rouse public opinion in the service of that divination? Such a view of political leadership makes a mockery of the reasoned and sober deliberation that is the heart of republican government." Additionally, excessive expectations for presidents create unachievable standards for leadership and assure that presidents will fail to meet them. The result is a vicious cycle wherein presidents and candidates feel even more pressure to break the deadlock with a stronger vision and still more ambitious leadership. Thus is the door opened for the soft demagogue, the "kind of public figure who will exploit citizens' impatience with the difficult tasks involved in sustaining a healthy constitutional democracy."[27]

These first two problems of the modern presidency are largely concerned with policy outcomes and how the presidency can disrupt or adversely influence the process of legislation or the public discourse that is concomitant with the legislative process. The third main drawback involves the impact of the modern presidency on the democratic process and representation in the United States. At least since Andrew Jackson, but particularly in this century, presidents have been regarded as champions of the people, direct representatives of the American public. Because no other federal leader (with the exception of the vice president) is elected by the nation as a whole, the president is seen as singularly equipped to be democratic leader par excellence. Some scholars, however, are coming to the realization that this characterization may, in fact, be a mischaracterization.

Robert Dahl, America's premier theorist of democracy, has recently described the development of the modern presidency as having wrought a "pseudodemocratization" of the presidency, which he defines as "change taken with the ostensible and perhaps even actual purpose of enhancing the democratic process that in practice retains the aura of its democratic justification and yet has the effect, intended or unintended, of weakening the democratic process." There are two main problems of pseudodemocratization, according to Dahl. One, remarked upon above, is the tendency of a president-dominated process to subvert the deliberation necessary to create good public policy. The second problem, though, is particularly relevant to democracy and representation in the United States. For Dahl, the democratic process and representation of the public requires a full-bodied participation of the people and/or their representatives. Democracy ideally "provides ordinary people with the opportunities to discover what public policies and activities are best for themselves and for others and to insure that collective decisions conform with . . . the policies they believe best for themselves and for others."[28]

Although we have been schooled in the twentieth century to believe that presidents are our democratic agents, that they in some way help Americans "realize" democracy, Dahl points out that the modern presidency may in fact be providing a hollow form of democracy. Along these same lines, Bruce Miroff has observed that contemporary presidents tend to "monopolize the public space" and "[w]hen one political figure dominates this space, and engrosses its proceedings, the possibilities for a democratic politics are greatly diminished." Additionally, Landy and Milkis argue that a "president must not do so much for them [the public] that the very concept of democratic citizen becomes vacuous."[29] But when, as the modern presidency counsels, we begin to look to the presidency to solve all problems, when we cede all civic obligations to the presidency, we lose sight of our role as citizens in the democratic process and the roles of the other branches of government. The drawback is not only that we become civically disengaged but also that we become skeptical and disaffected when the constitutional system does not work as quickly, efficiently, and boldly as presidents have promised.

There are numerous explanations for civic anomie.[30] Certainly, however, the modern presidency—and its "monopolization of the public space"—is partly to blame. When presidents consume most of the political oxygen, there is little for citizens and citizen groups to breathe. And for many Americans, given the welter of political information swirling about them, it is far easier to hope that one man (or woman) can make some sense and order of the political world than to sift through the mountain of competing information and views themselves. Walter Lippmann long ago assailed the notion of the "omnicompetent citizen," the idea that citizens, especially in the complex modern world, can be engaged in politics in anything more than a very superficial manner.[31] Lippmann's advice is surely a necessary corrective to the Pollyanna view of democratic citizenship that American political lore has often inculcated, but it goes too far, is too pessimistic.

Americans are capable, as citizens, of more than simply selecting the better of two elite politicians or answering yes or no on an important political question of the day. They are capable of contributing to the deliberation and discussion of public issues, policy positions, the character of leaders, and more. There are many forums through which to engage the political world, moreover. Tocqueville's associations are still alive and well in America, providing an important linkage between citizens and their government, and there are numerous opportunities for citizens to make themselves heard by their local, state, and federal legislators.[32]

Yet, most citizens seem supremely uninterested in the Congress or their state legislatures. Many Americans cannot even name their U.S. congressman or senator, let alone state and local representatives. How times have changed since 1841, when President William Henry Harrison, without a hint of sarcasm, could opine in his inaugural address: "It is preposterous to suppose that a thought could for a moment have been entertained that the President, placed at the capital, in the center of the country, could better understand the wants and wishes of the people than their own immediate representatives, who spend a part of every year among them."[33] A critical reason that we are alienated from our legislators and our legislatures is that we are impatient with democracy. As John Hibbing and Elizabeth Theiss-Moore have put it, "The main reason the public is disgruntled with Congress and politics in Washington is the processes inherent in a democratic political system—debates, compromises, conflicting information, inefficiency, and slowness."[34] Ambivalence toward democracy also helps to explain the modern aversion to political parties. How often do Americans lament the "partisanship" that pervades Washington and call for "bipartisanship"?

Americans are intolerant of the conflict, disagreement, and argument that characterize democracy, legislatures, and political parties. Yet it is legislators and political parties, not the presidency, that remain the best hope for a substantive democratic politics and offer the possibility of democracy rather than pseudodemocracy. Presidents, of course, should be important players, but a system of democracy that is wholly dependent on a plebiscitary relationship between public and president is a facile system of democratic government. The nineteenth-century party presidency, as examined in this book, offers a template for a democratization of the presidency that is not a pseudodemocratization.

The Presidency, Political Parties, and Democratic Government

Contra modern presidents, party-period presidents were not impediments to the deliberative process, rarely engaged in demagoguery, and—because they did not "monopolize the public space"—allowed citizens more opportunities to chart the nation's policy course themselves. Presidents during the party period had considerable respect for the prerogatives of Congress in the process of lawmaking. They differed in the amount of pressure they placed on senators and representatives to support presidential policies, but few believed it their job to strong-arm Congress into following their policies. They allowed their congressional partisans to take the lead in policymaking, though they did, to varying degrees, play important roles in the process. Some, such as Benjamin Harrison, assumed a modest role in the legislative process, making recommendations, conferring with members at times, threatening the veto, and so forth. Others, such as James Polk, used the powers of patronage, the partisan newspapers, and individual lobbying to "persuade" fellow partisans in Congress to follow their policy direction. In either case, in the main, Congress and the parties were the primary directors of the legislative process. Presidents could wield important influence within the collectivity of their political parties—particularly by making policy recommendations in line with the party platform—but they rarely dominated the legislative agenda or subverted the deliberative process.

Further, party presidents very rarely engaged in demagogic speech of either the hard or soft variety. When Martin Van Buren helped to develop the mass party system, he did so in part to limit and temper presidential ambition. He believed that tying presidential candidates and presidents to parties, organizations with clear histories and principles, would have the likely effect of limiting presidents to moderate and "safe" policies. What is more, with strong political parties acting as the conduits between the people and the presidency, presidents would have little reason to be constantly courting the favor of the people; party leaders—legislators, state leaders, and loyalists—would take care of shoring up support and popularity. When presidents did appeal to the people, they did so as champions of rather moderate party principles. Thus, demagoguery was of little concern during the party era.

Finally, the party presidency, because it did not dominate the public space in the nineteenth century, allowed for a more substantial participation by citizens than does the modern presidency. Americans today assume that the modern presidency is a supremely democratic office, an office of the people, yet although presidents do seek to create a direct connection with the American people, this effort often amounts to a rather hollow pseudodemocratization. Presidents in the nineteenth century, by contrast, rarely pretended to be the people's preeminent spokesmen; consequently, party presidents were facilitators of democratic participation more than modern, plebiscitary presidents are. Sometimes, to be sure, party presidents were important figures in the rallying of the nineteenth-century public, but they were more regularly one of many leaders who awakened, engaged, and exhorted the people.

Sidney Milkis has well captured the nineteenth-century party system's facilitation of democratic participation and the consequent decline of participation with the development of the plebiscitary presidency:

> Progressive reformers had good reasons for viewing political parties and the provincial liberties they upheld as an obstacle to economic and political justice. But they failed to appreciate the purpose these parties served as effective channels of democratic participation. Representative government is essentially fostered by public speech, by political discussion that

most effectively occurs in the legislature and local community. Civic involvement is enervated by a political process dominated by executive action, which can strengthen and lead but cannot replace the decentralizing
institutions as the home of representative government. . . . [T]he advent
of progressive democracy strengthened the national purpose, but public
debate and legislative authorization, activities that are the essence of popular rule, were displaced as the center of government activity.[35]

The party presidency respected the fundamental values of popular rule:
representation, accountability, and deliberation. The plebiscitary presidency, while pretending to serve them more frequently undermines core
democratic values. A democracy based on presidential personality, rhetoric, and plebiscite is a far cry from a substantial and full-bodied democracy.

That the nineteenth-century party system, at least ideally, served the
values of representation, accountability, and deliberation attests to a fas-
cinating characteristic of the system: the mass political parties that
democratized politics and the presidency did so in a way that was still
fundamentally compatible with constitutional values. Certainly, the presidency was brought into much closer relationship with the public and
the Congress than the founders had desired, but this connection with
the public was not generally used to inflate the importance of the presidency. Rather, political parties—that bugbear of the founders—while
bringing the people closer to the presidency, also kept the presidency
largely within its constitutional boundaries. As Arthur Schlesinger Jr.
has said: "As the parties wasted away, the Presidency stood out in solitary majesty as the central focus of political emotion, the ever potent
symbol of national community. When parties were strong and media
weak, Presidents were objects of respect but not of veneration. There
were no great personal cults of Rutherford B. Hayes and Benjamin Harrison."[36]

When the parties were strong, they were elevated above all other actors in the political system, including the president. James Bryce commented in 1888: "In America the great moving forces are the parties.
The government counts for less than in Europe, the parties count for
more."[37] And although there was always some tension between presidents (and presidential candidates) and their parties in the nineteenth
century, presidents were typically deferential to constitutional roles and
thus to congressional and local prerogatives.[38] As evidenced most sharply

in their inaugural messages, nineteenth-century presidents saw party support as giving direction to presidential conduct only within the bounds of the Constitution and their party's principles. Party victory and support would give presidents a popular will to follow and tie them closely to the public, but as James Garfield so elegantly phrased it in his inaugural address, "To interpret and to execute that will *in accordance with the Constitution* is the paramount duty of the Executive."[39] Presidents would not use popular, partisan support to subvert or even stretch the Constitution; nor would they enlist such support to elevate the presidency above other actors in the political system.

As the parties declined in importance, though, the presidency's role in the political system changed markedly. The president, to use Schlesinger's idiom, became an "object of veneration" and began to loom ever larger on the political landscape. In Ceaser's words, the parties that had "in the past imposed constraints on the president's authority and actions" were increasingly less able to do so, and presidents began to establish stronger and more direct and personal ties to the people.[40] Once the president became democratic leader par excellence, he was as a matter of course accorded a new and enlarged role in the political system. Simultaneously, the power of Congress—and thus its deliberative and representational strengths—dwindled. Yet this new presidential role, although conflicting in important respects with the one established by the Constitution, was largely considered legitimate because ostensibly "democratic" in foundation.

Strong parties—or revitalized parties—seem a necessary condition for bringing the presidency back into constitutional balance with Congress and the public. It is not simply adventitious that the strong party era, the party period, was also an era in which there was high voter turnout and civic engagement, decentralization of power, and presidential respect for the prerogatives of Congress. Although there are certainly reasons beyond the decline of parties for the sorry state of the national legislature's public prestige and power, a discussion of the necessity and possibility of reinvigorating that legislature and the public's attachment to it, is beyond the scope of this book. My analysis, however, is absolutely relevant to the possible revitalization of the political parties, which is almost certainly crucial to such a project. Indeed, the party presidency described in the preceding pages, if it can have any relevance to current politics, requires that the parties regain at least some of their former strength. In the contemporary political environment, can parties again be the premier organizations for marshaling the people into the political process, educating them, and bringing their voices to bear on public matters?

Contemporary Political Parties: Revitalization or Continued Decline?

Especially since the 1970s, numerous scholars and commentators have administered last rites to U.S. political parties and the party system; David Broder's *The Party's Over* is only the most well known of these studies.[41] The theme of these works is that the American party system has been in serious and substantial decline since the 1960s; some scholars, such as Joel Silbey and Sidney Milkis, have argued that the decline started far earlier. Whatever date they assign, most agree that the heyday of the American party system is long past and point to signs of party atrophy across the board: in the electorate, in party organization, and in the government. The diagnosis offered by William J. Keefe is typical: "Unquestionably, the party-in-the-electorate has never been weaker. Partisanship is at low ebb. Candidates and incumbents dominate the electoral system. Party coalitions, the quintessence of American parties, have atrophied. . . . Party control of government continues to be uneven and unpredictable, and programmatic responsibility, which is occasionally impressive, is typically elusive and erratic."[42]

Many of these findings appear difficult to refute, since the signs of party decline seem to be ubiquitous. Split-ticket voting, the prominence of divided government, the rise of "independent" voters, the replacement of party workers with media professionals and candidate loyalists, and the continued distrust of parties expressed in opinion polls are all highly suggestive of the enervation of the political parties. Given this putatively overwhelming evidence that the parties are in significant decline, a call for a party presidency and a reinvigoration of the political parties would seem to be, at best, an intellectual exercise lacking in practical and historical sense.

The "decline of party" leitmotif, however, so prominent in the literature, has recently come under attack by scholars and commentators who emphasize the resurgence of political parties, especially in the last decade of the twentieth century. Even by the mid-1980s, some studies were noting a revitalization particularly of the party organizations, the most prominent being Xandra Kayden and Eddie Mahe's *The Party Goes On,* which explicitly confronted the work of Broder and company.[43] Focusing predominantly on the resurgence of party organization, however, Kayden and Mahe seemed to accept that parties had lost ground with the electorate and in government, whereas later writers would argue that parties did not decline substantially in the electorate or in the government. For instance, Gerald Pomper has argued provocatively that because of recent changes in political parties and congressional government, "we are developing, almost unnoticed, institutions of semiparliamentary, semiresponsible government."[44] Yet despite this round of much-needed revisionism, few scholars today argue that parties have returned to their nineteenth-century dominance. Most, rather, see signs of uneven revitalization: that is, resurgence in some areas, amid continuing decline or stasis in other areas.

The most obvious signs of party revitalization are, of course, to be found in the national party organizations; the party-as-organization is alive and well in the twenty-first century. Since the early 1990s, most notably through effective exploitation of campaign finance loopholes, the national parties have become financial behemoths capable of raising astounding sums through "soft money" contributions. They spend this money promoting candidates for federal offices, their expenditures far exceeding those envisioned by the Federal Election Campaign Act of the 1970s. With the rising costs of media and campaign communications, money is at a premium in elections, and thus the financial muscle of the parties has never mattered more. Accompanying the development of the national parties into sophisticated fund-raising apparatuses has been the professionalization of campaigns. The national party organizations are no longer loose collections of local and state leaders assembling for intermittent national political contests but rather a staff of highly skilled and trained campaign professionals, political tacticians, and fund-raisers. State parties have evidenced some of these same traits but are clearly outgunned by the national parties, which tend to dominate the party universe, at least when it comes to federal offices.[45]

To be sure, party organizations have not completely reclaimed such former powers as the control of nominations and the dispensing of patronage; their resurgence has not been total. As John Aldrich has argued, a new form of party organization has developed in recent years, "one that is 'in service' to its ambitious politicians but not 'in control' of them as the mass party sought to be."[46] What is more, interest groups, political action committees (PACs), corporations, and unions maintain independent influences on the electoral and legislative processes; they do not work simply through the parties and organizational leaders. Still, it is the ability to raise and distribute large sums of money to party candidates that is making the parties organizationally strong and influential again. Although not on a par with the strong, local party organizations of the past, which in their heyday monopolized the political arena, modern party organizations are clearly significant, if not hegemonic, forces in the American political system. In fact, the most important distinction between party organizations today and yesterday is probably one not of power but of the locus of that power. Traditionally, they were strong and influential at the local and state levels; the vaunted party organizations of today are the national and congressional party committees. This shift in the locus of power has been credited with allowing the parties to become more nationalized and programmatic in their policies—usually considered a favorable trend. That nationalization, however, has been of a piece with the declining influence of state and local parties, which is unquestionably tied to the overall decline of political involvement and participation over the past half-century.

The success of the national party organizations in recent years has coincided with the strengthening of partisanship in government, particularly in the U.S. Congress. For instance, although the 1970s witnessed an increase in the number and power of subcommittees in the House, there was also a concomitant strengthening of the party leadership, a centralization of power that culminated in the election of Newt Gingrich to the position of Speaker, a man who would in 1995 have scholars recalling Uncle Joe Cannon, the autocratic Republican Speaker from nearly a century earlier. But it is a mistake to attribute Gingrich's consolidation of power, however brief, to his own dynamic personality; that was surely a necessary but not sufficient condition. Also critical to the consolidation of power in the Speaker and party leadership in the 104th Congress was the growing partisanship among members of the House. The Senate experienced a similar partisanization of its membership. Indeed, as Pomper has noted, "In 1969, party conflict (a majority of Republicans opposing a majority of Democrats) was evident on only about a third of all roll calls. By 1993 . . . partisanship rose to two-thirds of both House and Senate votes," and in 1995, in both houses, "party unity" for the Republicans was around 90 percent for all roll calls.[47]

Although Republican unity waned over time—in 1998, Newt Gingrich was forced to resign his Speakership and his congressional seat—it still remained much stronger than in previous years, and Congress continued to be a highly partisan institution, Democrats and Republicans, Senate and House. And notwithstanding President Clinton's "triangulation"—charting a policy direction that included both Democratic and Republican ideas—and frequent appeals to the virtues of bipartisanship, the Clinton era (particularly its last six years) was perhaps one of the most partisan periods in the history of the United States. The president frequently demonized Republicans and rallied Democrats against the Republican policy agenda; the Republicans, for their part, persistently attempted to roll back many of the policies of the Democratic Congresses that had so long controlled Washington policymaking and maintained a red alert for Clinton gaffes, failures, and scandals. Obviously, this partisanship among elites in government came to a head in the impeachment of the president in 1998. But any who think it is a thing of the past need only recall the bitterly divided and contested election of 2000 and the partisan rancor that continues to pervade Washington, most particularly in the bitter judicial nomination battles in the Senate in 2003.

There can be no question that the strong partisan character of the national government in the 1990s had both positive and negative implications. Undoubtedly, the bitterness—the "politics of personal destruction," to use the phrase du jour—and the gridlock that predominated were problematic. Yet at the same time, thanks to increasing partisanship, Americans were treated to a real, sometimes passionate, debate about the ends, purposes, and scope of government. As Gerald Pomper has said, the political parties "are currently conducting a great national dialogue on the purpose of American government and the goals of the American community. However it is resolved, that dialogue is a societal emblem of the personal and serious conversation that makes political parties essential to meaningful democracy in America."[48]

But is anyone listening to this "great national dialogue" besides politicians, the media elite, and academics? Much of the research on parties-in-the-electorate would suggest that less and less of the mass public is paying attention these days.[49] John Aldrich has said in a major study of political parties, the "most persuasive evidence of the 'decline of parties' thesis is the changes in the public's identification with the political party, and in its relevance."[50] Indeed, it is in the electorate that parties seem incapable of effecting a comeback; because of voters' persistent aversion to the two major parties and their tendency to choose the candidate over the party, the revitalization of the parties is incomplete and uneven. Numerous contemporary surveys of public opinion show high levels of dissatisfaction with the present political parties and a desire for a third-party alternative.[51] What is more, overwhelming majorities of Americans agree that "the best rule in voting is to pick a candidate regardless of party label."[52] Our muscular national party organizations are central forces in national elections and policymaking, yet as they elect and reelect their candidates, they do not close the deal by forging long-term and intense attachments to voters.

There have been three major facets to this decline of party-in-the-electorate since the 1950s. The first is the lack of identification with one of the major political parties. In recent years the Democrats and Republicans have divided electoral supporters (at roughly one-third apiece) with the "independents." As William Keefe has said, "It is by no means an unusual survey that turns up more independents than either Democrats or Republicans. Many voters, moreover, change their party identification over a short period of time, thus contributing to further partisan instability." There is some dispute, to be sure, over exactly what constitutes an "independent" voter, and there are criticisms that many surveys include Democratic or Republican "leaners" among their independents, thus inflating their number; "pure" independents, in fact, constitute only 6 to 12 percent of the population.[53] Even so, independents who lean toward one party or the other are still professing independence and evidence the waning strength of attachment to parties. In other words, these numbers are suggestive of a decline in strong partisan identification and intensity in the electorate. Of a piece with this decrease is the aforementioned desire of the American public for a third-party alternative.

The second major facet of the decline relates directly to this unanchoring of the electorate: the rise of split-ticket voting in federal elections. Many Americans routinely vote for a president of one party and a House or Senate member of the opposition party, and this trend holds also for state elections. One recent estimate holds that in presidential elections, nearly two of three voters split their tickets between the presidential and congressional offices.[54] Driven mainly by candidate-centered campaigns and incumbency advantage, write Marjorie Hershey and Paul Beck, voters generally do not "split their tickets out of a conscious desire to create a divided government."[55] Nevertheless, one notable outcome of split-ticket voting is a high incidence of divided government (in twenty-six of the thirty-two years from 1969 to 2001). Although David Mayhew has provided a necessary corrective to some of the excessive claims about the gridlock that accompanies divided government, there is no question that divided government does prevent parties from serving the ends of responsibility and accountability to the voters.[56] When parties can point fingers at each other and, believably, claim that but for the other party they would have achieved their goals, it becomes very difficult for voters to assess blame and assign responsibility for government policies or inaction. The people cannot hold their government responsible and accountable for its actions. Thus, ironically, while partisanship is strong within the government, because of waning party sentiment in the electorate, neither party is likely to control the House, the Senate, and the presidency. Sharp, elite partisanship within the context of a divided government provides the basis for a governance of bitterness, demagoguery, and investigations, as in the Clinton era, post-1994.

The third and final facet of the declining party electorate has been the resultant decline in voting turnout over much of the twentieth century—with the exception of the New Deal period. From the record levels of the late 1800s, higher than 80 percent, voter turnout in the United States dropped to roughly 50 percent of eligible voters in presidential elections and considerably less, 35 to 40 percent, in congressional off-year elections. Although there are numerous reasons for the decline of voting in the United States, few scholars doubt that without strong political parties, the high levels of participation in earlier eras would not have been achievable. Only with the partisan realignment and, therefore, resurgence of political parties in the 1930s did turnout and interest approach its nineteenth-century levels. As Joel Silbey has pointed out, "For a time during the New Deal years, there was evidence that political parties still had a strong kick, reminiscent of an earlier era and perhaps suggestive of a return to dominance by them."[57] But by the 1970s the resurgence of voter interest wrought by the New Deal political system had waned, with turnout approaching again its pre-1930s norm of roughly 50 percent turnout in presidential elections.[58]

Although parties, then, have experienced a resurgence in their organizational and governing capacities in recent years, they have not achieved similar or consistent gains in electoral loyalty and support. Furthermore, the gains made in organization and government, though impressive, have not been complete; parties are not the dominant political actors that they once were. Adapting to a candidate-centered political environment, they have made themselves significant actors but less as principled, popular organizations than as institutions specializing in "servicing" politicians' ambitions. Given this adaptation, it is not surprising that today's parties fail to stoke voter interest in the manner of the earlier decentralized and locally rooted parties which, as Sidney Milkis has noted, "by enticing Americans into neighborhood organizations and patronage practices beyond their tiny private orbits, . . . helped to show individuals the connection between their private interests and public concerns."[59] Modern parties surely help politicians win office and organize the government, but they do not excel in bringing Americans to the polls or into the political process.

Although any strengthening of political parties was discounted by commentators only a few decades ago, there has been a resurgence, however uneven; what is more, there is no reason to believe that it will not continue. A reconsideration of the party model of presidential leadership is therefore appropriate. The normative case for such a model, as presented above, can be argued in any political era, but its persuasiveness is increased in a political era that is amenable or at least not inhospitable to party presidential leadership.

The Party Presidency and the Future of Presidential Leadership

The revitalization of the political parties undoubtedly had an influence on the office of president in the late 1980s and 1990s. The strong organizational capacities of the national parties assured in those presidential nomination seasons that the choice made by party leaders and the party elite was the final choice for the party. The hand-wringing that accompanied the nomination of Jimmy Carter—over whether party primary reforms had fundamentally shifted the balance of power from party leaders to the mass public or rank-and-file partisans—turned out to be overblown and premature. What is more, thanks to the impressive fund-raising abilities of the national parties, their expenditures of soft money and get-out-the-vote drives, they played a critical role in general elections, for all the scholarly talk about presidential candidates and presidents who establish personal organizations and campaigns. These trends, which bode well for reestablishing presidential restraint, should be nurtured and cultivated. Candidates who are tied to traditional organizations and their issues and who do not gain support primarily through "outsider" appeals to the mass public become presidents who are more likely to work with partisans in Congress and other party leaders to achieve mutually defined goals.

Stronger parties mean, all things being equal, that presidents will be more easily held accountable, that Congress will assume a larger role in the legislative, representational process, and that presidential action and rhetoric will be moderated. But will parties be able to reconnect with voters and actually establish themselves in the traditions, and hearts, of the people again? If they cannot reconnect, can parties that are strong organizationally and governmentally still be capable of exerting a salutary affect on presidential leadership? The answer to the latter question is yes, but only under specific conditions. Even if parties cannot reestablish themselves with the people and thus cannot robustly represent voters, an elite-based party system that reins in presidents and preserves the constitutional balance of power should be welcomed. Although the people may have only a limited role in this sort of political system—largely that of approving or rejecting parties and their candidates—the values that are preserved—deliberation and accountability—would be an improvement on the current system, which does not promote participation and citizenship either. Under the illusory popularization, or pseudodemocratization, of the presidency, the public is said to be involved and participating through presidential leadership; however, this vicarious participation is hardly a robust and substantial participation. Even in the 2000 election, an election with no incumbent president, only a little more than 50 percent of the eligible electorate bothered to turn out.

But an elite-based party system can control and discipline presidents, and serve the values of accountability and deliberation, only if unified government becomes more common than it is today. No necessary logic dictates that Americans will have divided government when party loyalties are weak. The 2000 election is a case in point: Republicans gained unified control, albeit by the slimmest of margins, after six years of divided government.[60] Although they lost their majority in the Senate early in the 107th Congress (with Vermont senator Jim Jeffords's switch from Republican to Independent), Republicans regained majority control in the 2002 midterm elections. Moreover, there is no necessary reason to believe that Republicans will not retain unified government in 2004, or that Democrats will not assume majority control of Congress and the presidency in 2004 or 2008. In fact, if the national parties continue to increase their financial power and their influence on federal elections, they may be capable of effecting more cooperation, in elections and governing, between the popular institutions. Indeed, more institutional cooperation at the electoral stage, tying congressional and presidential candidates to the collectivity of the political party, would certainly increase the chances of electing unified party majorities. Voters would not have to be "strong" or "loyal" Democrats or Republicans to render a judgment as to the relative merits and potentials of the (unified) parties.

Nevertheless, even though there is no iron law of divided government in the current era of weak party loyalty, divided government has been the norm and does appear to be strongly correlated with weakened party loyalty in the electorate. Absent dominant party organizations to force solidarity among institutions, an electorate without firm loyalties to the political parties has a strong likelihood of producing divided government, which does not well serve the value of accountability; each party, and institution, can blame the other for policy failures and missteps. Congress and president have far less incentive, when divided by party affiliation, to see themselves as part of a common enterprise and undertaking. As Sarah Binder has said, speaking of growing partisanship in Congress in recent years, "Resurgent legislative parties are unlikely to lead to greater government responsiveness to the public's agenda—particularly in an era of divided government."[61] Moreover, divided government naturally leads a president to engage in dramatic acts of rhetorical leadership in order to exert influence on the opposition party in Congress and to increase his own power and authority in the political system; thus is (congressional) deliberation jeopardized as well.

To foster disciplined and accountable presidential leadership, therefore, an elite-based party system must more often than not produce unified party government. If the increasing organizational strength of the parties cannot do so, party resurgence will have a limited affect on presidential leadership. To foster proper presidential leadership, party resurgence may, of necessity, have to extend to the party-in-the-electorate. Not only would a revitalized electorate help to create a party system that serves the values of accountability and deliberation, but the party system would also serve the cherished democratic value of citizen representation, a value sorely lacking in the contemporary political world. Who would not like to see the mass public intimately involved in establishing the traditions, issues, and policies of the political parties, in communicating with their legislative representatives and contributing to the deliberative process, and in holding their leaders and parties accountable?

Although a revitalization of the party electorate seems at the moment a quixotic dream, there is no telling how Americans might respond if parties could be relieved of the stigma of corruption. Curbing soft money might be a first strong step; parties could retain a critical role in the electoral system, even with regulation or elimination of soft money.[62] Whether the McCain-Feingold campaign finance reform legislation, passed in 2001, which eliminates party soft money while increasing hard-money contributions, will help on this front remains to be seen. Competing predictions of party reinvigoration and party decay have been offered, but until the new system governs a round of elections (the 2004 election will be the first under its rules), there will be no solid base of evidence from which to generalize. In any case, congressional consideration of campaign finance reform in recent years has started an important national debate over the role and scope of political parties in American society. All challenges in the courts, evaluations of the new finance system, and possible further attempts at reform will continue this debate and ideally result in an appreciation of the possibilities for political parties in the American political system.

Even readers sympathetic to the arguments offered here may ultimately balk at the diminution of presidential authority and leadership that a revitalized "party presidency" would entail. The modern world is a far different place from that of the nineteenth century, they will say, and the need for unilateral, strong presidential leadership is much greater today; a restrained and moderated party presidency may have been ideal when government was largely in the business of "distribution," but with its numerous functions today—particularly in foreign affairs—government can not sustain a dearth of presidential leadership. Yet this problem is not as challenging as it first appears. It is clear that the country can never fully return to the practices and values of the party period. Particularly, the "dark horse" or the merely "available" candidate, with little qualification or ambition, is undoubtedly an anachronism. Returning to the values of party-period presidential leadership will not reduce high expectations and standards for modern candidates.

Harvey Mansfield is correct to point out a key conflict between statesmanship and party government: that statesmanship is exercised by great individuals who can engage in bold actions, whereas party government is "attuned to lesser capacities," being the outcome of collectivity, compromise, and moderation.[63] But the problem that party presidential leadership seeks to address is the surfeit of grand leadership claims in the modern political arena. To say that a revisiting of the values of the party period risks a lack of statesmanship and the institution of a "brokership" presidency is to underestimate the power of the modern understanding of the presidency.[64] Even with a return to the values of the party constitution, there will be strong presidential leadership. In other words, any such return cannot but be partial. Ideally, though, presidents might temper their leadership claims, preferring, more often than not, to work with the collectivity of their political party rather than strike out on their own in novel and bold directions.

Interestingly, it is a twentieth-century president, a modern president, who provides perhaps the best model of what a modernized party presidential leadership might look like. Although Woodrow Wilson is consistently credited with modernizing the presidency and being a towering figure in the White House, his continuing adherence to the party model of presidential leadership while in office is just as notable. Contrary to the dominant interpretation of his presidency, he did, with a few notable exceptions, conduct himself prudently as president, working largely within the system (with his political party and with the Congress) to promote his policies. But he also understood that presidents would need to take on a more active leadership role within their political parties and the country to meet the demands of a changing and more complicated political and economic world. It should come as no surprise that Cleveland's administrations, among others, were a model for Wilson's views on leadership.[65] Although parties and Congress often lacked direction and could be exceedingly slow and prone to inaction, on his view, a president would not seek to dominate his party or Congress on all issues; in fact, the president would defer on many issues to his party and partisans in Congress, nudging them but not prodding too hard. On the few issues or policies that a president believed critical, he would use the power and position of the office, particularly its connection with the American people, to help ensure the success of his viewpoint. Yet it cannot be overemphasized that these instances of dramatic leadership would be rare and coupled with give-and-take with congressional leaders and other interested parties. Presidential leadership would thus remain largely one of reconciling competing viewpoints, showing a respect for deliberation and the incorporation of numerous and diverse perspectives.

Wilson, then, cuts a model for a modernized version of presidential party leadership, retaining its essence but also recognizing the demands of the modern world for periodic expressions of dominant executive power and rhetoric. This brand of leadership prizes political parties and party government and shows respect for constitutional place and prerogative. It allows legislatures, political parties, and citizens to do much of the work of democracy. It avoids routine displays of popular, rhetorical leadership but unhesitatingly assumes great responsibility and public leadership at critical junctures and on challenging issues. Although much of Wilson's concern for party government and constitutionalism was lost on his successors (and later historians and political scientists), his successful melding of party presidential leadership with modern rhetorical leadership augurs the continuing possibilities for the party model in the modern era.

And just as Wilson helped to create a newer, bolder style of leadership, future presidents, and candidates for the presidency, will shoulder the burden of forging models of presidential leadership for the twenty-first century. Some have suggested that the changing character of the domestic and international spheres in recent decades portend a diminished scope for the presidency in coming years, and the inabilities of recent presidents to exercise strong and dramatic leadership would seem to strengthen these claims.[66] Presidential aspirations to greatness and acts of bold leadership have not abated, however, nor have presidential candidates ceased to make wildly unrealistic promises of leadership to the American people. Ultimately, a critical component in forging a presidency and a style of presidential leadership that respects the values of representation, accountability, deliberation, and, in appropriate circumstances, energy, will be presidents and presidential candidates themselves. Paradoxically, a moderation of presidential leadership may be possible only with the aid of bold and strong presidential leadership.[67]

Appendix One
Campaign Biographies as Data Sources

Among plausible ways to examine the electoral environment of the party period, one might conceivably study the partisan newspapers and pamphlets that proliferated prior to each election. Alternatively, one might study the speeches of the major stump speakers of the parties. Yet each of these methods is problematic in terms of finding consistent data over time. Partisan newspapers and campaign tracts are often lost to the dustbin of history or are excessively difficult to procure. Speeches, an obviously oral art form, were often not recorded consistently for all presidential canvasses in the time period under consideration.

One source of information which is rather consistent and readily available is campaign biographies of presidential candidates. They were a very important aspect of the nineteenth-century political milieu, and soon after 1824 they became obligatory.[1] Since they were obviously attempts to sell the candidates to the American public, analyzing them with an eye for what they considered marketable traits offers a window onto the American political system of the time. The images that are constructed of the candidates, the issues (if any) that are stressed or elided, the party associations that are withheld or proffered in campaign biographies can be very important measures of political values and conventions,

especially regarding the president's role in the political system. Usually written after the nominating conventions, the biographies were
informed by the political context and ferment of the ongoing campaign; they reflect the milieu markedly and thus would appear to offer a way to gauge the electoral environment, the issues, and the aspects of the candidates that held prime place in the campaigns of the
party period.

Yet one might offer two challenges: were the often large and pon-
derous campaign biographies really in the hands of the people? And, relatedly, were they in fact important to the canvass; did they actually
stress those things that found a prominent place in the campaigns?[2]
First, although it is difficult to trace their actual influence on the electorate, this does not mean that campaign biographies were not in the
hands of the mass electorate; they were not merely elitist publications.
The great length of some suggests that not all were meant for mass
distribution, yet the pamphlet-like quality of others certainly implies
a wide distribution. Even large size does not preclude their having
reached the public indirectly: biographies were widely reported in re-
views or campaign accounts throughout the country. Those that did not
get into the hands of the electorate directly may have reached their
destination via the party newspapers.[3] It seems reasonable to conclude
that a significant slice of the American public generally was aware of the
campaign biographies and those aspects of the candidates which they
emphasized.

Even if the biographies did not actually reach the hands of the people,
I would contend that they are nevertheless accurate reflectors of the electoral and political environment. First, their authors certainly saw themselves as providing a service for the masses; as Nathaniel Hawthorne put
it in his biography of Franklin Pierce, they were "intended to operate
upon the minds of multitudes, during a presidential canvass."[4] Likewise,
the author of an 1888 biography of Benjamin Harrison explains, "The
subject of this sketch has just reached that point in a career for the Presidency, and it is to at least partially gratify the hunger of the multitude
for information of the man that these pages are respectfully offered
them."[5] And a biography of Horatio Seymour declares, "It is eminently
proper that they [the people] should know the events of his previous life,
in order that they may be enabled to form from them an intelligent opinion as to his qualifications for the position to which he aspires."[6]

Statements like these, which could be produced for nearly all the biographies I use, indicate that the authors certainly had a mass audience in mind, which is perhaps even more important than whether the biographies actually got into the hands of the public. If they were written as if they would be widely read and distributed, it would be surprising if they were not laden with popular language and guided by popular assumptions. They would in all likelihood traffic in assumptions, sentiments, and ideas specific to the time period. Campaign biographies would still be important gauges of the broad political culture in the nineteenth century even if they were not read by a majority of citizens.

Further, historians have found them essential for setting and establishing the terms of the campaigns. As Michael Heale has pointed out, "Once a *Life* had been published, it was quarried shamelessly and repeatedly by other authors and editors. The same material, the same presentation, the same anecdotes, even the same paragraphs, sentences and phrases recurred endlessly."[7] Such repetition is really not surprising, considering that the biographies were often crafted in consultation with the candidates and the major players in the party and were generally written by party functionaries or individuals beholden to the candidate and the party.[8] In fact, a number of authors are candid enough to admit in their prefaces that the candidate had been consulted and had provided materials for the construction of the biography.[9]

Indeed, a comparison of the usually multiple biographies of a candidate reveals much more similarity than difference, and comparison with speeches, pamphlets, and other campaign tracts also suggests that they were quite representative of the issues and ideas prominent in the general campaign.[10] In other words, the biographies appear to be clearly representative of the political context of their times. (Incidentally, the similarity of those for the same candidate means that one need not canvass *all* the biographies in a given campaign to get a sense for the electoral milieu at that time; one need study only a select few for each election cycle.)

Accepting the campaign biography as prime data, then, I moved on to a detailed and systematic analysis of a broad universe of biographies, sixty for the period studied (the full list can be found below). I approached their analysis by first constructing an idealized "constitutional campaign biography," enumerating its likely major features by working from a counterfactual question: If campaign biographies had accompanied the first presidential elections (those closest to the founding and, hence, the founding norms), what would they have looked like?

Consistent with the founding doctrines, such a biography would presumably have stressed the character, reputation, firmness, and independence of the candidate. As the founders were suspicious of popular influence, candidates would not have been expected to make "pledges" or promises in their biographies; they would need to remain independent in office and have flexibility to make right, rather than popular, decisions. What would matter for purposes of election would be how well a candidate for the presidency had proved himself in other stations of life, whether he had acted with resolve, probity, patriotism, and impartiality in whatever occupations preceded his call to presidential service.

Furthermore, those candidates would certainly not have pledged to act with a political party when in office or to carry through, with the aid of congressional party members, a party platform. To do so would not only have violated the "pledge" restriction but would have allied the candidate with a party, that bête noire of the founding period. Additionally, it would have confounded the workings of the separation of powers, designed to produce tension and conflict rather than harmony between the presidency and the popular branch. After all, the president was that force which, though ultimately dependent on the people (at least indirectly), would act to mitigate and temper the people's will as transmitted through the Congress, the people's branch. These early biographies, then, would have sought to champion (in Hamilton's phrase) "characters preeminent for ability and virtue."[11]

After constructing this constitutional campaign biography template, I proceeded to examine the universe of biographies to see how well they fit the template. This process was largely qualitative and interpretive, rather than quantitative (although I did employ one rough quantitative measure). Not only would the scope of a content analysis have been unmanageable (sixty biographies, many of them over three hundred pages), but it would not have been tremendously heuristic, at least on my view. Counting instances of words and phrases cannot fully gauge emphasis, tone, and placement of phrases and ideas—facets understood chiefly through interpretive research yet deemed far more valuable to the examination of party-period elections. The full list of campaign biographies follows.

Bibliography of Campaign Biographies

Note: Titles are in alphabetical order by election; some excessively long ones have been shortened.

1836

Emmons, William. *Biography of Martin Van Buren.* Washington, D.C.: Jacob Gideon Jr., 1835.

Hall, James. *A Memoir of the Public Services of William Henry Harrison.* Philadelphia: Edward C. Biddle, 1836.

Holland, William. *The Life and Political Opinions of Martin Van Buren.* Hartford, Conn.: Belknap & Hamersley, 1836.

Jackson, Isaac Rand. *A Sketch of the Life and Public Services of William Henry Harrison.* New York: Harper & Brothers, 1836.

1840

Cushing, Caleb. *Outlines of the Life and Public Services, Civil and Military, of William Henry Harrison.* Boston: Weeks, Jordan, 1840.

Dawson, Moses. *Sketches of the Life of Martin Van Buren, President of the United States.* Cincinnati: J. W. Ely, 1840.

Hildreth, Richard. *The People's Presidential Candidate; or the Life of William Henry Harrison.* Boston: Weeks, Jordan, 1840.

"A Workingman." *More Than One Hundred Reasons Why William Henry Harrison Should and Will Have the Support of the Democracy.* Boston: Tuttle, Dennet & Chisholm, 1840.

1844

Biographical Sketches of the Democratic Candidates for the Presidency and Vice Presidency. N.p., n.d. [1844?].

[Collins, George C.] *Fifty Reasons Why the Hon. Henry Clay Should Be Elected President.* Baltimore, Md.: Murphy, 1844.

[Hickman, George.] *The Life and Public Services of the Hon. James Knox Polk.* Baltimore, Md.: N. Hickman, 1844.

Sargent, Nathan. *Life of Henry Clay.* Philadelphia: R. G. Berford, 1844.

1848

Fry, J. Reese. *A Life of General Zachary Taylor.* Philadelphia: Grigg, Elliot, 1848.

[Hickman, George.] *The Life and Public Services of General Lewis Cass.* Baltimore, Md.: N. Hickman, 1848.

Poore, Benjamin Perley. *Life of Gen. Zachary Taylor.* Boston: Stacy, Richardson, 1848.

Sketch of the Life and Public Services of Gen. Lewis Cass. Washington, D.C.: Congressional Globe Office, 1848.

1852

Bartlett, D. W. *The Life of Gen. Franklin Pierce.* Auburn, [N.Y.]: Derby & Miller, 1852.

Deering, Edward. *Life of General Scott.* New York: C. A. Alvord, 1852.

Hawthorne, Nathaniel. *The Life of Franklin Pierce.* Boston: Ticknor, Reed & Fields, 1852.

Headley, J. T. *The Lives of Winfield Scott and Andrew Jackson.* New York: Charles Scribner, 1852.

The Presidency: Winfield Scott—Franklin Pierce; Their Qualifications and Fitness for That High Office. Washington, D.C.: Towers, 1852.

1856

Bigelow, John. *Memoir of the Life and Public Services of John Charles Fremont.* New York: Derby & Jackson, 1856.

Jerome, C. *Life of James Buchanan.* Claremont, N.H.: Tracy, Kenney, 1856.

Hall, Benjamin. *The Republican Party and Its Presidential Candidates.* New York: Miller, Orton & Mulligan, 1856.

Horton, R. G. *The Life and Public Services of James Buchanan.* New York: Derby & Jackson, 1856.

1860

Bartlett, D. W. *The Life and Public Services of Hon. Abraham Lincoln.* New York: H. Dayton, 1860.

[Hinton, Richard Josiah.] *The Life and Public Services of Hon. Abraham Lincoln.* Boston: Thayer & Eldridge, 1860.

Sheahan, James. *The Life of Stephen Douglas.* New York: Harper & Brothers, 1860.

Warden, Robert. *A Voter's Version of the Life and Character of Stephen Arnold Douglas.* Columbus, Ohio: Follett, Foster, 1860.

1864

A Brief Sketch of the Life and History of General McClellan. N.p. [New York?], n.d. [1864?].

The Life and Public Services of Gen. Geo. B. McClellan: Campaign Document, No. 4. N.p., n.d. [1864?].

Raymond, Henry. *The Life of Abraham Lincoln.* New York: National Union Executive Committee, [1864].

[Williamson, David Brainerd.] *Life and Public Services of Abraham Lincoln.* Philadelphia: T. B. Peterson & Brothers, 1864.

1868

Croly, David. *Seymour and Blair: Their Lives and Services.* New York: Richardson, 1868.

Howland, Edward. *Grant as a Soldier and Statesman.* Hartford: J. B. Burr, 1868.

McCabe, James D., Jr. *The Life and Public Services of Horatio Seymour.* New York: United States Publishing Company, 1868.

Mansfield, Edward. *Popular and Authentic Lives of Ulysses S. Grant and Schuyler Colfax.* Cincinnati: R. W. Carroll, 1868.

1872

Conkling, Roscoe. *The Presidential Battle of 1872: Grant and His Defamers.* N.p., n.d. [1872?]

Parton, James. *The Life of Horace Greeley.* Boston: James R. Osgood, 1872.

Phelps, Charles A. *Life and Public Services of Ulysses S. Grant.* Boston: Lee & Shepard, 1872.

The True Issues of the Presidential Campaign: Speeches of Horace Greeley. N.p., n.d. [1872?].

1876

Cook, Theodore. *The Life and Public Services of Hon. Samuel J. Tilden.* New York: Appleton, 1876.

Howells, William Dean. *Sketch of the Life and Character of Rutherford B. Hayes.* New York: Hurd & Houghton, 1876.

1880

Brisbin, James. *The Early Life and Public Career of James A. Garfield.* Philadelphia: H. W. Kelley, 1880.

Coffin, Charles. *The Life of James Garfield.* Boston: James H. Earle, 1880.

Cole, J. R. *The Life and Public Services of Winfield Scott Hancock.* Cincinnati, Ohio: Douglass Brothers, 1880.

Goodrich, Frederick. *The Life and Public Services of Winfield Scott Hancock.* Intro. Frederick O. Prince. Boston: Lee & Shepard, 1880.

1884

Craig, Hugh. *The Biography and Public Services of Hon. James G. Blaine.* New York: H. S. Goodspeed, 1884.

Goodrich, Frederick. *The Life and Public Services of Grover Cleveland.* Intro. Frederick O. Prince. Portland: H. Hallett, 1884.

King, Pendleton. *The Life and Public Services of Grover Cleveland*. New York: Putnam, 1884.

Ramsdell, Henry. *Life and Public Services of Hon. James G. Blaine*. New York: Phillips & Burrows, 1884.

Welch, Deshler. *Stephen Grover Cleveland*. New York: John W. Lovell, 1884.

1888

Hensel, W. U., with Geo. Parker. *Life and Public Services of Grover Cleveland*. Philadelphia: Hubbard Brothers, 1888.

Northrop, Henry Davenport. *The Life and Public Services of Gen. Benjamin Harrison, the Great American Statesman*. Philadelphia: John C. Winston, 1888.

Stoddard, William. *The Lives of the Presidents: Grover Cleveland*. New York: Frederick A. Stokes & Brother, 1888.

Wallace, Gen. Lew. *Life of Gen. Benjamin Harrison*. Philadelphia: H. L. Warren, 1888.

1892

Campbell-Copeland, Thomas. *Harrison and Reid: Their Lives and Record*. New York: Charles L. Webster, 1892.

Grady, Colonel John Randolph. *The Life and Public Services of the Great Reform President, Grover Cleveland*. Philadelphia: National Publishing Company, 1892.

Wallace, Gen. Lew. *The Life and Public Services of Hon. Benjamin Harrison*. N.p.: Edgewood, 1892.

Parker, George. *A Life of Grover Cleveland*. New York: Cassell, 1892.

Appendix Two
Selection of Cases for Chapters 5 and 6

The presidencies of Polk, Taylor, Grant, Benjamin Harrison, and Cleveland fit the necessary criteria for a study of the party period: they adequately represent the time span; they duly represent the major parties across time; and these men all came to the office through a normal presidential election. Although the presidency of Andrew Jackson might seem worthy of study, his administration was more a "pre-party" than a party one: he helped to establish the rough parameters of the mass party system, but he ultimately stepped aside, allowing the system to grow and function without his leadership and influence. The founding of this party system during the Jackson years is an important story and may provide insights into presidential leadership and its relationship to parties; however, the main aim of this book is to understand the contours of presidential leadership once the party system had more or less taken firm root. Even under Martin Van Buren it was still only taking shape; hence, he presided over a more fluid partisan universe, an interstitial period before the hardening of partisanship. And since William Henry Harrison served only a month in office, it made good sense to begin with James Polk, whose tenure constituted the first complete administration of the full-blown party period.

Zachary Taylor was selected somewhat by default: he was a Whig, and he lived at least a bit longer than the only other Whig president, William Henry Harrison. Because it was necessary to span the party period fully, the administrations of Pierce and Buchanan were not examined, nor was Lincoln's. Eliminating Pierce and Buchanan from the sample was not controversial (since I already had a Democrat from the antebellum period), but the decision to omit Lincoln requires more justification.

Lincoln might seem an obvious choice for more detailed study, considering the bold leadership one tends to associate with him. He might, in fact, seem a perfect choice, his strength during the party period perhaps suggesting that party presidents were normally restrained by their parties but also capable of strong action when necessary. This suggestion would certainly help to make the case—a case that needs to be advanced if party presidential leadership is to have any modern-day applicability—that party presidents could, when the situation dictated, rise to the occasion as statesmen and bold leaders.[1]

Yet however much light Lincoln's presidency might shed on presidential leadership and political parties, it obscures more than it reveals about the essence of party-era presidential leadership. Because most of his strong leadership came in the midst of a bitter and bloody civil war, a situation unique in American history, it is of necessity sui generis. Of course, the support for many of his actions (some after the fact) by his political party was helpful to Lincoln, but in his wartime decisions he did not see himself as advocating Republican or party positions so much as maintaining the Union. (What is more, political opposition in time of war is often tepid and hesitant, the minority party acting more in unity with the majority party than is usual.) In any case, the Republican platform of 1860 became essentially beside the point once Fort Sumter was attacked. The remainder of Lincoln's tenure would be spent not redeeming 1860 pledges but keeping the Union intact. Thus the popular relationship between the president and the people, conducted through parties and elections—my main focus—is not ripe for analysis in Lincoln's case. Nor is a consideration of only his domestic legislative actions particularly enlightening. As David Donald has put it, regarding matters of domestic policy—non-war-related issues—Lincoln was a "Whig in the White House."[2] Since I had already chosen Zachary Taylor and U. S. Grant, there was little need to consider an additional "passive" president.

Grant's presidency was the next suitable selection: the first full presidency following the Civil War, after the political system had begun to tend toward normal again. Because of considerations of space, I focused only on Grant's first term in office. Since Rutherford B. Hayes was chosen by the House of Representatives in a disputed election, his presidency was winnowed out of the sample; also weeded out was James Garfield, who died not long after assuming office in 1881. Grover Cleveland, the winner in 1884 and 1892 and the only Democrat elected between 1856 and 1912, was a natural selection. I chose to emphasize his second term for two reasons: (1) again, considerations of space, and (2) the variety offered by a second-term presidency. Benjamin Harrison, the twenty-third president, sandwiched between the two Cleveland terms, rounds out the sample. His presidency is important, among other reasons, because it permits analysis of a more "ordinary" Republican administration. Ulysses S. Grant, after all, was not a politician, and he took office after a bitter Civil War. These facts are partly what make him an interesting case for examination, yet his administration may also provide a prejudicial view of Republican presidents of the nineteenth century; it is therefore important to look at Harrison's term to get a balanced picture of the presidency under the Republican Party.

Notes

Introduction

1. See Sidney M. Milkis, *The President and the Parties* (New York: Oxford University Press, 1993), pp. 5–7.

2. Theodore Roosevelt, *The Autobiography of Theodore Roosevelt,* ed. Wayne Andrews (New York: Scribner, 1958), p. 197.

3. Sidney M. Milkis, *Political Parties and Constitutional Government* (Baltimore, Md.: Johns Hopkins University Press, 1999), p. 184.

4. See John H. Aldrich, *Why Parties? The Origin and Transformation of Political Parties in America* (Chicago: University of Chicago Press, 1995), pp. 244–245.

5. See, for example, Jeffrey Tulis, *The Rhetorical Presidency* (Princeton: Princeton University Press, 1987).

6. See, however, Stephen Skowronek, *The Politics Presidents Make* (Cambridge: Belknap Press of Harvard University Press, 1993), and Milkis, *Political Parties,* for rich and textured analyses of presidential history. See also Richard J. Ellis, introduction to *Speaking to the People: The Rhetorical Presidency in Historical Perspective,* ed. Richard J. Ellis (Amherst: University of Massachusetts Press, 1998), for a critique of the common understanding of presidential history.

7. The following works are among the most important to these debates: James Ceaser, *Presidential Selection: Theory and Development* (Princeton: Princeton University Press, 1979); James Ceaser, Glenn Thurow, Jeffrey Tulis, and Joseph Bessette, "The Rise of the Rhetorical Presidency," in *Rethinking*

the Presidency, ed. Thomas Cronin (Boston: Little, Brown, 1982); Tulis, *Rhetorical Presidency;* Samuel Kernell, *Going Public,* 2d ed. (Washington, D.C.: Congressional Quarterly Press, 1993); Elmer Cornwell, *Presidential Leadership of Public Opinion* (Bloomington: Indiana University Press, 1965); George C. Edwards III, *The Public Presidency: The Pursuit of Public Support* (New York: St. Martin's Press, 1983); and Theodore Lowi, *The Personal President* (Ithaca, N.Y.: Cornell University Press, 1985). Most of these writers accept the premise that the presidency of the nineteenth century was "traditional" and nonpublic and that the twentieth-century presidency is "modern" and "plebiscitary." Some writers, however, have taken issue with, if not overturned, this conception. See, for instance, the essays in Ellis, *Speaking to the People.*

8. See "The New Nationalism, Speech at Osawatomie, 31 August 1910," in Theodore Roosevelt, *The New Nationalism,* intro. William E. Leuchtenburg (Englewood Cliffs, N.J.: Prentice-Hall, 1961), p. 36.

9. *Federalist* No. 71, in *The Federalist,* ed. Henry Cabot Lodge (New York: Putnam, 1888), p. 446.

10. Marc Landy and Sidney M. Milkis, *Presidential Greatness* (Lawrence: University Press of Kansas, 2000), p. 10.

11. Stephen Skowronek, review of *The Rhetorical Presidency* by Jeffrey Tulis, *Review of Politics* 49 (1987): 432.

12. Joel Silbey, *The American Political Nation* (Stanford, Calif.: Stanford University Press, 1991).

13. Those who have written about the lack of public appeals in the nineteenth century, however, have often given short shrift to the revolutionary administration of Andrew Jackson or have made far too big a deal of Johnson's impeachment (often construing it primarily as a result of his demagogic rhetoric, which in fact constituted only one of many charges). See R. V. Remini, *The Revolutionary Age of Andrew Jackson* (New York: Harper & Row, 1976); and David Nichols, *The Myth of the Modern Presidency* (University Park: Pennsylvania State University Press, 1994).

14. The classic work of this type is Anthony Downs, *An Economic Theory of Democracy* (New York: Harper & Row, 1957).

15. John Gerring, *Party Ideologies in America, 1828–1996* (New York: Cambridge University Press, 1998), p. 6.

16. Silbey, *American Political Nation,* pp. 1 (quoting Morton Keller), 7, 190; Michael F. Holt, *The Rise and Fall of the American Whig Party* (New York: Oxford University Press, 1999), p. 83; Gerring, *Party Ideologies,* p. 12.

17. But see Maurice Duverger, *Political Parties* (New York: Wiley, 1963), for an alternative understanding of the historical role and development of parties.

18. James Ceaser glimpsed this point some years ago in his study of the evolution of the presidential selection system. He chose to see the glass of democracy as half empty, however; that is, he chose to see the development of political parties as not representing a major break with the founders' understanding of the political system, as I do in this book. See Milkis, *Political Parties,* pp. 2–4,

for a view similar to mine; see *Presidential Selection,* pp. 166–169 for Ceaser's thoughts on the development of the party system and founding doctrine.

19. Susan Herbst, "On the Disappearance of Groups: 19th- and Early 20th-Century Conceptions of Public Opinion," in *Public Opinion and the Communication of Consent,* ed. Theodore Glasser and Charles T. Salmon (New York: Guilford Press, 1995), pp. 95–96.

20. Quoted in Richard Hofstadter, *The Idea of a Party System* (Berkeley: University of California Press, 1967), p. 269.

21. A. James Reichley, *The Life of the Parties* (New York: Free Press, 1992), p. 432. As I explain later in this chapter and throughout the book, presidents' relationships with their parties were not uniform; they took two ideal-typical forms. First, parties promoted men to office who were expected to follow (and defer to) the party's agenda and platform while in office. These presidents were elected to carry through the people's will as expressed in the election, not by aggressive leadership but rather by deference to prominent party leaders. Second, parties promoted men to office who saw themselves less as party *agents* than as party *leaders.* These men did not try merely to rubber-stamp congressional party actions and the ideas of party leaders but assumed a much more active role in promoting the party agenda (regarded as the "people's will") and working with and rallying Congress to pass legislation. As either agent or leader, the president was connected with the public, even though this connection was established through the party rather than directly and immediately.

22. Assuredly, many voters and party leaders wanted their party to win the presidency because of the rich store of patronage that accompanied a presidential victory, but this motive was not, as some commentators suggest, the summum bonum of presidential elections in the nineteenth century. (The issue of the spoils system and the corruption of the parties is addressed more fully in the conclusion.)

23. Tulis, *Rhetorical Presidency;* James MacGregor Burns, *The Power to Lead* (New York: Simon & Schuster, 1984), p. 131.

24. For an excellent treatment of the development of democracy in the United States, see Robert Wiebe, *Self-Rule: A Cultural History of American Democracy* (Chicago: University of Chicago Press, 1995). See also Richard L. McCormick, *The Party Period and Public Policy* (New York: Oxford University Press, 1986), p. 163, which notes the democratic advance represented by the party conventions of the nineteenth century.

25. I am indebted to Sidney Milkis for this conceptual and linguistic formulation.

26. Landy and Milkis, *Presidential Greatness,* pp. 9, 10.

27. See Milkis, *President and the Parties,* on the development of national administrative power and the removal of decisions from the arena of political action and debate.

28. See American Political Science Association, *Toward a More Responsible Two-Party System* (New York: Rinehart, 1950).

29. On the origin of the "mandate" concept in American presidential poli-

tics, see Richard J. Ellis and Stephen Kirk, "Presidential Mandates in the Nineteenth Century: Conceptual Change and Institutional Development," *Studies in American Political Development* 9 (spring 1995): 117–186.

30. Although his is not a part of my sample of presidencies, I also briefly show how these trends continued in the administration of William McKinley.

Chapter One

1. James MacGregor Burns, *The Power to Lead* (New York: Simon & Schuster, 1984), p. 131. Although a discussion and analysis of a broad range of figures associated with the development of the "party constitution" would be a desideratum, it is ultimately unnecessary for my purposes. Van Buren is an important enough figure, and his recollections and writings quite rich enough, to furnish an adequate understanding. Moreover, key secondary analyses can flesh out the few lacunae in the party story which result from a focus on Van Buren alone.

2. This discussion is indebted to the excellent study by Ralph Ketcham of the early presidency, *Presidents above Party* (Chapel Hill: University of North Carolina Press, 1984).

3. Quoted in ibid., p. 60.

4. To be sure, Bolingbroke had in mind a monarch, one who would act in the public interest and transcend party divisions. The founders republicanized this notion, which, it should be said, was espoused not only by Bolingbroke but by other writers for centuries. Nonetheless, Bolingbroke was a most articulate spokesman of this style of leadership and was likely read by many of the founders. See Ketcham, *Presidents above Party,* pp. 67–68.

5. *Federalist* No. 10, in *The Federalist,* ed. Henry Cabot Lodge (New York: G. P. Putnam's Sons, 1888), pp. 52–53.

6. Richard Hofstadter, *The Idea of a Party System* (Berkeley: University of California Press, 1969), p. 64; *Federalist* No. 10, p. 52.

7. *Federalist* No. 68, pp. 426–427.

8. *Federalist* No. 71, pp. 446, 449.

9. *Federalist* No. 73, p. 458.

10. Ibid., p. 461.

11. *Federalist* No. 76, p. 473.

12. Hofstadter, *Idea of a Party System.* The following discussion is indebted to Hofstadter.

13. Ketcham, *Presidents above Party,* pp. 66, 84.

14. Even though some of the early presidents, most particularly Jefferson, acted in a partisan manner while in office (e.g., making requests of Congress for party policies and programs), their partisanship was in the service of ultimately ending the influence of parties in the political system. Their actions should be distinguished from those of later partisan presidents, who were not looking to transcend or eradicate partisanship.

15. "Washington's Farewell Address," in *The Statesman's Manual,* ed. Edwin Williams (New York: Edward Walker, 1849), p. 74 (emphasis added).

16. Details of each of the early presidencies would take me too far afield (although those of Monroe and John Quincy Adams are discussed below). The reader is referred to two masterly studies: Hofstadter, *Idea of a Party System;* and Ketcham, *Presidents above Party.*

17. Ralph Volney Harlow, *The History of Legislative Methods in the Period before 1825* (New Haven: Yale University Press, 1917), p. 121.

18. Again, it should be stressed that Van Buren did not create the party system on his own. It would have developed even without him; see R. V. Remini, *Martin Van Buren and the Making of the Democratic Party* (New York: Columbia University Press, 1959), pp. 167–167. Yet he was very important to its development and was probably also its most articulate spokesman. See Hofstadter, *Idea of a Party System,* for a more exhaustive discussion of Van Buren's experiences in party politics.

19. Martin Van Buren, *Inquiry into the Origin and Course of Political Parties in the United States* (1867; New York: Augustus M. Kelley, 1967), p. 7.

20. Ibid., pp. 3–4.

21. Remini, *Martin Van Buren,* p. 117.

22. Ibid., p. 118.

23. Quoted in ibid., p. 126.

24. See *The Autobiography of Martin Van Buren,* ed. John Fitzpatrick, vol. 2 of American Historical Association, *Annual Report for the Year 1918* (Washington, D.C., 1920), p. 125: "Doubtless excesses frequently attend them [parties] and produce many evils, but not so many as are prevented by the maintenance of their organization and vigilance."

25. Ibid.

26. Hofstadter, *Idea of a Party System,* p. 31.

27. James Ceaser, *Presidential Selection: Theory and Development* (Princeton: Princeton University Press, 1979), p. 135.

28. Ibid., pp. 156–158.

29. Robert Wiebe, *Self-Rule: A Cultural History of American Democracy* (Chicago: University of Chicago Press, 1995), p. 29.

30. Burns, *Power to Lead,* p. 130.

31. Ibid., p. 131.

32. It is important to note that the electoral college system had turned into a partisan contest almost immediately with the development of the first party system, but with Van Buren and the second party system in the 1820s and 1830s, partisanization of the electoral college was considered a far less undesirable trend.

33. Sidney M. Milkis and Michael Nelson, *The American Presidency: Origins and Development, 1776–1998,* 3d ed. (Washington, D.C.: Congressional Quarterly Press, 1999), p. 121. See Jeffrey Tulis, *The Rhetorical Presidency* (Princeton: Princeton University Press, 1987), pp. 39–40, on the original constitutional de-

sign's suggestion of a deliberative role for the veto (though it would be little employed before Jackson).

34. See, for instance, Tulis, *Rhetorical Presidency,* pp. 50–51.

35. The party constitution did serve to temper direct demagogic appeals by presidents and presidential candidates but nonetheless offered more possibility for passionate appeals to the populace than the original Constitution. One must not assume that the parties were always moderate in their principles and platforms. They were probably, for the most part, rather reasonable in their principles, yet at times they capitalized on passionate issues and emotional topics (the Republican platform of 1856 is certainly not free of such rhetoric). Therefore, although the two-party system did prevent leaders from assuming power by capitalizing on segments of opinion in the population which were unrepresented (or underrepresented) in the two major parties, it did not necessarily prevent emotional and passionate party appeals to the people. The important distinction, though, was between an individual candidate's or president's direct, unmediated relationship with the people and his indirect relationship *through the party* with the people. The possibility for demagoguery would be much more substantial in the former than in the latter case.

36. Marc Landy and Sidney M. Milkis, *Presidential Greatness* (Lawrence: University Press of Kansas, 2000), p. 10.

37. Richard P. McCormick, for example, argues that the campaign of 1840 brought the two-party system to its fruition; see "Political Development and the Second Party System," in *The American Party Systems,* 2d ed., ed. William Nisbet Chambers and Walter Dean Burnham (New York: Oxford University Press, 1975).

38. James Bryce, *The American Commonwealth* (Indianapolis: Liberty Fund, 1995), 2:876.

39. Michael McGerr, *The Decline of Popular Politics* (New York: Oxford University Press, 1986), p. 26; E. E. Schattschneider, *Party Government* (New York: Rinehart, 1942), p. 136; Wiebe, *Self-Rule,* p. 72.

40. Wiebe, *Self-Rule,* p. 80; see also p. 66.

41. Ibid., p. 83. I am playing off Wiebe's notion of the People—"For that instant, they were the American People"—substituting "Party" for "People."

42. Joel Silbey, *The American Political Nation* (Stanford, Calif.: Stanford University Press, 1991), p. 87.

43. "Magnification" is the felicitous term Schattschneider (*Party Government,* p. 136) employs to discuss this phenomenon.

44. Richard P. McCormick, *The Presidential Game* (New York: Oxford University Press, 1982), p. 183.

Chapter Two

1. See Richard P. McCormick, *The Presidential Game* (New York: Oxford University Press, 1982), for this line of argument.

2. See appendix 1 for a defense of campaign biographies as the prime source of data for this and the next chapter, followed by the full list of biographies examined.

3. Nathan Sargent, *Life of Henry Clay* (Philadelphia: R. G. Berford, 1844), p. 21. (Subsequent citations of most campaign biographies shorten title to *Life of* with candidate's surname.)

4. Theodore Cook, *The Life and Public Services of Hon. Samuel H. Tilden . . .* (New York: D. Appleton, 1876), p. 67.

5. Isaac Rand Jackson, *A Sketch of the Life and Public Services of William Henry Harrison* (New York: Harper & Brothers, 1836), p. 31; Nathaniel Hawthorne, *The Life of Franklin Pierce* (Boston: Ticknor, Reed & Fields, 1852), p. 132; [Richard Josiah Hinton,] *The Life and Public Services of Hon. Abraham Lincoln . . .* (Boston: Thayer & Eldridge, 1860), p. 12; Frederick Goodrich, *The Life and Public Services of Winfield Scott Hancock* (Boston: Lee & Shepard, 1880), p. 279; Hugh Craig, *The Biography and Public Services of Hon. James G. Blaine . . .* (New York: H. S. Goodspeed, 1884), p. 300.

6. William Holland, *The Life and Political Opinions of Martin Van Buren* (Hartford, Conn.: Belknap & Hamersley, 1836), p. 360; J. Reese Fry, *A Life of Gen. Zachary Taylor* (Philadelphia: Grigg, Elliot, 1848), p. 324; D. W. Bartlett, *The Life of Gen. Franklin Pierce* (Auburn, [N.Y.]: Derby & Miller, 1852), p. 133; Pendleton King, *The Life and Public Services of Grover Cleveland* (New York: Putnam, 1884), p. 14.

7. Caleb Cushing, *Outlines of the Life and Public Services, Civil and Military, of William Henry Harrison* (Boston: Weeks, Jordan, 1840), p. 63. (The expression "free and untrammeled" appears in several biographies of Harrison; it seems to have been a catchphrase.)

8. "A Workingman," *More Than One Hundred Reasons Why William Henry Harrison Should and Will Have the Support of the Democracy . . .* (Boston: Tuttle, Dennet & Chisholm, 1840), pp. 4–5; Fry, *Life of Taylor,* p. 324.

9. [David Brainerd Williamson], *Life and Public Services of Abraham Lincoln* (Philadelphia: T. B. Peterson & Brothers, 1864), p. 179; James Parton, *The Life of Horace Greeley . . .* (Boston: James R. Osgood, 1872), p. 253; William O. Stoddard, *The Lives of the Presidents: Grover Cleveland* (New York: Frederick A. Stokes & Brother, 1888), p. 262.

10. "A Workingman," *More Than One Hundred Reasons,* p. 14; *The Presidency: Winfield Scott—Franklin Pierce; Their Qualifications and Fitness for That High Office* (Washington, D.C.: Towers, 1852), p. 14; J. R. Cole, *The Life and Public Services of Winfield Scott Hancock* (Cincinnati: Douglass Brothers, 1880), p. 5.

11. It hardly needs mentioning that in most biographies there is much that is not "political," such as stories about the candidate's childhood or family or schooling; this is to be expected from biography, after all. Yet in nearly every biography, significant space (often at the beginning or end) is devoted to the candidate's political opinions, the upcoming campaign, and the nature of the presidential office. It is this space, and the content and extent of it, which is most

important for my purposes. Consequently, a rigorous content analysis of the biographies would have been not only prohibitively time-consuming but inappropriate. To be sure, the rough amount of text devoted to political issues and viewpoints is important and is noted where relevant. But *what* is said is sometimes just as, or even more, important than *how much* is said.

12. Although not directly cited in the following section, Joel Silbey, *The American Political Nation, 1838–1892* (Stanford, Calif.: Stanford University Press, 1991), was very much an inspiration in my conceptualization and understanding of the issues dealt with here.

13. R. G. Horton, *The Life and Public Services of James Buchanan* . . . (New York: Derby & Jackson, 1856), p. vi.

14. Substantive issues, those that are timely and controversial and about which contestants for office would presumably differ, allowed voters a real choice in the directing of government; they could determine from his opinions and principles that the election of one candidate would give certain policies a better chance of being passed (or at least championed) than if another candidate won. For instance, individuals voting for James Polk in 1844 could reasonably presume, because of his own and his biographers' statements, that he would work for the annexation of Texas. This is a substantive issue position. Likewise, voting for a candidate pledged to "strict construction" of the Constitution, a common Democratic position in the nineteenth century, would ostensibly increase the likelihood of government policies favoring a strict reading of the Constitution. By contrast, a hollow issue is something so accepted or so general as to be meaningless as a basis for choice on the part of the voters. Consider this statement: "Now . . . there is a clearly defined contest in behalf of pure government, led by a man [Grover Cleveland] who, if elected, will surely give it to us so far as he can" (King, *Life of Cleveland*, p. iii). Although this statement has the markings of a pledge or political opinion, it is clearly noncontroversial: Who does not want "pure government"? The hollow issue is a close cousin to the appeal to the people based upon the character and virtue of the candidates: both reserve prime governing decisions for leaders and offer the people little opportunity to assume the reins of government.

15. William Burlie Brown, *The People's Choice: The Presidential Image in Campaign Biography* (Baton Rouge: Louisiana State University Press, 1960), p. 13.

16. The race was actually four-way, with the Whigs running three candidates: Daniel Webster, Hugh White, and William Henry Harrison (clearly the front runner); through this strategy they hoped to split the vote and send the election to the House of Representatives. See Robert J. Dinkin, *Campaigning in America: A History of Election Practices* (New York: Greenwood Press, 1989), p. 48.

17. Holland, *Life of Van Buren*, p. 261.

18. James Hall, *A Memoir of the Public Services of William Henry Harrison* . . . (Philadelphia: Edward C. Biddle, 1836), p. 65; Richard Hildreth *The People's Presidential Candidate; or the Life of William Henry Harrison*, 3d ed. (Boston: Weeks, Jordan, 1840), p. 120.

19. *Niles' National Register,* February 8, 1840, p. 379.

20. Quoted in William Nisbet Chambers, "Election of 1840," in *History of American Presidential Elections, 1789–1968,* 4 vols., ed. Arthur Schlesinger Jr. (New York: Chelsea House, 1971), p. 678 (hereafter, *Presidential Elections*). This bit of information, incidentally, illustrates that findings from the campaign biographies must be checked against solid historical and contextual work. In this case, the biographies were in all likelihood published before Harrison's canvass of the voters and did not, therefore, allude to these speeches.

21. "An Irish Adopted Citizen" [George C. Collins], *Fifty Reasons Why the Hon. Henry Clay Should Be Elected President of the United States* (Baltimore, Md.: Murphy, 1844), pp. 15, 18.

22. *Biographical Sketches of the Democratic Candidates for the Presidency and Vice Presidency: James Polk, of Tennessee* (N.p., n.d., [1844?]), pp. 2, 3; [George Hickman,] *The Life and Public Services of the Hon. James Knox Polk . . .* (Baltimore, Md.: N. Hickman, 1844).

23. The elections of 1848, 1852, and 1860 exhibit the same traits and characteristics as the 1844 and 1856 elections.

24. Benjamin Hall, *The Republican Party and Its Presidential Candidates . . .* (New York: Miller, Orton & Mulligan, 1856), pp. 468–469; C. Jerome, *Life of James Buchanan* (Claremont, N.H.: Tracy, Kenney, 1856), p. 31.

25. Edward Mansfield, *Popular and Authentic Lives of Ulysses S. Grant . . .* (Cincinnati: R. W. Carroll, 1868), p. 371.

26. David Croly, *Seymour and Blair: Their Lives and Services* (New York: Richardson, 1868), p. 195; Parton, *Life of Greeley,* p. 492.

27. James Brisbin, *The Early Life and Public Career of James Garfield* (Philadelphia: H. W. Kelley, 1880), pp. 283–284; Henry Ramsdell, *Life and Public Services of Hon. James G. Blaine* (New York: Phillips & Burrows, 1884, p. 87.

28. Stoddard, *Life of Cleveland,* p. 247; Gen. Lew. Wallace, *Life of Gen. Benjamin Harrison* (Philadelphia: H. L. Warren, 1888), p. 256.

29. I conducted a rudimentary content analysis by counting the number of paragraphs (in shorter works) or chapters (in longer works) that dealt with "political issues" and dividing that figure by the total number of paragraphs or chapters. Those with less than 20 percent political content were labeled "low"; between 20 and 50 percent, "moderate"; and more than 50 percent, "high." This surely rough-hewn but not insignificant measure yielded only sixteen of the sixty biographies in which the discussion of the political opinions and principles of the candidates was minimal or "low." That ten of those were biographies of three military candidates—William Henry Harrison, Zachary Taylor, and Ulysses S. Grant—strengthens my claim of a political norm that promoted or at least sanctioned the declaration of political principles by (or on the behalf of) candidates in the nineteenth century.

30. Holland, *Life of Van Buren,* pp. iii–iv.

31. Cushing, *Life of Harrison,* p. 66; see also James Hall, *Memoir of Harrison,* p. 317. Again, it is important to remark that although the campaign biographies

do distance Harrison from the Whigs, his own speeches during the campaign sought to identify him more closely with the Whig Party and its programs. See William Nisbet Chambers, "Election of 1840," pp. 678–679.

32. Collins, *Fifty Reasons,* pp. 2–5.

33. Hickman, *Life of Polk,* pp. 9, 16.

34. Fry, *Life of Taylor,* p. 324; Benjamin Perley Poore, *Life of Gen. Zachary Taylor, the Whig Candidate for the Presidency* . . . (Boston: Stacy, Richardson, 1848), pp. 12, 15.

35. *Sketch of the Life and Public Services of Gen. Lewis Cass* (Washington, D.C.: Congressional Globe Office, 1848), p. 8; [George Hickman,] *The Life and Public Services of General Lewis Cass* . . . (Baltimore, Md.: N. Hickman, 1848), pp. 72, 38.

36. Bartlett, *Life of Pierce,* p. 122.

37. *The Presidency: Winfield Scott—Franklin Pierce,* pp. 14, 16.

38. Jerome, *Life of Buchanan,* p. 37.

39. Hall, *Republican Party,* p. 501.

40. Hinton, *Life of Lincoln,* pp. 9–10.

41. Robert Warden, *A Voter's Version of the Life and Character of Stephen Arnold Douglas* (Columbus, Ohio: Follett, Foster, 1860), p. 92. Of course, the Breckenridge faction disputed that Douglas was true to the "doctrines of the democratic party": that is, he was not an adequately representative "Democrat," which helps explain his defeat in 1860. Nevertheless, for my purposes, the point still stands that Douglas was associated rather strongly with a political party, if a disintegrating one.

42. *A Brief Sketch of the Life and History of General McClellan* . . . (N.p., n.d. [1864?]), p. 9.

43. Williamson, *Life of Lincoln,* p. 179.

44. Croly, *Seymour and Blair,* p. 17.

45. See William Gillette, "Election of 1872," in Schlesinger, *Presidential Elections,* pp. 1303–1330, for a good discussion of the bizarre nomination of Horace Greeley in 1872.

46. Parton, *Life of Greeley,* p. 153.

47. Gillette, "Election of 1872," pp. 1313, 1326.

48. It is important to note that Greeley was in an important sense anticipating the plebiscitary electoral behavior that would not become prominent until the twentieth century. His campaign was a different style of communicating with the public or, rather, a mixture of styles. Whereas James Buchanan is reported to have said in 1856 that he became the Democratic platform once nominated, Greeley referred to the Liberal Republican platform and "my platform" interchangeably; see *The True Issues of the Presidential Campaign. Speeches of Horace Greeley* (N.p., n.d. [1872?]). Furthermore, Greeley's canvass of several states, clearly at odds with the constitutional notion of presidential campaigning, was also partially at odds with the party constitution notion in that constraints on the candidate were loosened. Candidates could begin to build individual bases of power independent of the party and thereby undercut its power and influence.

The party no longer dominated as completely the linkage between candidate and public.

49. Cook, *Life of Tilden,* pp. 7–8, 348.

50. William Dean Howells, *Sketch of the Life and Character of Rutherford B. Hayes* (New York: Hurd & Houghton, 1876), pp. 27, 104.

51. Goodrich, *Life of Hancock,* p. 212.

52. Brisbin, *Life of Garfield,* n.p.

53. Stoddard, *Life of Cleveland,* p. 39; Craig, *Biography of Blaine,* p. 137; Henry Davenport Northrop, *The Life and Public Services of Gen. Benjamin Harrison, The Great American Statesman* (Philadelphia: John C. Winston, 1888), p. iv.

54. Most obviously, party affiliation was rather weak in the case of the famous war heroes who ran for president, particularly William Henry Harrison and Ulysses S. Grant. Similarly, the Civil War provided a strong incentive for candidates to transcend party. Furthermore, parties differed in their tendencies toward strong expression of party sympathy. Whigs, and to a lesser extent Republicans, were more likely than Democrats to downplay or even denigrate partisanship on the part of their presidential candidates, as well as keep them on the sidelines during the canvasses. See Terri Bimes, "The Metamorphosis of Presidential Populism" (Ph.D. diss., Yale University, 1999), on these differences in political style and in the willingness of candidates and presidents to make strong appeals to public opinion.

55. Holland, *Life of Van Buren,* p. 77.

56. Cook, *Life of Tilden,* p. 4; Sargent, *Life of Clay,* p. 31; Parton, *Life of Greeley,* p. 495.

57. Frederick O. Prince, introduction to Frederick Goodrich, *The Life and Public Services of Grover Cleveland . . .* (Portland, Maine: H. Hallett, 1884), p. 8.

58. Quoted in Barlett, *Life of Pierce,* p. 290.

59. Quoted in Thomas Campbell-Copeland, *Harrison and Reid* (New York: Charles L. Webster, 1892), p. 14.

60. Quoted in Hinton, *Life of Lincoln,* p. 83. Although Lincoln's words came in the midst of a Senate campaign, such sentiments were not meant to be exclusive and indeed closely reflected beliefs that Lincoln would take with him to the White House.

61. Hickman, *Life of Cass,* p. 37; Wallace, *Life of Harrison,* p. 247; W. U. Hensel with Geo. Parker, *Life and Public Services of Grover Cleveland* (Philadelphia: Hubbard Brothers, 1888), p. 288.

62. Ramsdell, *Life of Blaine,* p. 377; Mansfield, *Lives of Grant,* p. 420.

63. Quoted in Henry Raymond, *The Life of Abraham Lincoln . . .* (New York: National Union Executive Committee, [1864]), p. 73.

64. These candidates' biographies did not include letters of acceptance, nor do the appendixes in Schlesinger, *Presidential Elections;* letters are included for nearly all others.

65. Dinkin, *Campaigning in America,* p. 52; Schlesinger, *Presidential Elections,* pp. 616–638.

66. Schlesinger, *Presidential Elections,* pp. 809, 900.

67. As a slight counter to this claim, Clay did release several letters (as did Polk) with the aim of influencing the campaign. These letters, however, had less to do with candidates setting the terms for the campaigns than with candidates allaying the fears of their would-be supporters regarding their political views. See Paul Bergeron, *The Presidency of James K. Polk* (Lawrence: University Press of Kansas, 1987), pp. 18–19.

68. James Polk, "Letter of Acceptance," in *Niles' National Register,* July 6, 1844, p. 294.

69. Quoted in Raymond, *Life of Lincoln,* p. 72.

70. Bartlett, *Life of Pierce,* p. 257; *The Works of James Buchanan,* comp. and ed. John Bassett Moore (New York: Antiquarian Press, 1960), 10:81.

71. Quoted in D. W. Bartlett, *The Life and Public Services of Hon. Abraham Lincoln . . .* (New York: H. Dayton Publisher, 1860), p. 356.

72. Schlesinger, *Presidential Elections,* p. 1538; Brisbin, *Life of Garfield,* p. 528.

73. Schlesinger, *Presidential Elections,* p. 1746.

74. Quoted in Mansfield, *Lives of Grant,* p. 421.

75. Quoted in Parton, *Life of Greeley,* pp. 547–548.

Chapter Three

1. Quoted in Richard P. McCormick, *The Presidential Game: The Origins of American Presidential Politics* (New York: Oxford University Press, 1982), p. 186.

2. See James Ceaser, *Presidential Selection: Theory and Development* (Princeton: Princeton University Press, 1979), pp. 123–169 for Martin Van Buren's views on parties and presidential selection.

3. It should be stressed that I am focusing on the impact of antipartyism only on the presidency, not on such other political institutions as Congress. Although the legislative branch was not immune to the rising antiparty rhetoric and philosophy, it was not affected with the same intensity or force as the presidency. After all, at the same time that presidents such as Grover Cleveland began stressing their independence of party, partisanship was at an all-time high in Congress, which appears to have reacted differently to the significant antiparty criticism of the late nineteenth century. Perhaps because, as Sidney Milkis has pointed out in *The President and the Parties* (New York: Oxford University Press, 1993), pp. 5–7, the presidency has always had an uneasy relationship with the party system, it was much easier for presidents to jettison partisanship and declare themselves leaders of *all* the people. Conversely, although constituents may criticize Congress or party in general, they usually reserve praise for *their* congressman and *their* partisan, which may help explain why party could still be a dominating force in Congress during an era of significant criticism of party. In any case, I am concerned here only with the influence of antipartyism on the presidency; what is more, I do not take the different reaction of Congress to this antipartyism as

an obviation of my claims about the presidency. See Karen Orren and Stephen Skowronek, "Beyond the Iconography of Order: Notes for a 'New Institutionalism,'" in *The Dynamics of American Politics: Approaches and Interpretations,* ed. Lawrence C. Dodd and Calvin Jillson (Boulder, Colo.: Westview Press, 1994), pp. 320–323, on the ways that institutions react and evolve differently in similar circumstances and contexts.

4. Gil Troy, *See How They Ran: The Changing Role of the Presidential Candidate,* rev. and exp. ed. (Cambridge: Harvard University Press, 1996), p. 45, admirably shows how party functionaries linked the candidates with both the party and the people: "In the eyes of the audience the stump speaker became the candidate himself, even the party itself, energizing principles and party affiliation."

5. See Joel Silbey, *The American Political Nation* (Stanford, Calif.: Stanford University Press, 1991), p. 38.

6. Benjamin Perley Poore, *Life of Gen. Zachary Taylor, the Whig Candidate for the Presidency* (Boston: Stacy, Richardson, 1848), p. 15. See Troy, *See How They Ran,* p. 48, on Taylor's submission to the party logic.

7. See Michael F. Holt, *The Rise and Fall of the American Whig Party* (New York: Oxford University Press, 1999), p. 290.

8. Quoted in Troy, *See How They Ran,* p. 48.

9. Zachary Taylor, "Taylor's 'Second Allison Letter,' Sept. 4, 1848," in *History of American Presidential Elections,* 4 vols., ed. Arthur Schlesinger Jr. (New York: Chelsea House Publishers, 1971), p. 917 (hereafter, *Presidential Elections*).

10. Troy, *See How They Ran,* p. 50.

11. *The Presidency: Winfield Scott—Franklin Pierce; Their Qualifications and Fitness for That High Office* (Washington, D.C.: Towers, 1852), p. 16.

12. Roy and Jeannette Nichols, "Election of 1852," in Schlesinger, *Presidential Elections,* p. 948. The term "mute candidate" is used by Troy in *See How They Ran.*

13. Quoted in Troy, *See How They Ran,* p. 51. As Troy puts it in the same paragraph, "Strong parties gorged on passive candidates and a weakened presidency."

14. Silbey, *American Political Nation,* p. 43. See also Daniel Walker Howe, *The Political Culture of the American Whigs* (Chicago: University of Chicago Press, 1979), pp. 7–8, 141–143. The Whigs most likely took this tortuous course in part because of pragmatic politics (they began as a somewhat disparate collection of anti-Jacksonians and had to be careful not to alienate members of the coalition through strong statements of political principle) and also because of their party ideology, which contained a conscious disdain of the Democrats' ostensible pandering to the people.

15. Michael Wallace, "Ideologies of Party in the Early Republic" (Ph.D. diss., Columbia University, 1973), quoted in Silbey, *American Political Nation,* p. 43.

16. See Thomas Brown, *Politics and Statesmanship: Essays on the American Whig Party* (New York: Columbia University Press, 1985), p. 70.

17. Nathan Sargent, *Life of Henry Clay* (Philadelphia: R. G. Berford, 1844),

p. 31; William Nisbet Chambers, "Election of 1840," in Schlesinger, *Presidential Elections,* p. 665.

18. Maurice G. Baxter, *Henry Clay and the American System* (Lexington: University Press of Kentucky, 1995), p. 157.

19. Brown, *Politics and Statesmanship,* p. 70.

20. Howe, *Political Culture,* p. 91.

21. Holt, *Rise and Fall,* p. 137.

22. See ibid., 161.

23. Howe, *Political Culture,* p. 142; Holt, *Rise and Fall,* p. 121; "An Irish Adopted Citizen" [George C. Collins], *Fifty Reasons Why the Hon. Henry Clay Should Be Elected President of the United States* (Baltimore, Md.: Murphy, 1844), p. 37; Sargent, *Life of Clay,* p. 31; Brown, *Politics and Statesmanship,* p. 43.

24. Brown, *Politics and Statesmanship,* p. 30.

25. From the *American Review: A Whig Journal,* November 1846, quoted in Silbey, *American Political Nation,* p. 43.

26. This change in attitude over time is perhaps best seen in an anonymous Whig tract from 1848 called "The Necessity of Party," discussed in Holt, *Rise and Fall,* p. 349.

27. James MacGregor Burns, *The Power to Lead* (New York: Simon & Schuster, 1984), p. 134. See also Richard Hofstadter, *The Idea of a Party System* (Berkeley: University of California Press, 1969), p. 268.

28. Quoted in Richard Josiah Hinton, *The Life and Public Services of the Hon. Abraham Lincoln* (Boston: Thayer & Eldridge, 1860), p. 60.

29. Robert Warden, *A Voter's Version of the Life and Character of Stephen Arnold Douglas* (Columbus, Ohio: Follett, Foster, 1860), p. 92; D. W. Bartlett, *The Life and Public Services of Hon. Abraham Lincoln* (New York: H. Dayton, 1860), p. 142. Although some of Douglas's actions in the 1860 campaign squared with the antebellum party model, others constituted exceptions. For instance, much at variance with the party model—which preferred passive candidates—Douglas actively campaigned among the people. Furthermore, he (and his supporters) can be seen as having strong-armed the "popular sovereignty" plank into the Democratic platform. This candidate, then, was more a leader than a servant of his party, presaging trends that would strengthen after the war.

30. Richard L. McCormick, *The Party Period and Public Policy* (New York: Oxford University Press, 1986), pp. 168–169.

31. Matthew Josephson, *The Politicos: 1865–1896* (New York: Harcourt, Brace & World, 1938), p. 319.

32. Silbey, *American Political Nation,* p. 228.

33. Michael McGerr, *The Decline of Popular Politics* (New York: Oxford University Press, 1986), p. 43.

34. Theodore Cook, *The Life and Public Services of Hon. Samuel J. Tilden . . .* (New York: D. Appleton, 1868), pp. 327–328; W. U. Hensel, with Geo. Parker, *Life and Public Services of Grover Cleveland* (Philadelphia: Hubbard Brothers, 1888), p. 94.

35. "Speech of Hon. Carl Schurz before the Meeting of Independent Vot-

ers, Brooklyn, August 5, 1884," excerpted in Deshler Welch, *Stephen Grover Cleveland: A Sketch of His Life* (New York: John W. Lovell, 1884), p. 215.

36. Quoted in Cook, *Life of Tilden,* p. 102.

37. J. R. Cole, *The Life and Public Services of Winfield Scott Hancock* (Cincinnati, Ohio: Douglass Brothers, 1880), p. 5; James Brisbin, *The Early Life and Public Career of James A. Garfield* (Philadelphia: H. W. Kelley, 1880), p. 530; George Parker, *A Life of Grover Cleveland* (New York: Cassell, 1892), p. 138.

38. One might be inclined to conclude that the independence and antipartyism of the postwar period were in large part generated by a Democratic Party hungry for power, but such a conclusion would be incorrect. One must remember not only Grover Cleveland but the prominent Republicans who were also major figures in the Mugwump and independence movements—Horace Greeley and Carl Schurz being among the most notable. The following discussion of Liberal Republicanism should reinforce this point.

39. For a detailed analysis, see Earle Dudley Ross, *The Liberal Republican Movement* (New York: Holt, 1910).

40. See James Parton, *The Life of Horace Greeley* (Boston: James R. Osgood, 1872), pp. 253, 547–548.

41. Quoted in McGerr, *Decline of Popular Politics,* p. 56.

42. See James L. Sundquist, *Dynamics of the Party System,* rev. ed. (Washington, D.C.: Brookings Institution, 1983), pp. 106–169, on third-party movements in the post–Civil War period.

43. Troy, *See How They Ran,* p. 81.

44. Hugh Craig, *The Biography and Public Services of Hon. James G. Blaine* (New York: A. S. Goodspeed, 1884), p. 309. See, for a similar point, Mark D. Hirsh, "Election of 1884," in Schlesinger, *Presidential Elections,* p. 1564.

45. Hirsh, "Election of 1884," p. 1564.

46. *Newport-Observer,* October 9 1888, quoted in Troy, *See How They Ran,* p. 94.

47. Quoted in Welch, *Stephen Grover Cleveland,* p. 157.

48. "Speech of Hon. Carl Schurz," ibid., p. 211; Pendleton King, *Life and Public Services of Grover Cleveland* (New York: Putnam, 1884), p. 213.

49. Richard Welch, *The Presidencies of Grover Cleveland* (Lawrence: University Press of Kansas, 1988), p. 224.

50. McGerr, *Decline of Popular Politics,* pp. 108, 109–110.

51. Michael Schudson, *Discovering the News: A Social History of American Newspapers* (New York: Basic Books, 1978), p. 65. See also Troy, *See How They Ran,* pp. 83–84, on the changing role of the newspaper in party politics.

52. Frank Luther Mott, *American Journalism* (New York: Macmillan, 1941), p. 412; Schudson, *Discovering the News,* pp. 70–71.

53. McGerr, *Decline of Popular Politics,* p. 114.

54. Quoted in ibid., p. 117.

55. Mott, *American Journalism,* p. 412.

56. Troy, *See How They Ran,* p. 42.

57. Of course, Douglas canvassed the country himself in large part because

of the fragmentation of the Democratic Party. He did not have its full support, and thus the party could not be counted on, as it usually could, to marshal votes for the candidate. See Robert J. Dinkin, *Campaigning in America* (New York: Greenwood Press, 1989), p. 81.

58. Ibid., p. 68.

59. Ibid., p. 103. See also Troy, *See How They Ran*, p. 86.

60. Quoted in R. J. Horton, *The Life and Public Services of James Buchanan* (New York: Derby & Jackson, 1856), p. 415.

61. That Lincoln had an important role in crafting the Republican platform of 1864 is not necessarily inconsistent with my theory; the important part of the story is that he nevertheless thought it proper to act *publicly* as if he were simply obeying the dictates of the party and its platform drafters. The political culture was not yet amenable, at least on Lincoln's view, to large roles for candidates vis-à-vis their parties.

62. A way to substantiate this claim (at least impressionistically) is by examining the appendixes to elections in Schlesinger, *Presidential Elections*, containing items such as platforms, speeches, letters, etc. Very few acceptance letters prior to 1868 but most from 1868 to 1892 are included.

63. Quoted in *A Brief Sketch of the Life and History of General McClellan . . .* (N.p. [New York?], n.d. [1864?]), p. 10. See also Harold M. Hyman, "Election of 1864," in Schlesinger, *Presidential Elections*, p. 1172.

64. *The Democratic Platform*, "Campaign Document, No. 1" (N.p., n.d.).

65. Edward Howland, *Grant as a Soldier and Statesman* (Hartford: J. B. Burr, 1868), p. 637.

66. Quoted in James McCabe Jr., *The Life and Public Services of Horatio Seymour . . .* (New York: United States Publishing Company, 1868), pp. 284–285.

67. By contrast, Greeley's letter accepting the Democratic nomination in 1872 was more conventional: he did not rewrite the resolutions. Yet one still gets the sense that he did not see himself as entirely subordinate to party.

68. Quoted in Brisbin, *Life of Garfield*, p. 522.

69. Leonard Dinnerstein, "Election of 1880," in Schlesinger, *Presidential Elections*, pp. 1504–1505.

70. James Bryce, *The American Commonwealth* (Indianapolis: Liberty Fund, 1995) 2:867.

71. Henry Ramsdell, *Life and Public Services of Hon. James G. Blaine* (New York: Phillips & Burrows, 1884), p. 378.

72. Quoted in Craig, *Biography of Blaine*, p. 277.

73. William O. Stoddard, *Lives of the Presidents: Grover Cleveland* (New York: Frederick A. Stokes & Brother, 1888), p. 186.

74. Of course, Cleveland and other candidates at this time still did not, for the most part, promote themselves through campaign speeches and appearances. Yet by setting the terms for the campaign, at least in part, through the letter of acceptance, candidates were beginning to wrest control away from the party.

75. Troy, *See How They Ran*, p. 100. See Kathleen Hall Jamieson, "Accep-

tance Speeches," in *Encyclopedia of the American Presidency*, ed. Leonard W. Levy and Louis Fisher (New York: Simon & Schuster, 1994), p. 5.

76. Sidney Milkis, *Political Parties and Constitutional Government* (Baltimore, Md.: Johns Hopkins University Press, 1999), p. 65.

77. Troy, *See How They Ran*, p. 112.

78. Part of the confusion on this point most likely rests with the nineteenth-century mantra "Principles rather than persons, measures rather than men." The most obvious—and tempting—way of interpreting this phrase is within the context of the personality-versus-principles dichotomy so common to twentieth-century political analysis; however, I would argue that this interpretation largely misses the mark. In nineteenth-century political rhetoric the phrase denoted the tension between party subserviency and party independence on the part of candidates more commonly than the tension between issue and non-issue campaigns. To be sure, an independent candidate would almost perforce emphasize his personality more than would a subservient candidate, but issues and principles were not necessarily lost in the shuffle. The trade-off was not between issues and "emotion" (or non-issues); rather, it was between a "person" directing the campaign and a party (and its "principles") directing it. Indeed, a more concise formulation of the traditional mantra would be that made by the *North American Review* in 1892: "The Man, or The Platform?" Quoted in Troy, *See How They Ran*, p. 101.

79. McGerr, *Decline of Popular Politics;* Troy, *See How They Ran*, p. 94.

80. McGerr, *Decline of Popular Politics*, p. 177.

81. Jeffrey Tulis, *The Rhetorical Presidency* (Princeton: Princeton University Press, 1987), pp. 14–15.

82. A scholarly convention is that during the post–Civil War period, the Gilded Age, the pull of party was stronger than ever in the U.S. political system, with parties ostensibly at a peak they would never again reach. Yet some historians have noted that parties in the postwar period were not nearly as hegemonic as they might appear prima facie. There was undoubtedly a questioning of the existence and functions of parties: they came under attack from various sources, particularly at the presidential level. Moreover, the presidential candidates, whom the parties had previously restrained, were exerting more influence, increasingly competing with and even overshadowing their parties. See McCormick, *Party Period and Public Policy;* McGerr, *Decline of Popular Politics;* and Silbey, *American Political Nation*, esp. pp. 235–236.

83. Gerald Gamm and Renee Smith, "Presidents, Parties, and the Public: Evolving Patterns of Interaction, 1877–1929," in *Speaking to the People: The Rhetorical Presidency in Historical Perspective*, ed. Richard J. Ellis (Amherst: University of Massachusetts Press, 1998), p. 92. Gamm and Smith further clarify their point (p. 93): "Governing strategies, we contend, are the products of election strategies."

84. See Milkis, *Political Parties and Constitutional Government*, chap. 2, for an excellent discussion of the democratic linkages that parties provided between the people and government in the nineteenth century.

85. See *Letters of Grover Cleveland,* ed. Allan Nevins (Boston: Houghton Mifflin, 1933), for some examples of Cleveland's appeals to the people through public letters in his second term. See also Welch, *Presidencies of Cleveland,* pp. 213–224, on Cleveland's presidencies in the context of presidential history.

86. Joel Silbey, "Beyond Realignment and Realignment Theory, American Political Eras, 1789–1989," in *The End of Realignment? Interpreting American Electoral Eras,* ed. Byron E. Shafer (Madison: University of Wisconsin Press, 1991), p. 14.

87. Lewis L. Gould, *The Presidency of William McKinley* (Lawrence: University Press of Kansas, 1980), p. 137. Sidney Milkis and Michael Nelson in *The American Presidency, Origins and Development, 1776–1993,* 2d ed. (Washington, D.C.: Congressional Quarterly Press, 1994), p. 199, quite rightly point out that McKinley's administration "constituted an important preface to the more complete transformation of the executive that was about to take place in the twentieth century." See Stephen Skowronek, *Building a New American State* (New York: Cambridge University Press, 1982), p. 172, for a discussion of T. R.'s freedom because of Republican electoral security.

88. See Charles S. Olcott, *American Statesman: William McKinley* (1916; Boston: Houghton Mifflin, 1972), 2:295; and Gould, *Presidency of McKinley,* pp. 231, 251.

89. Interestingly, it is Tulis himself who has recently counseled thus. See his essay "Reflections on the Rhetorical Presidency in American Political Development," in Ellis, *Speaking to the People,* pp. 211–222.

90. Silbey, *American Political Nation,* p. 236.

Chapter Four

1. See, for instance, Jeffrey Tulis, *The Rhetorical Presidency* (Princeton: Princeton University Press, 1987), p. 50.

2. As with the campaign biographies and acceptance letters, I did not rigorously code the texts of inaugural addresses and attempt to quantify content in terms of words or themes; the more important task was the interpretive one of studying and comprehending the meanings conveyed by the president. Word and reference counts can be more helpful as supplemental support than as primary evidence; by themselves they are insufficient for dealing with the ambiguity and complexity of texts. I approached the inaugurals using questions as interpretive guideposts: How does the president see himself? Does he make impartial appeals and see himself as leader of all the people now that he is elevated to office? Is he beholden only to the Constitution? Or does he acknowledge his electoral behavior and any campaign commitments that he may have made? Does he mention elections and partisanship once he is supposedly "above the fray" in the White House? If so, what is his role as a partisan? In short, does the president see himself as party leader or party agent, constitutional officer, leader of all the people, or some combination of these roles? This does not mean, though, that the inaugurals were not systematically analyzed. I rather rigorously

mapped out the structure of arguments made and points emphasized; moreover, I also drew upon primary and secondary historical sources to locate these arguments within the context of the times and of each particular president's affectations and predilections. For example, Davis Newton Lott's annotated volume *The Inaugural Addresses of the American Presidents: From Washington to Kennedy* (New York: Holt, Rinehart & Winston, 1961) provides a background to each inaugural as well as helpful annotations. Moreover, I compared each inaugural with that president's party's platform to see whether it expressed loyalty to party principles. Finally, I used major biographies to contextualize the inaugurals and to compare my interpretations with those of presidential historians.

3. Although I offer original interpretations of twentieth-century addresses, I also rely on the work of Barbara Hinckley, *The Symbolic Presidency* (New York: Routledge, 1990), which analyzes different types of presidential speeches but spends a significant effort on the inaugural addresses of presidents after McKinley.

4. This is not the case with campaign biographies, which did not exist prior to 1824 and, after the late nineteenth century, became less important with the rise of the independent press and the changing nature of the presidential campaign.

5. See, for instance, Arthur Schlesinger Jr., ed., *The Chief Executive: Inaugural Addresses of the Presidents of the United States from George Washington to Lyndon B. Johnson* (New York: Crown, 1965), pp. iv–viii.

6. See Karlyn Kohrs Campbell and Kathleen Hall Jamieson, *Deeds Done in Words: Presidential Rhetoric and the Genres of Governance* (Chicago: University of Chicago Press, 1990); and David Ericson. "Presidential Inaugural Addresses and American Political Culture," *Presidential Studies Quarterly* 27, no. 4 (1997).

7. See Edward Chester, "Beyond the Rhetoric: A New Look at Presidential Inaugural Addresses," *Presidential Studies Quarterly* 10, no. 4 (1980); Tulis, *Rhetorical Presidency;* Hinckley, *Symbolic Presidency;* and Halford Ryan, ed., *The Inaugural Addresses of Twentieth-Century American Presidents* (Westport, Conn.: Praeger, 1993).

8. Louis Hartz, *The Liberal Tradition in America: An Interpretation of American Political Thought since the Revolution* (New York: Harcourt, Brace, 1955).

9. James Ceaser, Glen Thurow, Jeffrey Tulis, and Joseph Bessette, "The Rise of the Rhetorical Presidency," in *Rethinking the Presidency,* ed. Thomas Cronin (Boston: Little, Brown, 1982), pp. 238–239.

10. See Chester, "Beyond the Rhetoric," p. 576; and Tulis, *Rhetorical Presidency,* p. 51.

11. Tulis, *Rhetorical Presidency,* pp. 39–40, 47–48.

12. *Inaugural Addresses of the Presidents of the United States* (Washington, D.C.: Government Printing Office, 1974), p. 3 (hereafter, *Inaugural Addresses*).

13. See Lott, *Inaugural Addresses,* annotations on p. 7.

14. See Ralph Adams Brown, *The Presidency of John Adams* (Lawrence:

University Press of Kansas, 1975), p. 4, for a similar understanding of Adams's address.

15. *Inaugural Addresses,* pp. 9, 10–11.

16. Ibid., p. 14.

17. For a solid, capsule understanding of the constitutional model, see the excerpt from Glen Thurow's "Voice of the People: Speechmaking and the Modern Presidency," address delivered at Wake Forest University, October 1, 1979, quoted in Tulis, *Rhetorical Presidency,* pp. 48–49.

18. *Inaugural Addresses,* p. 14.

19. Michael Riccards, *The Ferocious Engine of Democracy* (Lanham, Md.: Madison Books, 1995), 1:53.

20. See Richard Hofstadter, *The Idea of a Party System* (Berkeley: University of California Press, 1967).

21. Forrest McDonald, *The Presidency of Thomas Jefferson* (Lawrence: University Press of Kansas, 1976), p. 26.

22. See especially Jefferson's second inaugural in *Inaugural Addresses,* p. 19.

23. *Inaugural Addresses,* pp. 25, 26. Madison's second inaugural address, however, deals almost solely with the War of 1812 and as such is something of an outlier in this discussion.

24. See Robert Allen Rutland, *The Presidency of James Madison* (Lawrence: University Press of Kansas, 1990), p. 20, for a complementary view.

25. *Inaugural Addresses,* pp. 36, 45. Although nineteenth-century presidents after Monroe (Van Buren, Harrison, Pierce, Hayes, Garfield, Cleveland, and McKinley) would speak of assuming a "trust," they did not see themselves only as trustees but stressed their closer connection with the views of the people. Moreover, by the time of Cleveland, the word "trust" appears to have taken on a considerably different meaning, as in his second inaugural: "Anxiety for the redemption of the pledges which my party has made and solicitude for the complete justification of the trust the people have reposed in us constrain me to remind those with whom I am to cooperate that we can succeed in doing the work which has been especially set before us only by the most sincere, harmonious, and disinterested effort" (*Inaugural Addresses,* p. 167). The people have entrusted them not as virtuous individuals but as partisans wedded to principles and a course of action.

26. *Inaugural Addresses,* p. 29; Noble E. Cunningham, *The Presidency of James Monroe* (Lawrence: University Press of Kansas, 1996), pp. 29–30. Cunningham suggests that Monroe's first address "was not particularly memorable" and that it was vague and noncontroversial. This description holds for the second as well.

27. *Inaugural Addresses,* pp. 35, 45.

28. Ralph Ketcham, *Presidents above Party* (Chapel Hill: University of North Carolina Press, 1984), p. 129.

29. *Inaugural Addresses,* pp. 47, 49. See also Mary W. M. Hargreaves, *The Presidency of John Quincy Adams* (Lawrence: University Press of Kansas, 1985), pp. 47–48.

30. Ketcham, *Presidents above Party,* pp. 137–140; *Inaugural Addresses,* p. 52.

31. See Sidney M. Milkis and Michael Nelson, *The American Presidency: Origins and Development, 1776–1993,* 2d ed. (Washington, D.C.: Congressional Quarterly Press, 1994), pp. 123–125; Donald B. Cole, *The Presidency of Andrew Jackson* (Lawrence: University Press of Kansas, 1993), pp. 33, 183.

32. See Richard J. Ellis and Stephen Kirk, "Presidential Mandates in the Nineteenth Century: Conceptual Change and Institutional Development," *Studies in American Political Development* 9, no. 1 (1995): 117–186, for an excellent analysis of the rise of the presidential mandate and the popularization of presidential elections. I reach a slightly different conclusion regarding the Whigs, however: I find that the Whigs, albeit reluctantly, embraced the "mandate" concept, whereas Ellis and Kirk emphasize Whig resistance.

33. Hinckley, *Symbolic Presidency,* p. 10.

34. *Inaugural Addresses,* p. 55; Robert V. Remini, *Martin Van Buren and the Making of the Democratic Party* (New York: Columbia University Press, 1951), pp. 196–198.

35. *Inaugural Addresses,* p. 57.

36. Of course, as already noted, the extension of suffrage was only to white males, not women or people of color. Even so, the changes between the system that developed in the 1830s and the one that came before it were dramatic and should be seen as an extension of democracy. See Robert Wiebe, *Self-Rule: A Cultural History of American Democracy* (Chicago: University of Chicago Press, 1995).

37. *Inaugural Addresses,* p. 68.

38. Ibid., pp. 66, 68.

39. Ibid., p. 67.

40. Ibid., pp. 76, 71–72. Norma Lois Peterson, *The Presidencies of William Henry Harrison and John Tyler* (Lawrence: University Press of Kansas, 1989), p. 35, notes that Harrison's inaugural is to an important extent a reiteration of his campaign pledges, many of which revolved around limiting the executive and returning to a more "constitutional" notion of government (although he does discuss Whig economic policy briefly). Harrison and the Whigs favored decreasing the power of the executive and making Congress supreme, which would seem to imply that the president would be returned to his original role of constitutional clerk. The irony is that Harrison's upright constitutionalism and anti-executive doctrine had a very popular base: as Whig party philosophy they had been validated in the recent election. As Milkis and Nelson phrase it, "By accepting and expanding upon the Democrats' successful campaign techniques, the Whigs in effect ratified the Jacksonian concept of the president as popular leader" (*American Presidency,* p. 136). The Constitution was indeed, throughout the nineteenth century, an object of popular contention. How it should be interpreted, how the branches of government should operate, how slavery in the territories should be addressed are all questions about the Constitution that were at various times subject to the whim of the ballot box. Daniel Walker Howe, for instance, opines that

"one reason historians have disparaged the alleged lack of issues in the 1840 campaign is that they have refused to take opposition to the executive seriously as an issue"; see *The Political Culture of the American Whigs* (Chicago: University of Chicago Press, 1979), p. 90. Excessive attention to constitutional referents in inaugurals, then, can distract one from essential changes that occurred as presidents continued to discuss and analyze the Constitution. To say that because nineteenth-century presidents talked about constitutional matters they were not popular leaders is to miss the point: articulations and musings about the Constitution had become subjects of popular concern and popular mandates.

41. *Inaugural Addresses*, pp. 85–86.

42. Ibid., p. 86.

43. Howe, *Political Culture*, p. 8. See also Peterson, *Presidencies of Harrison and Tyler*, pp. 38–39.

44. Tulis, *Rhetorical Presidency*, p. 50; *Inaugural Addresses*, p. 90.

45. *Inaugural Addresses*, pp. 95, 98 (emphasis added).

46. Ibid., pp. 90–97.

47. Ibid., pp. 100, 101.

48. From "Appendix to 1848 Election," in *History of American Presidential Elections*, 4 vols., ed. Arthur Schlesinger Jr. (New York: Chelsea House, 1971), p. 901 (hereafter, *Presidential Elections*).

49. Lott, *Inaugural Addresses*, p. 99.

50. *Inaugural Addresses*, pp. 105, 107, 108–109. For Pierce's approval of the Compromise of 1850, see also Nathaniel Hawthorne, *Life of Franklin Pierce* (Boston: Ticknor, Reed, & Fields, 1852), pp. 110–111.

51. *Inaugural Addresses*, pp. 111–112.

52. Ibid., pp. 114–115, 112.

53. On the tense environment surrounding Lincoln's accession to the presidency, see David Herbert Donald, *Lincoln* (New York: Simon & Schuster, 1995), pp. 257–284.

54. *Inaugural Addresses*, pp. 119–120.

55. Ibid., p. 125.

56. Bruce Miroff, *Icons of Democracy: American Leaders as Heroes, Aristocrats, Dissenters, and Democrats* (New York: Basic Books, 1993), p. 104.

57. One can speculate, with Murray Edelman, *The Symbolic Uses of Politics* (1967; Urbana: University of Chicago Press, 1985), p. 76, that the development of a complex, industrial-bureaucratic society may have helped to create a seemingly perpetual crisis situation, one conducive to strong leadership: "As the world can neither be understood nor influenced, attachment to reassuring abstract symbols rather than one's own efforts becomes chronic. And what symbol can be more reassuring than the incumbent of a high position who knows what to do and is willing to act, especially when others are bewildered and alone?"

58. John Hope Franklin, "Election of 1868," in Schlesinger, *Presidential Elections*, p. 1251.

59. A mild exception is perhaps his brief discussion of federalism in the second inaugural; see *Inaugural Addresses*, p. 133.

60. Ibid., pp. 129, 132.

61. See Riccards, *Ferocious Engine,* p. 315, among others.

62. *Inaugural Addresses,* pp. 136, 137. Many have pointed out that Hayes's advocacy of this policy was part of a deal with Democrats that allowed him to be elected. See Milkis and Nelson, *American Presidency,* p. 182.

63. *Inaugural Addresses,* pp. 135–136.

64. See Lott, *Inaugural Addresses,* annotation on p. 137.

65. Of Hayes's inaugural, Ari Hoogenboom has observed: "For the most part, he reiterated his letter of acceptance." See *The Presidency of Rutherford B. Hayes* (Lawrence: University Press of Kansas, 1988), p. 53.

66. *Inaugural Addresses,* p. 138.

67. Ibid., pp. 144, 143–144, 146. As Justus D. Doenecke has pointed out, "Garfield strongly supported the provision of the 1880 Republican platform that stressed 'the duty of the National Government' to aid education, maintaining during the campaign that such aid could resolve the South's difficulties." See *The Presidencies of James A. Garfield and Chester A. Arthur* (Lawrence: University Press of Kansas, 1981), p. 48.

68. *Inaugural Addresses,* p. 142.

69. Ibid., pp. 149–152.

70. Ibid., pp. 150, 151.

71. Ibid., pp. 155–156, 159, 160. Cleveland, as is well known, had made quite a reputation for himself as one more than willing to veto pension claims. See Richard E. Welch Jr., *The Presidencies of Grover Cleveland* (Lawrence: University Press of Kansas, 1988), pp. 62–63.

72. *Inaugural Addresses,* p. 161. Although Harrison does talk about the executive primarily implementing the laws of Congress when inveighing against corporate monopolies and discriminating implementation of federal laws, he does not say at any time that he is outlining his philosophy of the executive. Thus, one can only infer and speculate as to his model of presidential leadership.

73. Second inaugurals appear to differ in tone and conceptualization from first inaugurals, regardless of party affiliation. Presidents seem to personalize the office to a far greater degree the second time and are less concerned with articulating principles, since that has already been done in the first inaugural. One striking attribute of the party period is that very few presidents were elected to second terms, or even sought them—a fact consistent with the party-era mantra of "Principles Rather Than Persons." See Campbell and Jamieson, *Deeds Done in Words,* pp. 34–35, on inaugurals given by incumbent presidents.

74. *Inaugural Addresses,* p. 163.

75. See Robert F. Wesser, "Election of 1888," in Schlesinger, *Presidential Elections,* p. 1618.

76. *Inaugural Addresses,* pp. 164, 166.

77. Ibid., p. 164.

78. Ibid., pp. 171–172, 175, 176.

79. Ibid., pp. 176, 98.

80. Ibid., pp. 178, 179 (emphasis added).

81. Ibid., pp. 179–180.

82. Lott, *Inaugural Addresses*, annotation on p. 180; *Inaugural Addresses*, p. 179.

83. Milkis and Nelson, *American Presidency*, p. 199; Charles S. Olcott, *American Statesman: William McKinley* (1916; Boston: Houghton Mifflin, 1972), 2:294.

84. As a number of authors have focused on twentieth-century inaugural addresses, I offer original insights where relevant but also rely on works such as Hinckley, *Symbolic Presidency;* Tulis, *Rhetorical Presidency;* Ceaser et al., "The Rise of the Rhetorical Presidency"; and Chester, "Beyond the Rhetoric."

85. Hinckley, *Symbolic Presidency*, 110–111.

86. *Inaugural Addresses*, p. 184.

87. See Milkis and Nelson, *American Presidency*, pp. 224–225; Hinckley, *Symbolic Presidency*, p. 109, table 5.1.

88. *Inaugural Addresses*, p. 188. For the five references, see pp. 187, 188, 189, 193, 197.

89. See Hinckley, *Symbolic Presidency*, p. 109, table 5.1. Wilson's first inaugural mentions Congress only once (*Inaugural Addresses*, p. 199).

90. Again, Hinckley's data are instructive: just like T. R., Wilson was very likely to use the pronoun "we" (*Symbolic Presidency*, p. 109, table 5.1).

91. *Inaugural Addresses*, pp. 202, 205.

92. *Inaugural Addresses*, pp. 214, 219–220, 232.

93. Hinckley, *Symbolic Presidency*, p. 109, table 5.1; *Inaugural Addresses*, p. 222.

94. Hinckley, *Symbolic Presidency*, p. 40, table 2.1.

95. Jimmy Carter, "Inaugural Address," in *Inaugural Addresses of the Presidents of the United States* (Washington, D.C.: Government Printing Office, 1989; Bartleby.com, 2001), www.bartleby.com/124/ [January 8, 2001], ¶ 8.

96. Although F. D. R. did mention the Constitution three times (Chester, "Beyond the Rhetoric," p. 576), in his first address writes Hinckley (*Symbolic Presidency*, p. 111), he referred to it to "prepare for the statement that he [might] need to take extra-constitutional actions to meet the emergency" (the Great Depression).

97. *Inaugural Addresses*, p. 269; *Inaugural Addresses* (Bartleby.com edition), ¶s 18 and 19, 42.

98. Hinckley, *Symbolic Presidency*, p. 65. Hinckley is referring to economic and foreign policy addresses as well as inaugurals, but there are no substantial differences in this regard.

99. *Inaugural Addresses* (Bartleby.com edition), see ¶s 17–19, 24, 27. Reagan and Clinton also were somewhat willing to discuss parties and partisanship in their inaugurals, and not always to denigrate them. Clinton, too, stressed the need for compromise more than have other modern presidents, particularly in his 1997 address, which found him facing a Congress controlled by the opposition party.

100. *Inaugural Addresses*, pp. 239, 241.

101. I chose these four papers for several reasons. Each was a major daily newspaper in a large city and thus had a substantial influence on elite and public opinion. They also represent the major party viewpoints: the *Intelligencer*, Whig; the *Sun*, Democratic; the *Tribune*, Whig and then Republican; the *Evening Star* in many ways independent, nonpartisan. I examined the *Intelligencer* from 1825 to 1869, the *Sun* from 1841 to 1917, the *New York Tribune* from 1845 to 1917, and the *Evening Star* from 1853 to 1917. In every case I started with the earliest publication year in which an inaugural address was given and ended with the papers' coverage of Wilson's second inaugural in 1917 (except the *Intelligencer*, which ceased publication before Grant's second inaugural). Although I focus primarily on the party period, I examined newspapers through 1917 in order to identify further the early twentieth-century changes.

I examined each newspaper's coverage, in toto, for two weeks surrounding each inaugural, generally starting with late February (just in case word began to leak out prior to the actual address) and continuing through March 11–14, depending on the inauguration date. Although I scrutinized the papers' coverage in full, I found in editorial opinion the most candid and thoughtful analyses of the addresses and their meaning and function; my research leans heavily on this editorial commentary. I made no attempt to "code" these texts, choosing to rely on the actual words of the editors and my own interpretations.

102. In my universe of cases, this means coverage in the *National Intelligencer*, the only paper of the four publishing before 1841, of the inaugurals of Adams, Jackson, and Van Buren. It is important to note that the *Intelligencer*, March 5, 1829, pointedly remarks on Jackson's inaugural reference to "reform" and speculates as to the partisan qualities of the phrase and sentiment.

103. *Sun*, March 6, 1841; *Intelligencer*, March 5, 9, and 11, 1841. The *Intelligencer* also covers the Whig press and its swarming to Washington as well as opinions from numerous Whig journals around the country regarding the inaugural (March 8 and 11, 1841).

104. *Sun*, March 5, 1845; *Intelligencer*, March 6, 1845; *Tribune*, March 4, 1845.

105. *Sun*, March 5, 1849 (the paper also notes on March 6 the troubling passage in the inaugural supporting "internal improvements," that favored policy of the Whigs); *Intelligencer*, March 9 and 12, 1849 (see also the March 9, 10 and 15 editions for other quotations). The *Tribune* curiously provides almost no analysis of the inaugural beyond mere reportage (though of course the microfilm record of the newspaper may be incomplete).

106. See *Sun*, March 5 and 7, 1853; and *Star*, March 5, 1853. On March 11, 1853, the *Star* does print a parody of Pierce that is strongly partisan, said to be written by a Whig editor of the *New Orleans Crescent*.

107. *Tribune*, March 5, 1853. The *Intelligencer*, March 5, 1853, notes that Pierce has thus far "received in advance no small share of the confidence of the party which opposed his election . . . [and that party continues] to put the most favorable construction upon his acts." Parties are obviously critical players, even at the presidential level.

108. *Star,* March 5, 1857. The *Sun* acknowledges similarly the principles articulated in the address, and there can be no doubt to readers that these are Democratic principles (see March 5 and 7, 1857).

109. *Intelligencer,* March 6, 1857; *Tribune,* March 6 and 9, 1857. Incidentally, the *Star* March 6, 1857, quotes the *Washington Union* as to the strong power of the party and the platform over Buchanan's actions: "Mr. Buchanan recognizes the obligatory character of the Democratic platform. . . . Whether that [the soon-to-come *Dred Scott*] decision (which will probably be made to-day) shall accord with the individual opinion of Mr. Buchanan or not, he stands ready to acquiesce, and to carry it out as the doctrine of the democratic party."

110. *Star,* March 5, 1861; *Tribune,* March 7, 1861; *Intelligencer,* March 7, 1861; *Sun,* March 7, 1861.

111. *Sun,* March 7, 1865; *Intelligencer,* March 6, 1865. See also *Star,* March 4, and *Tribune,* March 6, 1865.

112. *Star,* March 5, 1869; *Sun,* March 5, 1869.

113. *Tribune,* March 5, 1869; *Intelligencer,* March 4, 1869.

114. See *Sun,* March 4 and 5, 1873; *Tribune,* March 5, 1873; and *Star,* March 5, 1873.

115. *Star,* March 6, 1877; *Sun,* March 6, 1877; *Tribune,* March 5, 1877 (cf. March 8, 1877).

116. *Sun,* March 5, 1881; *Star,* March 5, 1881; *Tribune,* March 5, 1881. On March 7, 1881, the *Tribune* notes that the new administration "means a united Republican party."

117. *Sun,* March 4, 1885; *Star,* March 7, 1885; *Tribune,* March 5, 1885. See also *Star,* March 5, 1885: "President Cleveland's inaugural address was one that might have been written by the champion of either party, and yet it was, in the truest sense, a party document."

118. *Sun,* March 4, 1889; *Tribune,* March 5, 1889. See also *Star,* March 5, 1889, which strongly links Harrison's preelection statements with his inaugural and assumed future conduct in office.

119. *Sun,* March 7, 1893; *Tribune,* March 5, 1893; *Sun,* March 4, 1893.

120. See, for instance, *Sun,* March 4, 1897; *Tribune,* March 5, 1901; and *Star,* March 5, 1897.

121. *Star,* March 4, 1901; *Tribune,* March 5, 1901.

122. See, for instance, *Tribune,* March 5, 1905; *Sun,* March 5 and 8, 1913; and *Star,* March 6, 1917. Consistent with my inaugural analysis as well, the newspapers all interpret Taft's address as a thoroughly partisan document. Incidentally, it is instructive to note that from little more than one page before the Civil War, coverage of inaugurations grew considerably thereafter. By the time of McKinley's inauguration, newspapers were devoting pages and pages for several days to the address, the new cabinet, the inauguration balls, and so forth. The press and the public were clearly eager for stories about presidents even before Theodore Roosevelt came to office. Undoubtedly, he was far more skilled than his predecessors at using the press and more interested in adu-

lation and coverage, but the system was already amenable to "heroic" and personal leadership.

Chapter Five

1. These data were drawn from Michael J. Malbin, "Presidential Proposals to Congress and Related Roll Call Votes, 1789–1993," in Elaine K. Swift, Robert G. Brookshire, David T. Canon, Evelyn C. Fink, John R. Hibbing, Brian D. Humes, Michael J. Malbin, and Kenneth C. Martis, *Relational Database of the U.S. Congress, 1789–1993* (Ann Arbor, Mich.: ICPSR, forthcoming). The "proposal" data consist of presidents' requests, through formal communications (i.e., annual and special messages), for congressional action.

2. Rather than determining the proportion of presidential requests that coincide with party pledges or are clearly partisan, I examined how many party pledges and planks were recommended by the presidents (and how aggressively). After all, a number of presidential requests were very minor (e.g., a recommendation for the surveying of new territories) or revolved around treaties and foreign relations, which were almost entirely out of the purview of partisan politics in the nineteenth century. Thus, party pledge recommendations may constitute only a fraction of the presidential requests yet can often lead to the most important, controversial, and momentous of public decisions. Thus, it seemed invidious to measure partisan requests in proportion to total presidential requests. Since the party view suggests that presidents honor their platforms, whether they did so is the prime empirical question, not whether their requests were predominantly partisan.

3. The best are James E. Pollard, *The Presidents and the Press* (New York: Macmillan, 1947); and John Tebbel and Sarah Miles Watts, *The Press and the Presidency* (New York: Oxford University Press, 1985). See also Mel Laracey, "Constitutionally Speaking: The Evolution of Going Public" (Ph.D. diss., University of Michigan, 1997). Given the difficulty of procuring copies of the major administrative organ or major partisan newspapers of each presidency, relying on the several solid studies of presidents' press relations for this evidence seems justifiable. Individual presidential biographies too can be helpful in discovering president's use of newspapers as a vehicle for leadership of the party.

4. Frank Luther Mott, *American Journalism* (New York: Macmillan, 1941), pp. 411–414.

5. One might ask why I do not make patronage or cabinet selection decisions a major thrust of my examination of presidents' relationships with their parties. Such decisions may at times be relevant to the narrative, and are included when germane. But most historians and presidential scholars are quite willing to grant that nineteenth-century presidents rewarded partisans with patronage and cabinet positions. What I aim to discover is whether partisan activity went beyond the "spoils system" or "patronage politics." Were these crass rewards the whole of the partisan story or just a prologue to a much more interesting and compelling tale?

6. See, for instance, Charles Sellers, *James K. Polk, Continentalist,*

1843–1846 (Princeton: Princeton University Press, 1966). Cf. Jeffrey Tulis, *The Rhetorical Presidency* (Princeton: Princeton University Press, 1987), p. 50, which downplays the innovative quality of Polk's administration.

7. I developed these nine planks from my own analysis but drew also on Edward Chester, *A Guide to Political Platforms* (Hamden, Conn.: Archon Books, 1977); and Daniel Feller, *The Public Lands in Jacksonian Politics* (Madison: University of Wisconsin Press, 1984).

8. See *The State of the Union Messages of the Presidents, 1790–1966,* ed. Fred L. Israel (New York: Chelsea House/Robert Hector, 1966), p. 656 (hereafter, *State of the Union*); Malbin, "Presidential Proposals."

9. *State of the Union,* p. 692.

10. Sellers, *James K. Polk,* p. 346.

11. *State of the Union,* pp. 741–744.

12. See Paul H. Bergeron, *The Presidency of James K. Polk* (Lawrence: University Press of Kansas, 1987), pp. 193–200, on Polk's internal improvements vetoes.

13. *A Compilation of the Messages and Papers of the Presidents, 1789–1897,* ed. James Richardson (Washington, D.C.: Bureau of National Literature and Arts, 1897), pp. 2311, 2314 (hereafter, *Messages and Papers*). See also Bergeron, *Presidency of James K. Polk,* pp. 195–196. Incidentally, Polk makes several references to Jackson in this message.

14. See "Appendix to Election of 1884," in *History of American Presidential Elections, 1789–1968,* 4 vols., ed. Arthur Schlesinger Jr. (New York: Chelsea House, 1971), p. 799 (hereafter, *Presidential Elections*).

15. *The Diary of James K. Polk during His Presidency,* ed. Milo Milton Quaife, 4 vols. (Chicago: A. C. McClurg, 1910), 3:249; *State of the Union,* p. 765.

16. Sellers, *James K. Polk,* pp. 325, 339.

17. *Washington Union,* May 9 1846, quoted in Sellers, *James K. Polk,* p. 446.

18. Sellers, *James K. Polk,* p. 347; Polk, *Diary,* 1:111–112, 4:205.

19. The Whigs had 105 members to the Democrats' 111 in the House, with 13 Free-Soilers holding the swing vote. In the Senate the Democrats had 34 members to the Whigs' 24 and the Free-Soilers' 2. See K. Jack Bauer, *Zachary Taylor: Soldier, Planter, Statesman of the Old Southwest* (Baton Rouge: Louisiana State University Press, 1985), p. 297.

20. Polk, *Diary,* 2:305–306.

21. *State of the Union,* pp. 743–744.

22. Ibid., p. 759. It is interesting that Secretary of State James Buchanan thought these denunciations inappropriate for an annual message, but he was in the minority on Polk's cabinet. See Polk, *Diary,* 4:218.

23. Polk, *Diary,* 4:225.

24. *State of the Union,* p. 767.

25. Ibid., pp. 767–768.

26. One might rightly ask what Polk means when he says "the people." On the one hand, these words about representing the "whole people" almost sound

as if he is disparaging partisanship and claiming the mantle of transcendent statesman. On the other hand, there is ambiguity in his phrase "the people of the whole Union, who elected him." Does he mean that he is responsible to *all* the people of the United States or to all those who in fact voted for and supported him? There is no definitive answer, for Polk does not clarify the phrase in his message, nor does he broach the subject at length in his diary. His inaugural address clearly suggests that he saw himself as acting for those who had elected (i.e., voted for) him; though Polk averred that he would not oppress Whigs or those who disagree with him, he would work for and promote the policies and success of his Democratic Party. Further, one must keep in mind that the very message in which he is laying out this theory of presidential leadership is certainly not a nonpartisan document. He is indeed appealing for unity on the slavery issue, but this is a unity best achieved through a rekindling of old party antagonisms. Polk is not making an appeal to *all* the people with his vilification of the American System and his championing of Democratic principles; rather, he is attempting to rally and unify Democrats and to get beyond the slavery controversies. Even as a "popular" president, he is largely attempting to cultivate the support of his fellow Democrats, aspiring not to the mantle of patriot king but to the more prosaic role of party leader.

27. Sellers, *James K. Polk,* p. 447.

28. For an in-depth discussion of these points, see Bergeron, *Presidency of James K. Polk,* pp. 23–39; and Sellers, *James K. Polk,* pp. 165–167, 173–186, 193–204.

29. Sellers, *James K. Polk,* pp. 130, 189, 191.

30. Polk, *Diary,* 2:347, 392, 341, 348.

31. Polk, *Diary,* 2:218.

32. Quoted in Sellers, *James K. Polk,* p. 447.

33. Ibid., pp. 447, 448.

34. A good discussion of the story is Pollard, *Presidents and the Press,* pp. 233–240. See also Laracey, "Constitutionally Speaking," pp. 94–101.

35. Quoted in Pollard, *Presidents and the Press,* pp. 235, 237.

36. Quoted in Tebbel and Watts, *Press and the Presidency,* p. 117. Andrew Jackson Donelson was the nephew of former president Andrew Jackson, and Polk thought he would be a unifying force for the party. Donelson did not accept the job. See Pollard, *Presidents and the Press,* p. 235.

37. Sellers, *James K. Polk,* p. 329.

38. See Laracey, "Constitutionally Speaking," pp. 96–97; Pollard, *Presidents and the Press,* pp. 241–242; Bergeron, *Presidency of James K. Polk,* p. 175; and, for an important window on the close consultations between Polk and Ritchie, Polk, *Diary,* 1:106; 3:237–238, 474; and 4:214–215.

39. Bergeron, *Presidency of James K. Polk,* pp. 175, 176–177.

40. Ibid., p. 122.

41. Quoted in Sellers, *James K. Polk,* p. 450.

42. Sellers, *James K. Polk,* p. 448.

43. See Bergeron, *Presidency of James K. Polk,* p. 182.

44. See Laracey, "Constitutionally Speaking."

45. Samuel Kernell, *Going Public: New Strategies of Presidential Leadership,* 2d ed. (Washington, D.C.: Congressional Quarterly Press, 1993), pp. xiii, 98, 39–41.

46. Pollard, *Presidents and the Press,* p. 252 (emphasis added).

47. Kernell, *Going Public,* p. 40.

48. See Stephen Skowronek, *The Politics Presidents Make* (Cambridge: Belknap Press of Harvard University Press, 1993), pp. 155–176.

49. See "Appendix to Election of 1848," in Schlesinger, *Presidential Elections,* p. 901.

50. See Elbert Smith, *The Presidencies of Zachary Taylor and Millard Fillmore* (Lawrence: University Press of Kansas, 1988), pp. 20–23; and Bauer, *Zachary Taylor,* p. 237.

51. Daniel Walker Howe, *The Political Culture of the American Whigs* (Chicago: University of Chicago Press, 1979), p. 16. See also Smith, *Presidencies of Zachary Taylor and Millard Fillmore,* pp. 246–247.

52. From the Whig Platform of 1844, in "Appendix to Election of 1844," Schlesinger, Jr., *Presidential Elections,* p. 807; see also Howe, *Political Culture,* p. 20.

53. Given Taylor's limited time in office and his small number of requests and recommendations, I consulted the Malbin database ("Presidential Proposals to Congress") as a reference point, but my analysis derives primarily from my own examination of Taylor's recommendations to and communications with Congress.

54. As matters of foreign policy were not often a source of consistent party agitation in the nineteenth century (parties at this time almost never developed platform planks addressing foreign affairs), and considering that Whigs did not campaign in 1848 on foreign policy issues, Taylor's special messages to Congress regarding dealings with other nations are not included in my analysis. Polk's involvement in the Mexican War led to one of the few instances when foreign affairs became the subject of heated partisan controversy.

55. See *State of the Union,* pp. 774–789.

56. Michael Heale, *The Presidential Quest* (New York: Longman, 1982), p. 127.

57. That his requests were supportive of Whig policies is not surprising, considering that his cabinet members, all Whigs, had an important influence on writing the message. See Holman Hamilton, *Zachary Taylor: Soldier in the White House* (New York: Bobbs-Merrill, 1951), p. 256; and Smith, *Presidencies of Zachary Taylor and Millard Fillmore,* p. 100.

58. *State of the Union,* p. 782.

59. Ibid.

60. Ibid., p. 783.

61. Although not a prominent Whig theme in the elections of 1844 and 1848, as Howe (*Political Culture,* p. 101) has pointed out, the development of the West through the railroad system was clearly a tenet of Whig political phi-

losophy. Howe also notes William Seward's championing of the railroads. It is interesting to speculate, then, whether Seward, a political confidant of sorts of Taylor, had something to do with this phrase in the annual message. For another linkage of Taylor and the Whigs with the development of a transcontinental railroad, see Hamilton, *Zachary Taylor,* p. 183.

62. *State of the Union,* p. 785.

63. Ibid., p. 788.

64. Ibid., p. 783.

65. Smith, *Presidencies of Zachary Taylor and Millard Fillmore,* pp. 96, 102.

66. Howe, *Political Culture,* p. 148.

67. Taylor did, however, at least halfheartedly, try to rally Whig support for his state admission plan. See, for instance, Bauer, *Zachary Taylor,* p. 309.

68. Quoted in Bauer, *Zachary Taylor,* p. 300.

69. Smith, *Presidencies of Zachary Taylor and Millard Fillmore,* pp. 59–60.

70. Bauer, *Zachary Taylor,* p. 255.

71. Hamilton, *Zachary Taylor,* pp. 167, 170. See also Bauer, *Zachary Taylor,* p. 259.

72. Michael Holt, however, emphasizes that Taylor and his supporters had the intention of ultimately building a new party, rather than sustaining the old Whig Party; if outward signs might indicate attempts to be a "partisan" president, it was as a president of a new, Taylor-oriented party; see *The Rise and Fall of the American Whig Party* (New York: Oxford University Press, 1999), p. 384. Be that as it may, Taylor's vision would be misguided and inapplicable in the partisan universe of the times.

73. Bauer, *Zachary Taylor,* pp. 262, 259–260.

74. Hamilton, *Zachary Taylor,* p. 167. See also Holt, *Rise and Fall,* p. 425.

75. Quoted in Bauer, *Zachary Taylor,* p. 265.

76. Quoted in Pollard, *Presidents and the Press,* p. 265. See also Smith, *Presidencies of Zachary Taylor and Millard Fillmore,* pp. 66, 140–141; Bauer, *Zachary Taylor,* pp. 262–265; and Hamilton, *Zachary Taylor,* pp. 203–217.

77. Hamilton, *Zachary Taylor,* p. 170.

78. It should be noted that Taylor's men did offer appointments to Clay's son and to Webster's son and brother-in-law in the hope of developing greater support from the Whig leaders. See Smith, *Presidencies of Zachary Taylor and Millard Fillmore,* pp. 65–66; Hamilton, *Zachary Taylor,* p. 206.

79. Quoted in Smith, *Presidencies of Zachary Taylor and Millard Fillmore,* p. 120.

80. Ibid., p. 141.

81. Pollard, *Presidents and the Press,* p. 262.

82. See Bauer, *Zachary Taylor,* p. 269; and Smith, *Presidencies of Zachary Taylor and Millard Fillmore,* p. 94.

83. Brainerd Dyer, *Zachary Taylor* (Baton Rouge: Louisiana State University, 1946), p. 401, quoted in Tulis, *Rhetorical Presidency,* p. 77.

84. See Tulis, *Rhetorical Presidency,* pp. 75–76; and Hamilton, *Zachary Taylor,* pp. 227–228.

85. Sidney M. Milkis and Michael Nelson, *The American Presidency: Origins and Development, 1776–1993,* 2d ed. (Washington, D.C.: Congressional Quarterly Press, 1994), p. 136.

86. See Hamilton, *Zachary Taylor,* p. 167.

87. See the Lincoln passage in Bruce Miroff, *Icons of Democracy: American Leaders as Heroes, Aristocrats, Dissenters, and Democrats* (New York: Basic Books, 1993), p. 112.

88. As Howe (*Political Culture,* p. 90), has put it regarding the election of 1840 and the Whigs' professed distrust of the executive, presidential deference to the wishes of Congress was a "safe enough commitment if a Harrison victory elected a Whig Congress on his coattails—as it did."

89. See Holt, *Rise and Fall,* p. 501.

90. Bauer, *Zachary Taylor,* p. 312.

Chapter Six

1. Henry Adams, *The Great Secession Winter of 1860–61 and Other Essays,* ed. George Hochfield (New York: A. S. Barnes, 1963), p. 195.

2. The phrase is attributed to Hamilton Fish in William S. McFeely, *Grant: A Biography* (New York: Norton, 1981), p. 274.

3. Louis A. Coolidge, *Ulysses S. Grant* (Boston: Houghton Mifflin, 1917), p. 428; Ari Hoogenboom, *The Presidency of Rutherford B. Hayes* (Lawrence: University Press of Kansas, 1988), p. 59.

4. No definitive historical analysis of the Grant presidency exists. Although scores of volumes have been written on his military career, little has been done exclusively on his presidency. (This sorry state of affairs will hopefully be rectified by a forthcoming contribution to the "Presidency Series" of the University Press of Kansas) Frank J. Scaturro's *President Grant Reconsidered* (Lanham, Md.: University Press of America, 1998) is a recent defense of Grant but written from a popular rather than scholarly perspective. The author is also president of the Grant Monument Association. Thus I have been forced to employ alternative works such as biographies of major senators during the Grant administration and members of his cabinet, most particularly Hamilton Fish.

5. See "Republican Platform of 1868" in *History of American Presidential Elections,* 4 vols., ed. Arthur Schlesinger Jr. (New York: Chelsea House, 1971), pp. 1270–1271 (hereafter, *Presidential Elections*).

6. Data on Grant's recommendations to the Forty-first and Forty-second Congresses were derived from Michael J. Malbin, "Presidential Proposals to Congress and Related Roll Call Votes, 1789–1993," in Elaine K. Swift, Robert G. Brookshire, David T. Canon, Evelyn C. Fink, John R. Hibbing, Brian D. Humes, Michael J. Malbin, and Kenneth C. Martis, *Relational Database of the U.S. Congress, 1789–1993* (Ann Arbor, Mich.: ICPSR, forthcoming).

7. Edward Chester, *A Guide to Political Platforms* (Hamden, Conn.: Archon Books, 1977), pp. 86–90.

8. *The State of the Union Messages of the Presidents, 1790–1966,* ed. Fred L. Israel (New York: Chelsea House/Robert Hector, 1966), p. 1189.

9. George H. Mayer, *The Republican Party, 1854–1966,* 2d ed. (New York: Oxford University Press, 1967), p. 177. See also Allan Nevins, *Hamilton Fish: The Inner History of the Grant Administration,* rev. ed., 2 vols. (New York: Frederick Ungar, 1957), pp. 289–293.

10. Nevins, *Hamilton Fish,* p. 293.

11. *A Compilation of the Messages and Papers of the Presidents, 1789–1897,* ed. James D. Richardson (Washington, D.C.: Bureau of National Literature and Art, 1897), pp. 4076–4077.

12. Coolidge, *Ulysses S. Grant,* pp. 339–341. See also Chester, *Guide to Political Platforms,* p. 87.

13. *State of the Union,* pp. 1190, 1214.

14. Coolidge, *Ulysses S. Grant,* pp. 452–455.

15. See *State of the Union,* pp. 1196–1197, 1202. Interestingly, these issues appear to have dropped out of Grant's annual messages (of the first term) after the second except for one minor reference to pensions in the fourth message. See *State of the Union,* p. 1251.

16. *State of the Union,* p. 1215.

17. McFeely, *Grant,* p. 385.

18. Sidney Milkis and Michael Nelson, *The American Presidency: Origins and Development, 1776–1993,* 2d ed. (Washington, D.C.: Congressional Quarterly Press, 1994), p. 179. See also David M. Jordan, *Roscoe Conkling of New York* (Ithaca, N.Y.: Cornell University Press, 1971), p. 123.

19. Wilfred E. Binkley, *President and Congress,* 3d ed. (New York: Vintage Books, 1962), pp. 170–171; Jordan, *Roscoe Conkling,* p. 123.

20. Matthew Josephson, *The Politicos, 1865–1896* (1938; New York: Harcourt, Brace & World, 1963), p. 84; Milkis and Nelson, *American Presidency,* p. 179; Adams, *Great Secession Winter,* p. 105.

21. *State of the Union,* pp. 1225–1226, 1231, 1241–1242, 1251. Grant's discussion of pensions can hardly be called a strong advocacy of liberal provisions for pensions; it reads more like an accountant's bookkeeping than a leader's championing of a cause.

22. *State of the Union,* pp. 1227–1229, 1248.

23. Coolidge, *Ulysses S. Grant,* p. 373.

24. *Messages and Papers,* p. 4081.

25. McFeely, *Grant,* p. 369.

26. As noted in the previous chapter, the *Union* denounced Congress for not acting promptly on Polk's first message, which was, it said, "Executive duty done in obedience to the popular mandate." This sentiment would have been wholly inapposite in talking about Grant and his messages.

27. As Matthew Josephson has put it (*Politicos,* pp. 85–86), early in Grant's first term the "famous 'Senatorial Clique' [Cameron, Morton, Chandler, and Conkling] working behind the scenes and behind the figurehead of Grant, now held absolute command over the ruling party and virtually ruled the country."

28. John Carpenter, *Ulysses S. Grant* (New York: Twayne, 1970), p. 114. See also Charles A. Phelps, *Life and Public Services of Ulysses S. Grant* (Boston: Lee & Shepard, 1872), pp. 323–324.

29. Although Grant was ultimately unsuccessful in instituting substantive civil service reform, it is interesting that this quite corrupt administration was responsible for early strides toward such reform. See Milkis and Nelson, *American Presidency*, pp. 180–182.

30. Carpenter, *Ulysses S. Grant*, p. 105.

31. See Adams, *Great Secession Winter*, pp. 97–100.

32. *State of the Union*, pp. 1202–1203.

33. Milkis and Nelson, *American Presidency*, pp. 179–182; see also Josephson, *Politicos*, p. 107. Again, let me stress that I have had to piece together this analysis from numerous biographies of Grant and members of his cabinet, and examinations of the party organizations at the time; needless to say, there are probably lacunae.

34. Josephson, *Politicos*, p. 78.

35. Coolidge, *Ulysses S. Grant*, p. 382.

36. Nevins, *Hamilton Fish*, p. 108; Carpenter, *Ulysses S. Grant*, p. 78.

37. Coolidge, *Ulysses S. Grant*, p. 275; McFeely, *Grant*, p. 291; Mayer, *Republican Party*, p. 175; Josephson, *Politicos*, pp. 83, 86.

38. Grant employed a military style of cabinet management; he allowed his subordinates much leeway and got directly involved in their business only on rare occasions. See Carpenter, *Ulysses S. Grant*, p. 93.

39. Mayer, *Republican Party*, p. 177.

40. Adams, *Great Secession Winter*, pp. 99–100.

41. Coolidge, *Ulysses S. Grant*, p. 287.

42. George F. Hoar, quoted in Binkley, *President and Congress*, p. 185.

43. Coolidge, *Ulysses S. Grant*, p. 320.

44. James E. Pollard, *The Presidents and the Press* (New York: Macmillan, 1947), p. 449; John Tebbel and Sarah Miles Watts, *The Press and the Presidency* (New York: Oxford University Press, 1985), p. 218.

45. Pollard, *Presidents and the Press*, p. 452.

46. Jordan, *Roscoe Conkling*, p. 171.

47. See *Inaugural Addresses of the Presidents of the United States* (Washington, D.C.: Government Printing Office, 1974), p. 129.

48. James W. Davis, *The American Presidency*, 2d ed. (Westport, Conn.: Praeger, 1995), p. 26.

49. Arthur Wallace Dunn, *From Harrison to Harding*, 2 vols. (New York: G. P. Putnam's Sons, 1922), 1:11.

50. Richard E. Welch Jr., *The Presidencies of Grover Cleveland* (Lawrence: University Press of Kansas, 1988), p. 83; Chester, *Guide to Political Platforms*, pp. 117–118; Homer E. Socolofsky and Allan B. Spetter, *The Presidency of Benjamin Harrison* (Lawrence: University Press of Kansas, 1987), pp. 11, 48.

51. See "Appendix to Election of 1888" in Schlesinger, *Presidential Elections*, pp. 1656–1660. See also Chester, *Guide to Political Platforms*, pp. 115–121.

52. Presidential request data for the Fifty-first and Fifty-second Congresses were derived from Malbin, "Presidential Proposals to Congress."

53. See *State of the Union*, pp. 1631, 1648–1649, 1643–1645, 1637. Regarding tariff legislation, there are, in fact, four requests in Harrison's first annual message, but two of these revolve around tightening the administration of the laws rather than changing their substance and are therefore not counted as substantial requests.

54. Socolofsky and Spetter, *Presidency of Benjamin Harrison*, p. 75.

55. Interestingly, although the postage issue would not receive attention in any of Harrison's messages, it did pop up again in the Republican platform of 1892, which said that reduction of postage was still a goal that the Republicans hoped would be realized in the near future. See "Appendix to Election of 1892," in Schlesinger, *Presidential Elections*, p. 1740.

56. *State of the Union*, pp. 1635, 1651.

57. See Socolofsky and Spetter, *Presidency of Benjamin Harrison*, pp. 47–76.

58. *State of the Union*, pp. 1656, 1664.

59. Harrison's annual messages attest to the steps he has taken to comply with extant civil service legislation, and he pursued a vigorous land policy in large part by treating with Indian tribes to secure more land for homesteaders and settlers. See Harold U. Faulkner, *Politics, Reform, and Expansion* (New York: Harper and Brothers, 1959), p. 111.

60. In fact, it would appear that the only planks from the 1888 platform that he did not speak to in one of these ways were the reduction of postage and federal aid for the education of blacks.

61. *State of the Union*, pp. 1666, 1668–1669.

62. Interestingly, Harrison also advocated several bills that were not part of the platform of 1888 but were nevertheless consistent Republican programs: developing an international bank, establishing a national bankruptcy law, and mandating federal safety regulations for freight trains. In fact, federal safety regulations would become a plank of the Republican platform of 1892. See *State of the Union*, pp. 1670–1675; and "Appendix to Election of 1892" in Schlesinger, *Presidential Elections*, p. 1739.

63. *State of the Union*, pp. 1674–1675, 1676.

64. Quoted in Thomas Campbell Copeland, *Harrison and Reid: Their Lives and Record* (New York: Charles L. Webster, 1892), p. 17.

65. Acceptance Letter of President Benjamin Harrison, September 3, 1892, in "Appendix to Election of 1888," in Schlesinger, *Presidential Elections*, p. 1746.

66. Mayer, *Republican Party*, p. 230.

67. Lynching prevention was not an actual part of the platform of 1888 but was clearly a partisan issue.

68. The Fifty-first Congress passed the Ocean Mail and Steamer Act of 1891 before it adjourned in March 1891.

69. *State of the Union*, pp. 1687–1704, 1711–1733.

70. Ibid., p. 1687.

71. Ibid., pp. 1711–1712.

72. Ibid., p. 1734.
73. Socolofsky and Spetter, *Presidency of Benjamin Harrison,* p. x.
74. Ibid., p. 47.
75. Ibid., p. 29.
76. Ibid., p. 34.
77. Dunn, *From Harrison to Harding,* 1:10; Mayer, *Republican Party,* p. 221.
78. Dunn, *From Harrison to Harding,* 1:85, 88; Socolofsky and Spetter, *Presidency of Benjamin Harrison,* p. 79.
79. Socolofsky and Spetter, *Presidency of Benjamin Harrison,* p. 48. Like Grant, Harrison wielded no significant vetoes that might be thought of as leadership of his party. And whether he was establishing new precedents is arguable; Jefferson had been notable for his quiet yet firm management of congressional partisans, particularly through "dinner parties." See Harold F. Bass Jr., "The President and the Parties," in *The President, the Public, and the Parties,* 2d ed. (Washington, D.C.: Congressional Quarterly Press, 1997), p. 32.
80. Socolofsky and Spetter, *Presidency of Benjamin Harrison,* pp. 58, 64; Mayer, *Republican Party,* p. 227; Dunn, *From Harrison to Harding,* 1:88.
81. Socolofsky and Spetter, *Presidency of Benjamin Harrison,* p. 9.
82. Pollard, *Presidents and the Press,* pp. 541–543.
83. Tebbel and Watts, *Press and the Presidency,* p. 283.
84. Ibid.
85. Jeffrey Tulis, *The Rhetorical Presidency* (Princeton: Princeton University Press, 1987), p. 64. Tulis acknowledges (p. 86) that Harrison did talk policy in some speeches on these tours, but he fails to note that one tour through the Midwest in October 1890 had the thinly veiled purpose of generating support for Republican candidates for the election of 1890. There is some similarity here to Taylor's "swing around the circle" in 1849, but it was aimed more at shoring up support for Whig candidates in state elections and for Whig policies in the Northeast in general. In Harrison's case, the clear aim was to influence congressional midterm elections.
86. Socolofsky and Spetter, *Presidency of Benjamin Harrison,* pp. 169–170.
87. The term "facilitator" in this context is borrowed from George Edwards and Stephen Wayne, *Presidential Leadership,* 4th ed. (New York: St. Martin's Press, 1997). Incidentally, the leadership styles of Taylor, Grant, and Harrison suggest that James Polk's famous statement about wanting "to be myself President of the U.S." does not adequately characterize the full ambit of presidential motivations and ambitions in the nineteenth-century party period. Stephen Skowronek, in *The Politics Presidents Make: Leadership from John Adams to George Bush* (Cambridge: Belknap Press of Harvard University Press, 1993), p. 12, has argued that Polk's sentiment is "an impulse that all presidents share." On my analysis, however, neither Taylor, Grant, nor Harrison (nor likely a number of other party presidents) seemed particularly concerned about leaving an important individual legacy or dominating the politics of the time. Benjamin Harrison would seem to be better described as wanting to be a good

party man or party servant rather than a great president in his own "individual" right.

88. Described in Tebbel and Watts, *Press and the Presidency*, p. 279.

89. Josephson, *Politicos*, p. 358.

90. Welch, *Presidencies of Grover Cleveland*, p. 60.

91. Ibid., p. 80.

92. Ibid., p. 85.

93. *Letters of Grover Cleveland*, ed. Allan Nevins (Boston: Houghton Mifflin, 1933), p. 246.

94. When Cleveland won the presidency in 1884, only the House of Representatives was controlled by his Democrats; the Republicans retained control of the Senate throughout his first term.

95. *Inaugural Addresses*, p. 166.

96. Quoted in Allan Nevins, *Grover Cleveland: A Study in Courage* (New York: Dodd, Mead, 1932), p. 563.

97. See "Appendix to Election of 1892," in Schlesinger, *Presidential Elections*, pp. 1733–1737. See also, Chester, *Guide to Political Platforms*, pp. 121–126.

98. Malbin, "Presidential Proposals to Congress."

99. *State of the Union*, pp. 1740, 1753–1754, 1759; 1767, 1783–1784, 1789. Cleveland's support of the Nicaraguan canal, at most a statement or two in each message, was particularly weak.

100. *State of the Union*, pp. 1809, 1802; 1842–1843, 1844, 1846, 1849, 1850–1852.

101. Ibid., pp. 1811–1812.

102. Ibid., p. 1760.

103. Ibid., pp. 1760–1761.

104. Ibid., pp. 1821, 1822.

105. Welch, *Presidencies of Grover Cleveland*, p. 25.

106. Davis, *American Presidency*, p. 309.

107. Quoted from Cleveland's letter accepting the Democratic nomination in 1892, "Appendix to Election of 1892," in Schlesinger, *Presidential Elections*, p. 1768. See also Theda Skocpol, *Protecting Soldiers and Mothers: The Political Origins of Social Policy in the United States* (Cambridge: Belknap Press of Harvard University Press, 1992), pp. 124–129, on the partisan nature of the pension system of the late nineteenth century and Cleveland's pension vetoes within this context.

108. It is instructive to note the range of executive action, in this case the wielding of the veto, that falls outside a party interpretation of the presidency. A significant number of presidential actions have little to do with party policy per se. For instance, a number of Cleveland's vetoes, and Harrison's for that matter, are more properly explained as the actions of an executive officer who is concerned with a spendthrift Congress rather than with party policy. Partisanship, then, while explaining much of nineteenth-century presidential behavior, does not account for it all.

109. See *Messages and Papers,* p. 5915.

110. Ibid., p. 5917.

111. It matters little that many of the votes for the Seigniorage Bill came from Cleveland's own Democratic Party. He can still be thought of as preserving through this veto the party standard as interpreted by himself and embodied in the platform of 1892, from which, he believed, silverite Democrats had unconscionably strayed.

112. Nevins, *Grover Cleveland,* pp. 725–726.

113. "Democratic Platform of 1892," in Schlesinger, *Presidential Elections,* p. 1736; *Messages and Papers,* p. 6191.

114. See James Ceaser, *Presidential Selection: Theory and Development* (Princeton: Princeton University Press, 1979), pp. 197–207, for Wilson's views on political parties and leadership.

115. Welch, *Presidencies of Grover Cleveland,* p. 115; Nevins, *Grover Cleveland,* p. 511.

116. Nevins, *Grover Cleveland,* p. 512; Welch, *Presidencies of Grover Cleveland,* pp. 215, 50, 115. Welch explains that Cleveland was quite in control of his cabinet during both presidential terms.

117. Welch, *Presidencies of Grover Cleveland,* p. 122.

118. Controlling the House in the nineteenth century, no mean task, was made much easier in the Fifty-first Congress with the adoption of the famous "Reed Rules," which allowed a willful majority party to control procedures much more easily.

119. Charles S. Hamlin, assistant secretary of the treasury, quoted in Nevins, *Grover Cleveland,* p. 542.

120. Nevins, *Grover Cleveland,* p. 544; Cleveland, *Letters,* p. 336.

121. Welch, *Presidencies of Grover Cleveland,* p. 132; Nevins, *Grover Cleveland,* p. 563.

122. Nevins, *Grover Cleveland,* pp. 573–574 (see Nevins's discussion of Cleveland's consultations with Senator James Jones), 580–581.

123. Ibid., p. 581; Cleveland, *Letters,* pp. 354–355.

124. Welch, *Presidencies of Grover Cleveland,* p. 136; Nevins, *Grover Cleveland,* pp. 582–583.

125. Nevins, *Grover Cleveland,* pp. 602–603, 608–609.

126. Welch, *Presidencies of Grover Cleveland,* p. 104. See also Pollard, *Presidents and the Press,* p. 500.

127. Quoted in George F. Parker, *Recollections of Grover Cleveland* (New York: Century, 1909), p. 361.

128. Nevins, *Grover Cleveland,* p. 515; Parker, *Recollections,* p. 360; Pollard, *Presidents and the Press,* p. 533.

129. Cleveland, *Letters,* pp. 386, 394–395.

130. Ibid., p. 441.

131. Nevins, *Grover Cleveland,* pp. 698, 708.

132. See ibid., p. 677, for Nevins's discussion of Cleveland's letter to Governor J. M. Stone of Mississippi and its publication in *Public Opinion* in May 1895.

133. Ibid., pp. 677–681.

134. Parker, *Recollections,* p. 336.

135. Ceaser, *Presidential Selection,* p. 199.

136. Welch, *Presidencies of Grover Cleveland,* p. 223. Welch adds that "Grover Cleveland's tenure provides the essential preface to the evolution of the modern presidency in the McKinley-Roosevelt administrations" (p. 224).

137. It should be pointed out that this characterization of presidential leadership in the party period is not necessarily at odds with the recent work of Stephen Skowronek and, in fact, would appear to be complementary. In *Politics Presidents Make,* Skowronek understands presidential leadership as a combination of constitutional, political, and secular forces. Although I see party decline occurring earlier than he does, I would not contest that parties remained strong enough in the twentieth century to continue to influence presidential leadership strategies. Nor would I contest that party-period presidents were constrained by constitutional norms, or that it mattered at what point in "political time" these presidents came to office. That Pierce and Buchanan were trying to lead a badly fraying Democratic coalition, undoubtedly shaped their possible leadership strategies. I am more concerned, however, with a secular influence on presidential leadership—nineteenth-century parties—than with parties or political coalitions in general. Therefore, I am attuned more to the commonalities of the period and how these presidents *tried* to act, consistent with the norms and rules of the period, rather than how they did act, given the hand that was dealt them or the stage of political time in which they found themselves.

Conclusion

1. James MacGregor Burns, *The Power to Lead* (New York: Simon & Schuster, 1984), p. 131.

2. Anthony Downs, *An Economic Theory of Democracy* (New York: Harper & Row, 1957), p. 28; emphasis in the original; Richard P. McCormick, *The Presidential Game: The Origins of American Politics* (New York: Oxford University Press, 1982), p. 166, quoted in Joel Silbey, *The Partisan Imperative* (New York: Oxford University Press, 1985), p. 59.

3. This notion of parties as diverse coalitions is based on a discussion in John Aldrich, *Why Parties? The Origin and Transformation of Political Parties in America* (Chicago: University of Chicago Press, 1995), pp. 9–10.

4. The term "persuasions" comes from Marvin Meyers, *The Jacksonian Persuasion* (Stanford, Calif.: Stanford University Press, 1960).

5. Paul Allen Beck, *Party Politics in America,* 8th ed. (New York: Longman, 1997), pp. 9–10.

6. Silbey, *Partisan Imperative,* p. 63.

7. See, for instance, Daniel Walker Howe, *The Political Culture of the American Whigs* (Chicago: University of Chicago Press, 1979); Meyers, *Jacksonian Persuasion;* Eric Foner, *Free Soil, Free Labor, Free Men: The Ideology of the Republican Party before the Civil War* (London: Oxford University Press, 1970); Joel

Silbey, *The American Political Nation* (Stanford, Calif.: Stanford University Press, 1991); and John Gerring, *Party Ideologies in America, 1828–1996* (New York: Cambridge University Press, 1998).

8. Gerring, *Party Ideologies,* pp. 10–11; Michael F. Holt, *The Rise and Fall of the American Whig Party* (New York: Oxford University Press, 1999), p. 90.

9. See Louis Hartz, *The Liberal Tradition in America* (New York: Harcourt, Brace, & World, 1955).

10. See William Riordon, *Plunkitt of Tammany Hall* (New York: Signet, 1995).

11. Matthew Josephson, *The Politicos, 1865–1896* (1938; New York: Harcourt, Brace & World, 1963), p. 100.

12. See Jeffrey Tulis, *The Rhetorical Presidency* (Princeton: Princeton University Press, 1987); and James Ceaser, *Presidential Selection: Theory and Development* (Princeton: Princeton University Press, 1979), for the constitutionalist perspective. See Burns, *Power to Lead*; and Bruce Miroff, "Monopolizing the Public Space: The President as a Problem for Democratic Politics," in *Rethinking the Presidency,* ed. Thomas Cronin (Boston: Little, Brown, 1982), for more popular, democratic critiques of the modern presidency.

13. The term "pseudodemocratization" comes from Robert A. Dahl, "Myth of the Presidential Mandate," in *Politicians and Party Politics,* ed. John C. Geer (Baltimore, Md.: Johns Hopkins University Press, 1998).

14. "The New Nationalism, Speech at Osawatomie, 31 August 1910," in Theodore Roosevelt, *The New Nationalism,* intro. William E. Leuchtenburg (Englewood Cliffs, N.J.: Prentice-Hall, 1961), p. 36 (emphasis added).

15. Theodore Roosevelt, "Address by Former President Theodore Roosevelt, Chicago, August 6, 1912," in *History of American Presidential Elections, 1789–1968,* 4 vols., ed. Arthur Schlesinger Jr. (New York: Chelsea House, 1971), p. 2221 (emphasis added).

16. See Tulis, *Rhetorical Presidency,* pp. 174–181, for a discussion of "crisis" and "normal" politics.

17. See, for instance, Tulis, *Rhetorical Presidency;* and Joseph Bessette, *The Mild Voice of Reason* (Chicago: University of Chicago Press, 1994).

18. Tulis, *Rhetorical Presidency,* pp. 37–38.

19. On Reagan's 1981 budget victory and the "supplanting" of deliberation, see ibid., pp. 196–197.

20. See Sidney M. Milkis and Michael Nelson, *The American Presidency: Origins and Development,* 3d ed. (Washington, D.C.: Congressional Quarterly Press, 1999), pp. 288–289.

21. This is of course an old tale, dating back to the presidency of Andrew Jackson, at the very least.

22. Bill Bradley, "March 1, 2000, Democratic Primary Presidential Debate," quoted in *Los Angeles Times,* Home Edition, p. 1, March 2, 2000.

23. William Howard Taft, *Our Chief Magistrate and His Powers* (New York: Columbia University Press, 1925), p. 12.

24. See Ceaser, *Presidential Selection,* pp. 318–327.

25. For instance, some of Clinton's criticisms regarding Republican plans to reform Medicare bordered on hard demagoguery, being largely attempts not to contribute to public debate but to prey on the fears and anxieties of elderly Americans for political benefit. And presidential candidate Pat Buchanan clearly engaged at times in what might be called hard demagoguery in his campaigns for the office.

26. Burns, *Power To Lead,* pp. 159–160.

27. Marc Landy and Sidney M. Milkis, *Presidential Greatness* (Lawrence: University Press of Kansas, 2000), p. 234; Sidney M. Milkis, *Political Parties and Constitutional Government* (Baltimore, Md.: Johns Hopkins University Press, 1999), p. 173.

28. Dahl, "Myth of the Presidential Mandate," pp. 253, 254.

29. Miroff, "Monopolizing the Public Space," p. 218; Marc K. Landy and Sidney M. Milkis, "Democratic Presidential Leadership: An Oxymoron?" (paper presented at the annual meeting of the American Political Science Association, Washington, D.C., 1997), p. 49.

30. See, for example, Robert D. Putnam, *Bowling Alone: The Collapse and Revival of American Community* (New York: Simon & Schuster, 2000).

31. See Walter Lippmann, *Public Opinion* (New York: Free Press, 1997).

32. Legislators, indeed, spend a large amount of their time worrying what their constituents may be thinking on public matters. A central part of their job consists in keeping open lines of communication with their constituents. See John W. Kingdon, *Congressmen's Voting Decisions,* 3d ed. (Ann Arbor: University of Michigan Press, 1989); and Richard Fenno, *Home Style: House Members in Their Districts* (New York: HarperCollins, 1978).

33. William Henry Harrison, "Inaugural Address," in *Inaugural Addresses of the Presidents of the United States* (Washington, D.C.: Government Printing Office, 1974), p. 76.

34. John R. Hibbing and Elizabeth Theiss-Morse, "Too Much of a Good Thing: More Representative Is Not Necessarily Better," in *The U.S. House of Representatives: Reform or Rebuild?* ed. Joseph F. Zimmerman and Wilma Rule (Westport, Conn.: Praeger, 2000), p. 129.

35. Milkis, *Political Parties,* p. 184.

36. Arthur Schlesinger Jr., *The Imperial Presidency* (Boston: Houghton Mifflin, 1973), p. 210.

37. James Bryce, *The American Commonwealth* (New York: Macmillan, 1933), 2:5.

38. Indeed, as I have noted throughout, the parties came into existence partly as a result of constitutional questions and disagreements (e.g., the Whig and Democratic disagreement over the constitutionality of internal improvements), and the Constitution thereby occupied a venerable position in their political philosophies.

39. James Garfield, "Inaugural Address," in *Inaugural Addresses,* p. 142 (emphasis added).

40. Ceaser, *Presidential Selection,* pp. 340–341.

41. David Broder, *The Party's Over: The Failure of Politics in America* (New York: Harper & Row, 1972). See also Walter Dean Burnham, "The End of Party Politics," *Transaction 7* (1969); Austin Ranney, "Political Parties: Reform and Decline," in *Both Ends of the Avenue,* ed. Anthony King (Washington, D.C.: American Enterprise Institute, 1978); Nelson W. Polsby, *Consequences of Party Reform* (New York: Oxford University Press, 1983); William Crotty, *American Parties in Decline,* 2d ed. (Boston: Little, Brown, 1984); and Martin P. Wattenberg, *The Decline of American Political Parties, 1952–1992* (Cambridge: Harvard University Press, 1994).

42. William J. Keefe, *Parties, Politics, and Public Policy in America*, 8th ed. (Washington, D.C.: Congressional Quarterly Press, 1998), p. 303; Silbey, *American Political Nation* and Milkis, *Political Parties.*

43. Xandra Kayden and Eddie Mahe Jr., *The Party Goes On: The Persistence of the Two-Party System in the United States* (New York: Basic Books, 1985).

44. Gerald Pomper, "Parliamentary Government in the United States?" in *The State of the Parties,* 3d ed., ed. John C. Green and Daniel M. Shea (Lanham, Md.: Rowman & Littlefield, 1999), p. 269.

45. See John F. Bibby, "State Party Organizations: Coping and Adapting to Candidate-Centered Politics and Nationalization," in *The Parties Respond,* 3d ed., ed. L. Sandy Maisel (Boulder, Colo.: Westview Press, 1998), p. 24. It may seem redundant to say that federal parties now have greater control over running federal elections. But in fact, for much of the life of the political party system, House and Senate candidates *and* presidential candidates were promoted in their states largely through the work and services of the *state* parties. Not until after the Civil War did national organizations develop that were more than organizations in title only.

46. Aldrich, *Why Parties?* p. 273.

47. Gerald Pomper, "The Alleged Decline of American Parties," in Geer, *Politicians and Party Politics,* p. 23.

48. Ibid., p. 36.

49. But see David G. Lawrence, "On the Resurgence of Party Identification in the 1990s," in *Political Parties: Decline or Resurgence?* ed. Jeffrey E. Cohen, Richard Fleischer, and Paul Kantor (Washington, D.C.: Congressional Quarterly Press, 2001), on recent scholarship that shows partisanship in the electorate to be strengthening somewhat.

50. Aldrich, *Why Parties?* p. 245.

51. See John F. Bibby and L. Sandy Maisel, *Two Parties—Or More?* (Boulder, Colo.: Westview Press, 1998), pp. 75–77, for a summary of opinion surveys from recent decades.

52. See Wattenberg, *Decline of Political Parties,* p. 22.

53. Keefe, *Parties in America,* pp. 197, 196.

54. Ibid., p. 276. See also Wattenberg, *Decline of Political Parties,* p. 20, for a similarly high number of individuals reporting that they split their tickets in presidential elections.

55. Marjorie Randon Hershey and Paul Allen Beck, *Party Politics in America,* 10th ed. (New York: Longman, 2003), p. 117.

56. David Mayhew, *Divided We Govern* (New Haven: Yale University Press, 1991).

57. Joel H. Silbey, "From 'Essential to the Existence of Our Institutions' to 'Rapacious Enemies of Honest and Responsible Government': The Rise and Fall of American Parties, 1790–2000," in Maisel, *Parties Respond,* p. 14. See also Michael McGerr, *The Decline of Popular Politics* (New York: Oxford University Press, 1986), pp. 6–9, on voter turnout and its decline in the twentieth century.

58. See Crotty, *Parties in Decline,* p. 7.

59. Milkis, *Political Parties,* p. 70.

60. The Senate was split 50–50, but Vice President Dick Cheney's tie-breaking vote gave Republicans control of the Senate and thus of Congress as well as the presidency.

61. Sarah Binder, "Can the Parties Govern?" in Cohen, Fleischer, and Kantor, *Political Parties,* p. 228.

62. Numerous sensible reform plans could either curtail or eliminate soft money without undermining the power of the political parties. These plans usually substantially raise the hard-money limits and free parties to contribute as much hard money as desired to their candidates. See, for instance, Norman J. Ornstein, Thomas E. Mann, Paul Taylor, Michael J. Malbin, and Anthony Corrado, "Reforming Campaign Finance," in *Campaign Finance Reform: A Sourcebook,* ed. Anthony Corrado, Thomas E. Mann, Daniel R. Ortiz, Trevor Potter, and Frank J. Sorauf (Washington, D.C.: Brookings Institution Press, 1997).

63. Harvey C. Mansfield Jr., *Statesmanship and Party Government* (Chicago: University of Chicago Press, 1965), p. 17.

64. The concept of the party president as a "broker" comes from Ceaser, *Presidential Selection.*

65. Terri Bimes and Stephen Skowronek, "Woodrow Wilson's Critique of Popular Leadership: Reassessing the Modern-Traditional Divide in Presidential History," in *Speaking to the People: The Rhetorical Presidency in Historical Perspective,* ed. Richard J. Ellis (Amherst: University of Massachusetts Press, 1998), pp. 160, 147.

66. See Jeffrey K. Tulis, "Today's Neo-Whig Presidency," in *Policy Visions: Reflections on Political and Social Issues from the Center for Economic and Policy Education at Saint Vincent College* 3, no. 2 (1998).

67. James Ceaser makes a similar point in *Presidential Selection,* p. 353.

Appendix One

1. William Burlie Brown, *The People's Choice: The Presidential Image in Campaign Biography* (Baton Rouge: Louisiana State University Press, 1960), p. xiv.

2. One might also feel inclined to quibble with using such "public" documents as campaign biographies (also inaugural addresses and annual messages) as the prime source of data on the electoral environment of the nineteenth century. After all, candidates, or their biographers, may have been forced by the

public context to be less than candid about the political system and the role of elections. To be sure, campaign biographies do not provide an exhaustive account of the electoral/political environment. But it is not the argument of this book that politicians never have ulterior motives for winning office, that they do not dissemble in public, or that they do not undercut the public good sometimes. Rather, my interest in changing political norms and conceptions requires a strong emphasis on publicly validated and accepted modes of action. Campaign biographies, then, as documents offered to the mass public, will likely reveal cultural norms regarding the office of the presidency and its relationship with the public. Moreover, the idiographic studies of individual presidencies in chapters 5 and 6, which focus on "private" as well as "public" presidential behavior, can serve as checks on the information derived from campaign literature.

3. For instance, the appendix to William Holland, *The Life and Political Opinions of Martin Van Buren* (Hartford, Conn.: Belknap & Hamersley, 1836), shows that the volume was reviewed in papers in New York, Pennsylvania, Tennessee, Maryland, and Connecticut. It would be surprising if this were not the case with many of the campaign biographies in the nineteenth century.

4. Nathaniel Hawthorne, *The Life of Franklin Pierce* (Boston: Ticknor, Reed & Fields, 1852), p. 3.

5. Gen. Lew. Wallace, *Life of Gen. Benjamin Harrison* (Philadelphia: H. L. Warren, 1888), p. 17.

6. James D. McCabe Jr., *The Life and Public Services of Horatio Seymour* (New York: United States Publishing Company, 1868), p. v.

7. Michael Heale, *The Presidential Quest* (New York: Longman, 1982), p. 159.

8. See Brown, *People's Choice,* pp. 3–14.

9. See, for instance, Charles Coffin, *The Life of James A. Garfield* (Boston: James H. Earle, 1880), p. 5; and William Dean Howells, *Sketch of the Life and Character of Rutherford B. Hayes* (New York: Hurd & Houghton, 1876), p. iii.

10. Prominent campaign speeches are often included in the appendixes of *History of American Presidential Elections, 1789–1968,* 4 vols., ed. Arthur Schlesinger Jr. (New York: Chelsea House, 1971); moreover, essays on each of the presidential elections by distinguished historians, also included in the Schlesinger volumes, are helpful in indicating the direction of the campaigns. Robert J. Dinkin's *Campaigning in America: A History of Election Practices* (New York: Greenwood Press, 1989), provided useful discussions of the elections against which to compare the biographies for representativeness.

11. *Federalist* No. 68, in *The Federalist,* ed. Henry Cabot Lodge (New York: Putnam, 1888), p. 427.

Appendix Two

1. See, for example, the chapter on Lincoln in Marc Landy and Sidney M. Milkis, *Presidential Greatness* (Lawrence: University Press of Kansas, 2000).

2. See David Donald, *Lincoln Reconsidered: Essays on the Civil War Era* (New York: Vintage Books, 1961), chap. 10.

Index

Michael J. Korzi is assistant professor of political science at Towson University. He received his B.A. from the University of Pittsburgh, Johnstown, his M.A. from Penn State University, and his Ph.D. from the University at Albany, State University of New York. He teaches and researches the presidency, public opinion, Congress, American political thought, and political philosophy. He has published articles in *Presidential Studies Quarterly*, *Polity*, and *Congress & the Presidency*. He resides in Towson, Maryland, with his wife, Dawn, and his two children, William and Samuel.